Mr. Robert G. Hinkle
110 Bell Rd
Fredericksbrg, VA 22405-3027

APPOINTMENT
CONGO

APPOINTMENT CONGO

by *Virginia Law Shell*

SHELL HOUSE, INC.
Lake Junaluska, NC 28745

This is Burleigh Law's story so primarily
it is dedicated to him. But it is also the
story of David, Paul, and Margaret Ann who
so wonderfully became a part of all that
their daddy did. To them I lovingly dedicate
this Appointment Congo.

Preface

"What ever happened?" is a question I often hear. People who came to know our family through the story of Burleigh Law's life and death wonder how the story has progressed.

Added to these interested friends were the frequent requests for a copy of *Appointment Congo*. Believing there is a message of hope for others who face tragedies and a witness of beauty as God has worked together all things in each of our lives for good, I have updated our story.

Whether it is an update to you or an introduction to our pilgrimage of faith, may it bring laughter, tears, joy and challenge in your own walk with our God.

Virginia Law Shell

September 1985
Lake Junaluska, N.C.

Foreword

THREE WEEKS AFTER BURLEIGH LAW ARRIVED IN THE central Congo in 1950, he was given the name *Uwandji Utshudi A Koi* ("Chief Leopard of the Artisans") by the Congolese at the mission station. Since to these people the leopard, not the lion, is king of the beasts, this was a name of high distinction.

Twelve years later, returning from furlough to a Congo now torn by violence, Burleigh Law knew he faced danger and even possible death. But he said, "If somewhere, someone must raise a white cross over my grave, I'd rather it be in the heart of the Congo."

In APPOINTMENT CONGO, Virginia Law, his wife, who shared his life in the Congo, has written about this dedicated man.

One of the great realities of Burleigh Law's early life was his desire to be a missionary in the Congo, but he had little interest in preaching so was uncertain how this desire could be realized. Although the early Protestant and Catholic missionaries, encouraged by the Belgian government, had been mostly concerned with setting up schools and hospitals, and, indeed, provided a large part of the teaching and medical forces in the country, their responsibilities had broadened over the years. Men trained in agriculture and in mechanics were badly needed.

Burleigh Law was a natural mechanic, and so it was that he received an appointment to the Congo by the Methodist Church as a lay missionary or, as he himself put it, "a jack-of-all-trades for the Lord." His wife and two young sons went with him.

Burleigh's charge was the construction of a 250-bed hospital at the Wembo Nyama mission station, the most ambitious building project ever attempted in central Congo. His unique mechanical abilities served him well as he coped with the moving of tons of heavy machinery from the river port to the construction site; with setting up a brick press, sawmill, and power plant; with locating and acquiring adequate building supplies; and with training men to run the machines. He also had a unique ability to enter into the lives of the Congolese people, and the witness he bore to his Christian faith as he worked with them was an effective proclamation of the gospel.

The whole Law family, which later included a girl born at the mission, entered with zest into their new life, thinking of the Congo as their permanent home. But the fifties were crucial years in the Congo's history. The tide of nationalism was sweeping other African colonies; change was in the wind and the Congo could not remain isolated. Organized political activity among the people, which had been nonexistent before, increased to such an extent that the Belgian government was forced to speed up its scheduled political reforms, and in June, 1960, the Congo became independent.

The new government was immediately faced with a series of crises. Because of a lack of enough schools above the primary grades, there were few educated Congolese trained and able to step into administrative and professional jobs, few who had ever been at all involved in governmental responsibility. Riots and disorder spread throughout the country. Katanga province seceded from the new republic, civil war broke out, and at the request of Premier Lumumba, a United Nations force was sent to help restore order. The breakdown in governmental authority resulted in the overthrow and eventual killing of Lumumba. Although a new government was finally formed, political and tribal rivalries continued to trigger fighting in many parts of the country between the government and United Nations forces and rebel armies.

The missionaries were caught in the middle. They were there to serve all people without regard to tribe or politics. But as the situation in the country deteriorated, some of the Congolese suspected them of favoring one tribe over another and of being sympathetic to the white man's world of colonialism. In some sections, the danger was extreme—stations were looted and burned, and missionaries forced to flee for their lives.

In 1960 at the time of independence, the Laws went on furlough. When time approached for their return, the internal situation in the Congo was still considered highly unstable. Some missionaries had gone back, but the Board of Missions would not risk sending families. Since the Congolese were urgently calling on the missionaries for help, it was decided that Burleigh should go back alone. His separation from his family was brief, however, and six months later, in the fall of 1962, the Law family had all returned to the Congo.

The new Congo was still a country of strife, of tension, of uncertainty. Essential services had deteriorated or were nonexistent. Burleigh was given the additional responsibility of piloting the mission plane, flying in supplies of food and medicine, and delivering the mail. Keeping open the lines of communication between isolated mission stations became his major concern. In August, 1964, in an attempt to rescue some missionaries held hostage, he was shot and killed by a rebel soldier.

Virginia Law has written a vivid, warm, sympathetic picture of the years she and her family spent in central Congo, of the Congolese people, and of the purpose and nature of the work of the church. She shows the development of the Congolese church, its contribution to the lives of the people and the faithfulness and ability of its leaders. She does not attempt to evaluate the political forces but gives an objective report on what independence meant to the Congolese and to the work of the mission. Primarily, however, this book is the inspiring story of her husband, Burleigh Law, missionary to Batetela land.

DR. TRACEY K. JONES
Associate General Secretary
World Division of the
Board of Missions of the
Methodist Church

Table of Contents

APPOINTMENT CONGO

Prologue

I SCANNED THE SKY, MISTY WITH DRY-SEASON HAZE. "WILL AIR Congo get in?" I asked.

"I think so, if the radio beacon is working," Burleigh answered.

It was summer, 1964, four years after the Congo had become an independent nation. My husband and I stood, each with his own thoughts, in the shade of a palm tree at the Lodja Airport in the heart of the Congo.

I was not sure I really wanted the plane to land. If it did, ten-year-old Margaret Ann and I would be off to America, going home for a vacation in the middle of our four-year term. I still could not believe that the tickets in my hand were real. Gifts from the Congo Government! In appreciation, I was told, for teaching in the secondary school. The new nation was desperately in need of teachers.

America seemed far away. Our sons, David, a freshman in college, and Paul, a senior in a boarding school, had been in the States for the past year. Excitement rushed through me as I thought of seeing them again. But it hurt to think of our reunion without their dad.

Again I urged Burleigh to join us. He smiled but

shook his head. "You know I couldn't go off and leave our Mission without a pilot."

It was the same answer he had given before. I did know, of course, that our small plane was essential to the work of the mission. And Burleigh was now the only pilot.

Past experience brought doubts that the Air Congo DC-3 would make it into this gravel-covered bush airport. The radio beacon was not dependable. Sometimes the operator, unaccustomed to responsibility, would take off for a visit to his home village, leaving the passenger plane unable to land for lack of ground contact.

This had happened only two weeks before. An Air Congo plane after circling helplessly overhead had then started off for another airport. Fortunately, Burleigh was there to meet some missionaries returning from a furlough. He rushed out to our small mission plane, a Cessna 210, and called the pilot in on its radio.

"We don't land anywhere these days without ground clearance," the pilot explained after landing. "Fighting is too general in the Congo."

Now, as if responding to my unspoken questions, Burleigh said, "I heard today on our Mission broadcast that the rebels are in Kindu."

"Too close," I thought. We were not quite sure who the rebels were and what their aims were. But we knew that their advance meant fierce fighting between opposing Congolese forces.

Now we heard the distant drone of the Air Congo plane. It drew nearer, circled the airport, and landed. Three Congolese workmen rolled out the fifty-gallon gas drums and used the hand pump to fill the tanks. So

I was to get off to America. I was still torn between going and staying. Burleigh sensed my mixed feelings.

"It's only for five weeks. Then you'll be back," he said. "These last two years have been pretty trying. It will be good for you to have a break. Besides, I'd rather you'd be home with your folks and the boys instead of being here alone while I'm doing so much flying among the stations."

I nodded agreement. "Yes, only five weeks."

The luggage went out to the plane. Margaret Ann ran up, kissed her dad good-bye, and rushed on in excitement to the plane. Burleigh lifted my left hand to his lips and kissed my new diamond ring, just a month old, his birthday gift to me. "An engagement ring after being married twenty-two years," he had teased. Now he was serious. "There are a million sparkles in this ring," he said. "Every sparkle tells you I love you. When you look at it, remember that."

Seated in the plane, I looked out. Burleigh stood with one foot propped up on the fence, his arms folded on his knee. The sun now shining through the haze brought out the gray streak in his wavy hair. After twenty-two years of marriage, I still considered him one of the best looking men I knew.

With the window separating us, for the first time I felt afraid. There were reports of intertribal fighting on many fronts, as well as advance by the rebels against the Congolese Nationalists. I knew Burleigh would not avoid danger to himself if he were called upon to help.

I remembered last year when tribal fighting was reported near Katako Kombe where three missionaries lived.

"I'd better go check on them tomorrow," Burleigh had said.

We knew this danger was real. The next morning we had our prayers together. Burleigh's confidence, his complete dedication to what he felt was his duty, reassured my heart. But when I heard the plane motor crank up as I walked to school to teach my class, the fear came back.

I stopped. I could not face my class so upset. I could not keep Burleigh from going. I would not try. But I was afraid for him. I felt trapped between two emotions.

Standing there in the middle of the Congo road, I had prayed earnestly. "Father, I don't want Burleigh to fly to Katako Kombe and maybe get caught up in tribal fighting. But I don't want to keep him from going. Help me to commit him into Your hands." My fear was gone. I didn't know that Burleigh would be safe; I did know, somehow, that he was in God's hands. I went on to school. Late that afternoon I heard the sweetest sound possible, the distant drone of a single-engine plane coming home.

Yes, the dangers in the Congo were real. But here we had experienced great joys and satisfactions, too.

I recalled what had happened when Burleigh had been flying from Katubwe to Lodja, about an hour's flight. There was no weather report from Lodja. Skies were clear at Katubwe when he took off. A short way out he noticed scattered thunderheads in the distance.

Thirty minutes out, these thunderheads rushed together. The sky closed in. Burleigh turned back toward Lusambo looking for the emergency strip. It was closed, too. Banking around, looking for an opening, he saw only one spot of blue in the whole sky. He headed for it; visibility seemed clear ahead.

But by then, Burleigh didn't know where he was. Depending on visual navigation, he searched for some landmark and noted some shining roofs off to the left. He turned toward them and saw a landing strip. Flying low, he circled to check it. It seemed clear so he landed.

He had hardly stopped the motor when a Landrover came racing up. A nurse jumped out. "I don't know where you came from or why you came here, but I know you are an answer to our prayers," she greeted him.

The nurse and one missionary couple, the Michees, had been isolated on this Scottish Plymouth Brethren Mission at Kole for more than three months. Due to the unsettled political situation, there was no mail service in, no transportation out. The roads were impassable; bridges were out. Then Mrs. Michee became seriously ill with a high fever. Added to all else was a fear of rabies. They were desperate with anxiety.

Early that morning they had called together the Christians of their village. They explained the serious situation. Then together they joined in praying, "Father, send us help."

To them, Burleigh was God's answer to their prayers. He quickly flew back to Wembo Nyama for a doctor, and before the sun had set, Dr. Hughlett was at Kole with the necessary skill and medicines to treat Mrs. Michee.

Now, sitting in the Air Congo plane, I said in my heart, "It has been a good twelve years in the Congo."

As the plane took off for America, I remembered how our life together and our work there had begun.

CHAPTER ONE

Butterscotch Pudding

I N THE FALL OF 1941 I HAD GONE NORTH FROM MY HOME IN Chipley, Florida, to Asbury College, a small liberal arts school in the rolling bluegrass hills just south of Lexington, Kentucky. I arrived with all the excitement and thrill of any college freshman. The school was known as the "Happy Hunting Ground" for finding preacher-husbands, since a large number of the male students were preparing for the ministry.

The very first night at school I started waiting tables to help pay expenses. I was so busy I failed to really notice anyone around me until the dining-room matron in her authoritative voice announced, "Burleigh Law will ask our blessing." Then from the end of my table, a resonant, sincere voice lifted in prayer, obviously addressing someone the speaker knew.

I turned to see who voiced this prayer of such reality. When he finished, the slim, tall young man with brown wavy hair sat down to eat. He talked with the boy next to him, smiled often, but he didn't look my way. I had to hurry on, for this was my first experience at waiting tables. Finally, I had the plates cleared and rushed to get the butterscotch pudding for dessert. Twenty dishes were carefully placed on a huge tray, and I started into the dining room, balancing the tray on my shoulder.

I still don't know how one can balance a tray and watch where he's going at the same time. Another "green" waiter had dropped a dish of pudding just ahead of me. I stepped right on it, and down I went.

There I sat, in the middle of the dining-room floor with twenty dishes of butterscotch pudding dribbling down over my head, off my chin, and onto my nicest yellow linen dress, the one I had picked out for what I had hoped would be my grand entrance.

A groaning "OOOOHHHHHHHHHHHHH" spread over the dining room. I started laughing. As I looked up, there at the end of the table I saw a genuine smile of mirth joining mine. I had, at least, been noticed.

Many months later Burleigh's best friend told me that the handsome six-foot senior had turned to him at the time and said, "She'll make some missionary a good wife."

Now I can but say, "Thank God for butterscotch pudding." It introduced me to Burleigh.

Soon school was off to a full swing. Every now and then I saw the young man, but he was always rushing about on business. Instead of escorting some girl, he seemed to be keeping company with a tool chest.

Then I realized how many times I'd heard the matron say, "Send for Burleigh."

"Your window is stuck tight?" "The radiator leaks?" "The lock won't work?"

Always the matron's answer to the problem was the same, "Send for Burleigh."

So, that tool chest was required not for a class but by a young man working his way through college. It looked as if the only way I'd get to meet him was to find something wrong in my room. The matron could then say, "Send for Burleigh." But how could I without tools derange something that would require tools to repair?

Before I had solved the riddle, a girl knocked at my door one day.

"Would you like to go with two fellows and me to a mission church?" she asked.

"Mission church? What's that?"

"It's a small church out in the hills where we go every Sunday afternoon to conduct services," she said.

So on that Sunday afternoon we stood on the dormitory steps in the bright sunlight, waiting for the two fellows to take us out to "preach the Gospel."

I turned to see my date approaching, not on a white steed, but in a six-year-old Chevrolet which was shining like the armor of Sir Galahad. He was Burleigh Law.

The next Sunday and the next, I went on these missions. Riding to and from a Sunday service and walking over rough hilly paths to speak to families are good ways to get to know a person. The better I knew Burleigh, the more I liked him.

One fall afternoon I asked him, "What do you plan to be?" Without fanfare, without hesitation he said, "I'm going to be a missionary to the Congo."

Somehow I knew he would be just that. I said, "I am thinking, too, of being a missionary." I wasn't fibbing, for when he mentioned it I began to think, "How wonderful!" My interest in a church-related vocation had begun four years before. But it was only after this conversation that I began to think seriously of the type of Christian vocation I wanted.

Now I had come face-to-face with a young man who knew what he wanted to do. Burleigh told me that afternoon about the two great realities in his life—his conversion and his "call."

Burleigh had been seventeen, a junior in high school in the steel-mill town of Weirton, West Virginia. His Methodist church was like many, a good social organization with a much better basketball team than prayer meetings. Burleigh went regularly with his parents.

Then there came to his church a most unimpressive-looking new minister, neither dashing nor elegant in speech nor even a good conversationalist. In trying to describe him to me, Burleigh searched for some explanation for the Reverend Robert Ling's influence on his life. Finally he said, "Well, he was just a man of God."

As Mr. Ling began his ministry at his new church, he announced a Youth Revival. Burleigh wasn't much interested in the revival part of the meeting, but he knew he'd have to go, and he did enjoy sitting in the back row with the other boys.

Burleigh could never remember just what was said on that Sunday evening, but slowly there came over him a feeling of uneasiness about his own idea of commitment to the Christian faith. He listened and thought as his pastor quietly spoke. Burleigh began to want for himself this sense of purpose which he sensed was in Mr. Ling. When the minister invited the young people who felt a need for Christ to come forward and kneel in prayer at the altar, Burleigh went. He prayed. At the end of the prayer he returned to his pew, but without any sense of peace. He felt more disturbed than ever, and he knew why.

That night, long after the family was asleep, Burleigh lay in bed, thinking. At breakfast the next morning he announced to his parents, "I'm not going to school today."

"Not going to school? Why?"

"I've got to go down to see the manager at the lumberyard. I've got a chest of tools to return."

"Tools from the lumberyard? How come?"

"The gang and I slipped in and got them the other night. We needed them to work on our cars. I knew we could've used yours, Dad—I don't know why but we just decided to get some of our own. Thought it would be fun, I guess."

Horrified, his parents heard the tale of their teen-age thief.

"Then I've got to see Mr. Ralston when he comes off the shift," Burleigh told them next.

"What about?"

Burleigh's face flushed. "To pay him for some gas I took out of his car."

The parents stared at their son.

He returned the tools and paid for the gasoline. That evening he knelt again at the church altar, asking for forgiveness. This time when he ended his prayer, he felt a sense of peace and forgiveness so deep and genuine that it never left him.

When Burleigh was graduated from high school, he

wanted to go to Asbury College where Mr. Ling had gone. But there wasn't money for college in the Law family.

As the time drew nearer, Burleigh did get a promise of a campus job in the Industrial Department, but that wouldn't pay the bills. Then he received a letter. Inside was only one small slip of paper which read, "Asbury College. Received of Rev. R. H. Ling, one hundred and twenty-five dollars, for Burleigh Law account."

With this financial start, Burleigh went to college. There were a few other gifts, but he worked long, hard hours to pay all his bills each term. Quarter after quarter, with hardly a dollar left over, he made his way.

Then came the second great turning point. Burleigh was taking a liberal arts course at the time. He had no visions of serving far away. He wanted to finish college, marry the girl back home, get a job in the steel mill, and serve God there. During his junior year at college, however, a missionary speaker came to the campus. Listening to him, hearing the need for workers overseas, Burleigh heard down in his heart yet another voice, "This is for you." From that time on, his call became clear.

About six weeks after our first stroll Burleigh appeared at my table. Shifting his weight restlessly from one foot to another he asked, "Virginia, would you like to go out with me on Thanksgiving?"

"Well, it would be nice," I said, which was the understatement of the year. Thus, we began dating.

Still the tool chest was a real hindrance. There always seemed to be someone "sending for Burleigh," usually just before a date. I grew accustomed to those smudged little notes arriving while I was putting on the finishing touches. "Sorry, but—the light plant isn't running right." "The boiler has blown a cap." Or, "The furnace needs extra stoking."

My friends thought I was silly to wait, but I would—sometimes a short time, sometimes a long time.

When the bell would ring, I would rush out to find Burleigh in his four-year-old suit, always neatly pressed.

During Burleigh's senior year, I was to be his date for the big Fine Arts program. I had put my hair up in rollers, manicured my nails, creamed my face. In midafternoon, my bell rang.

Burleigh was there with a beautiful red rosebud corsage. Sixteen roses! All I could say was, "Thank you! How beautiful." But my heart sang. I knew Burleigh could not afford to give corsages casually.

Just a few hours later, he said for the first time, "I love you."

I walked on clouds, I laughed, I beamed. This was the answer to all my dreams. Life had no tears for me. Or did it?

Suddenly I faced the ever-present reality—Burleigh's "Call." What was I going to do about that? That he would follow it I did not doubt, but what about me? I had no such clear call. Thinking about being a missionary and having a call were different. Could I go on his Call? I really didn't think so.

The thing for me to do was to pray for God to call me. I prayed and prayed; I pleaded, "Please, God, hurry up. Burleigh's going to Florida to work in a war plant." But no call.

Burleigh left at the end of winter quarter. He could

not stretch his money to cover the next quarter's bills. He had to earn more before he could finish college. The night before he left, I told him I'd give my answer when we met again in June. He did not dream of the reason for my delay, and I dared not tell him. I wanted to give God time before I had to admit my lack of heavenly vision.

As June grew nearer, I became desperate. It looked as if I'd have to say no to Burleigh. Deep within me I realized that I could never come between Burleigh and God's Call. Where, oh, where was mine?

Then a missionary speaker came to our campus. I doubted that he would be interested in my problem, but I had to tell someone.

Quietly the missionary talked with me. "God calls some persons in a very specific way. Some, He just leads. God called Burleigh, but He didn't need to call you. You have been waiting since you were a child, ready to know His will." He smiled. "Go on to the Congo with Burleigh."

Suddenly I knew this was my answer. I went alone to the prayer chapel in my dormitory and thanked God. Then there came to my heart a promise, "I will never do anything to come between Burleigh and God's Call for him. I will accept Burleigh's call as my call."

CHAPTER TWO

No Sacrifice

JUNE FINALLY CAME. MY PARENTS HAD MOVED TO EGLIN FIELD, Florida, during my freshman year in college. When Burleigh was leaving college to go into war work, they helped him get a job in the aircraft woodworking shop at Eglin Air Force Base.

It was wonderful just to be together again, even on this base. My parents soon realized how much the two of us liked each other. Although they thought him a fine young man, they also thought I should finish college before getting married.

My parents and I discussed this, but after all the talks Burleigh and I were married quietly in the Eglin Field chapel on August 23, 1942.

We found an apartment on the base and had the fun of buying furniture and fixing it up. I went to work as a file clerk. My entire check was deposited in the bank, and most of Burleigh's, too. We were determined to return to college so Burleigh could finish his senior year.

We became active in the churches near the base. Burleigh filled in as lay preacher when there was a shortage. Then he was invited to preach regularly one Sunday each month at Fort Walton Community Church.

He loved being pastor, but he didn't enjoy preparing his sermons. Something else always seemed to be taking his time. Usually it was some gadget or his car. One Saturday morning when I reminded him he hadn't prepared his sermon for the next day, he said, "OK. I'm just going out to check the spark plugs. I'll be back in a few minutes." But he worked on the car all day.

I was annoyed as we started to church Sunday morning. I wanted him to preach what the people would call "good sermons." After getting in the car Burleigh suggested, "Virginia, will you lead in prayer at the service?"

"No," I shocked him by replying, "I won't. With the little effort you've made this far, I think you'd better do the praying."

Burleigh prayed, but the prayer wasn't very fluent. Neither was his sermon that morning.

We were happy. Burleigh was getting raises at the base at every three-month period.

One morning as I worked at my desk, the captain from Burleigh's repair hangar walked in with the base chaplain. Suddenly I was afraid.

"I am sorry, Mrs. Law," the chaplain began. "Burleigh has met with an accident."

I waited, frozen.

"He caught his left hand in the shaper. He's at the hospital for an operation. I'm afraid they're going to have to take off his hand. His index finger is torn out completely. His middle finger is just hanging on."

I sat by myself in the waiting room of the hospital. Slowly the clock ticked off the minutes, each minute seeming like ten. After four hours a captain wearing the insignia of a doctor came up to me.

"I think the middle finger will be OK with care. We've spliced a piece of bone into it."

So they hadn't taken off his hand! "What about his index finger?" I asked.

"Well, I tried something. When your husband saw that his finger was severed, he wrapped it in a hand-kerchief and brought it along. I made him a stub. Time alone will tell whether it will be useful."

When I went in to see Burleigh he turned to me and said, "God sure did hear my prayer. Just when the other doctor was getting ready to take off both fingers, this young captain came in. They decided he would take over. He saved my fingers."

The doctor did save Burleigh's fingers. The stub en-abled him to grasp objects so he could continue to work with his hands.

Two months later he was "as good as new." He re-ceived a notice to call at the chief's office.

"We've decided to recommend you for the special eight-week course at Forest Products Laboratory in Madison, Wisconsin," Mr. Allen said. "This laboratory specializes in studies of woods and how to work them. It's a wonderful chance for you."

I wanted Burleigh to go and I wanted to go with him. But we were watching that bank account. It would cost just too much. He went alone; I waited out the lonely weeks.

The war was now at its height. Eglin Field was hum-ming with secret missions, restricted areas, off-limit signs. During this excitement Burleigh built wooden equipment and cabinets for strange, new airplanes not yet named in the newspapers.

Then one day he came home sick with disappointment. "That beautiful Mosquito cracked up coming in today."

"What's so special about that plane?" I asked.

"It's made mostly of wood. De Haviland built this one for the British. It could be the answer to the metal shortage."

Several days later Burleigh alone was given the assignment to rebuild the Mosquito! Highly secret blueprints arrived. For weeks Burleigh worked night and day; his excitement was contagious.

Months later Burleigh called me at work. "Mr. Allen says you can get permission to come over to watch the Mosquito take off."

We watched his Mosquito make another maiden flight. This one was flawless. Weeks later I again stood by him as he received a "Citation for Outstanding Service to the War Effort." Again Burleigh's salary took a jump, this time a big one.

Our weeks were filled with work at the base; our Sundays devoted to the churches. Burleigh became more and more active in preaching. The Eglin Field area had turned from an isolated spot into an overcrowded, underchurched one. Opportunities were unlimited.

We had been married over a year and a half. Every time Burleigh's name appeared on the induction list for military service, he was frozen to the job as an essential civilian. Then a recruitment officer offered him the opportunity to go to New Mexico to help open a wood-work shop at a new Air Force base. This meant another big advancement.

As we pondered this offer, another came from De Haviland. They needed a supervisor in the States for repairs of their Mosquito planes. Another real oppor-tunity for advancement! Another jump in salary! We discussed these offers.

During our indecision another summons from the Army arrived. Burleigh said, "I'm not going to let them ask for a deferment for me. This time I'm going to Camp Blanding to give the Army a try at me."

"Won't your left hand keep you out?"

"They are taking fellows worse off than I am."

"What if they don't take you? What about the offers?"

He looked straight into my eyes. "I'm going to resign and go on back to school. We have enough in the bank to see me through."

I was somewhat shocked. "But if you took either of these offers we could save more, and you could finish seminary as well as college."

Burleigh shook his head. "If I take either of these offers, I'll move into a bigger salary bracket. Then we may never go back. There will always be something else to lead us away—lead us away from the Congo."

I hated to admit it, but I knew that he was right. That paycheck was getting bigger both in amount and in temptation.

Burleigh reported to Camp Blanding and was rejected.

We were returning to college.

Burleigh took his resignation to Mr. Allen who could

hardly believe that Burleigh was actually turning his back on the job opportunities waiting for him. "Burleigh, what is the real reason you've decided to leave?"

Burleigh thought for a moment. "I feel that if I don't go now, I may find it harder to break away next time. And if I did, I might some day be tempted to feel that I had sacrificed to be a missionary."

CHAPTER THREE

Going, Going, Gone!

O NCE AGAIN BURLEIGH AND I WERE AT ASBURY, THIS TIME definitely to prepare for the mission field. But how should he prepare? What kind of work would he do?

Burleigh had visions of a missionary standing under a palm tree preaching the Gospel to people who had never heard the message. Wasn't Christ's great commission "Go ye—and make disciples of all men?" There was no doubt that Burleigh felt compelled to go, but how was he to make disciples? Preaching was the only way he knew. Yet, this way didn't really satisfy him. He was a mechanic, not a preacher.

By a stroke of good fortune, Dr. Alex Reid, a missionary with years of experience in the Congo, visited Asbury, and Burleigh was asked to drive him to an appointment in Louisville.

Riding with Dr. Reid, listening to him speak so enthusiastically of the challenge to "go and preach" as a missionary, Burleigh felt the conflict within him growing stronger. Then there was a sudden jerk, a cough or two, and the car stopped dead. Burleigh got out and pushed it to the side of the road.

"What's happened?" Dr. Reid asked, looking at his watch. They didn't have any time to lose.

Burleigh lifted the hood, quickly checked several things, then looked down the road. A filling station was not too far away. "I'll run and see if they have a condenser," he said, and off he raced.

In a few minutes he was back and quickly put in the new condenser. One whirl of the starter and the car was ready to go. In amazement Dr. Reid said, "My boy, what I wouldn't give to have you in the Congo!"

Dr. Reid talked of a different kind of missionary service; of a great need that a mechanic could fill. He told of a doctor who was often forced to operate by the light of a kerosene lamp because the light motor wouldn't run and no one knew how to repair it. Or, even worse, a motor would suddenly stop in midoperation. He told of ministers who spent hours trying but not knowing how to repair their cars. As Burleigh listened, for the first time he felt he knew where he was headed, and his heart rejoiced.

But there were still three years of seminary, and Burleigh had no love for the academic subjects so necessary for a seminary degree. I was making good progress picking up my liberal arts course where I had left it two years before, but Burleigh was having a struggle. Any excuse was enough to pull him away from his books, and excuses came rattling (or were pushed) into our yard daily. Student preachers, living on a shoestring and serving churches that provided those strings, would ask him just to take a look at this Chevy, or Ford, or other conveyance no manufacturer would claim.

This "look" always seemed to take hours, whether it was just an appraisal, advice, or repair work, and usually it was done just for the love of doing.

In March, 1945, we had our first baby, a boy we named David. With this family addition Burleigh of necessity became one of the "preacher boys" and served a student charge at Campbellsburg, Kentucky. Though sermonizing continued to be a burden to him, pastoral calling was a high joy because this led him to the lovely farms of his parishioners. At every stop there was sure to be some tractor, some milker, some truck that needed fixing. Most of his pastoral work was done standing on his head under the hood. The farmers learned to love "that preacher boy."

Burleigh still wasn't making much progress in seminary. We were perplexed about what we should do.

Two years slipped by. Another son, Paul, came.

Just at this time Bishop Booth, the resident bishop serving the Congo and other African countries, came to visit the campus and to talk to missionary candidates. He confirmed what Dr. Reid had said. "Our Mission surely does need help with mechanical work in the Congo. And we need it right now."

"Would I have to finish seminary?" Burleigh asked.

"I don't think so. Write to Dr. Mel Williams. List all your experience, including Civil Service. He can tell you what you'll need," Bishop Booth advised.

Later, when the Bishop was leaving the campus, he patted Burleigh on the shoulder. "I'll see you in the Congo," he said. That was just the word of encouragement that Burleigh needed. We were as good as off. Jokingly I have often said, "When Burleigh had the choice between going to the Congo or taking Greek, he gladly chose the Congo."

We wrote to Dr. Williams as Bishop Booth suggested.

Back came the reply that we were tentatively accepted —Burleigh for mechanical work and teaching industrial arts and I for general educational work. But Burleigh needed one year of teaching experience, and I must complete my degree.

I wrote home to my parents telling them of this new development. My letter arrived on a Saturday.

Sunday morning at church my parents sat next to the principal of Lively Technical Trade School, who remarked, "You wouldn't know where I could find a good auto mechanics teacher, would you?"

Indeed my mother did! The next Sunday Burleigh and I were in Tallahassee for an interview.

While Burleigh taught auto mechanics to returning veterans at Lively Trade School, I worked toward my A.B. degree at Florida State University.

The next spring, at Eastertime, Burleigh's mother died. Since she was only fifty-three and apparently in perfect health, none of us were prepared for this sudden loss.

This was my first close experience with death, and from Burleigh, who accepted it in quiet faith, I learned that it was not something terrible.

During the week before Mother's Day, I asked Burleigh, "Don't you want to send some flowers for your mother?"

"Send flowers where?" he asked.

"Out to the cemetery."

"She's not there," Burleigh said with such certainty that I felt my suggestion had been rather silly.

When Mother's Day arrived Burleigh picked up the checkbook for our tithe account and looked at the balance. "Is it all right with you if I put fifty dollars in a Missions special gift for Mother today?"

"Of course. That would please her."

Burleigh wrote out a check. "I'm putting flowers where she really is," he said.

One year in Florida was just what the Mission Board had wanted for each of us. We were over the big hurdle of convincing the Regional Personnel Committee of the Board of Missions that we were suitable candidates for service in the Congo. There remained a year of preparation at Kennedy School of Missions at Hartford, Connecticut, and a year of French study in Belgium, the usual procedure for missionaries going to the Congo.

At Kennedy, there were courses on many subjects for our enlightenment—anthropology, linguistics, political science. There were instructions on what clothing and supplies we should take with us.

But no course interested our family so much as "How to Keep Healthy in Hot Climates." The teacher had spent years on the mission field with her own family. She had reared her children there, so she understood not only the health hazards but the secret fears of a young mother going forth with two small sons. As a doctor, she could and did give competent advice and counsel. I'm sure she made more scholarly and profound statements, but the one I recalled many times for reassurance was, "After doing all you can to protect your family, just remember, worm medicine is much cheaper than psychiatric care."

David and Paul couldn't have cared less about worms or psychiatry, but they were enthralled by the ever-expanding first-aid kit. As the class progressed we added merthiolate, bandages, burn ointment, triangles, and compress squares. I practiced the five pressure points on the boys. We played broken leg. Their ribs were sore from artificial respiration. Nothing was left out.

And then came the climax! We added to this marvelous kit a real curved surgical needle and practiced sewing up beefsteak on the kitchen table. Then a hypodermic syringe, an instrument the boys knew all too well from firsthand experience as they completed their innoculation chart. A due respect for this kit was necessary. It was locked and set aside for "Mommie to use in the Congo when someone is sick." Nothing Daddy studied had nearly the appeal that Mommie's kit had.

Then suddenly Burleigh received word to go to New York for a meeting with the Board. The topic of discussion was the building of the Lambuth Memorial Hospital at Wembo Nyama, a mission station among the Batetela tribe in the central Congo. This was the biggest building project ever attempted in that area. Burleigh listened in while the architects discussed the plans with a few missionaries from Congo. The missionaries were uneasy. "We've just never attempted such a project," said one of the preachers who had done some building in the Congo.

"But you've got plenty of machinery to help you this time," he was reminded. Tons of it had already been shipped to the Congo: a well driller, a sawmill, a brick press, light plants, and power tools for the carpenter shop.

"That's fine," said the doubtful missionary, "but who's going to set them up and run them?"

"Burleigh, here," answered the Board Secretary.

Burleigh was startled. "What! Me run those machines?"

As the conversation progressed, Burleigh realized that the Board really was counting on him to install and operate that equipment. He was assailed by real self-doubt. He'd never had any experience with such machines. "I'm not an engineer. I'm just a jack-of-all-trades mechanic. Somebody's made a mistake."

"No, Burleigh," Dr. Archer answered with a confident smile, "I don't think anyone has made a mistake. We think you can handle those machines all right."

"But I've never told anybody I had such experience," Burleigh insisted, concerned lest his application might have overstated his ability.

"We know you haven't," Dr. Archer said, "but everywhere we've checked, those who know what you have done have agreed you could handle the job."

"But what if I can't? What happens then on the field?" Burleigh asked.

"Don't worry. Those cases of machinery have already reached the Congo, but they will be damaged by high water during the rainy season if they are not moved as soon as possible to the station at Wembo Nyama. If you don't get anything done but that one moving job, your going to the Congo will be worthwhile. Do what you can. Don't worry about what you can't do. You haven't misrepresented your ability to us, unless maybe in understating it. The Board's not afraid. Don't you be."

Burleigh left the conference without feeling entirely confident about his changing role in the Congo.

Then came word that we were not to complete the

year at Kennedy School of Missions. We were to make our plans to go directly to the Congo in February, skipping the year in Belgium.

During the Annual Meeting of the Board of Missions in December, 1949, we were formally commissioned as Missionaries to the Congo at Buck Hill Falls, Pennsylvania. We went to Florida for Christmas vacation and to tell our family "good-bye." While there, we were invited to visit several churches to speak. This was fun except for one thing. People were confused about the work of a "lay missionary."

"Not going to preach?" someone would ask.

"How's that, you didn't finish seminary?"

"I can't see no need to go that far from home if ye ain't gonna convert the heathen."

For the Board of Missions to send Burleigh all the way to the Congo just to work with machines—that just didn't seem right. One dear old man came up after a service and said, "I've got ten dollars here. Could you give me the name of some missionary who's preachin' the Gospel out there in Africa?"

So our first missionary job was to try to interpret lay missionary service as an essential part of the work of the church.

While in Florida, Burleigh received word to go to Philadelphia for two weeks to talk with the architects.

Burleigh went off, and shortly I received a distressing letter from him. "These architects think I'm going to build the hospital," he wrote. "I don't know how to build a hospital!"

Two weeks later the boys and I boarded the train in Jacksonville. This was real excitement for David and

Paul. Something terribly important was taking place. That night, with pajamas on and prayers said, they climbed up into their Pullman berth, the old-fashioned kind from which they could peep out between the curtains at the full train of elderly passengers returning from their winter in Florida. I went to the ladies' lounge to prepare for bed. I could hear the conversation going on in the car. Little boys, full of excitement, naturally draw attention.

"Where are you going?" someone asked.

"Congo," said David.

"What are you going to the Congo for?"

"My mommie's a doctor, and she's going to Congo to doctor folks."

"Yeah," said Paul, not to be outdone. "She'll sew you up if you get cut."

"Where's your daddy?" someone asked.

"He's gone to Philadelphia."

"Isn't he going to the Congo?"

"Sure, he's gonna build my mommie a hospital."

So the half-true, half-fanciful story grew while I stood half-dressed in the ladies' lounge, wondering if I should rush out and correct the image being created.

Then one woman said, "I could tell she was a doctor just by looking."

"Yes," added another, "such a professional bearing."

What should I do? Since it wasn't my error, I decided to leave well-enough alone.

When I returned to the car, I was met with very gracious smiles.

Once in bed, I gave one deep sigh of relief only to inhale another one of panic. This train was full of aging

passengers. What would I do if suddenly there came a
feeble call, "Doctor, Doctor!" Fortunately no such call
came.

Next morning Burleigh stood waiting to greet us.
David and Paul ran to his arms, and he lifted them both
at once. When he turned to kiss me, I could see the
troubled look in his eyes. As soon as we were alone he
said, "Those architects thought I was a trained engineer
coming to study those plans."

I could sense his uneasiness. He had applied as a
mechanic. Now suddenly he was supposed to build a
hospital, the biggest project ever attempted in the central Congo.

I tried to reassure him. "Well, the New York office
has all your references. They know your training and
experience. You've talked to Dr. Archer, so you aren't
misleading anyone."

Burleigh waited a few moments. "No, I haven't mis-
led anyone." He smiled, "Well, God may need a jack-
of-all-trades in the Congo, although I don't know why
me."

A few days later we were ready to leave the United
States. We arrived in New York and boarded our
freighter. A tugboat slowly pulled us away from the
docks into New York Harbor starting us on our way for
our first term of four years. As we stood at the rail, Burleigh put his arm around me. "I feel a part of some
great divine purpose," he said.

CHAPTER FOUR

First Glimpse of the Congo

L ATE IN THE AFTERNOON IN MARCH, 1950, WE ANCHORED some ten miles off the coast of the Congo, out of reach of its mosquitoes, to await the morning and our river pilot.

At six o'clock the next morning we stood watching our first close-up of the Congo. The dark, almost black-looking waters of the Congo River came rushing down into the blue ocean. Along the shores was heavy, deep-green, and aged-looking foliage hugging close to the river's edge. Taller bushes, palms, and other trees closed off any view beyond the river, though from time to time we could see grass-roofed huts standing where the foliage had been cleared away.

Slowly, as our freighter made its way up the river, the scenery changed. Gradually the green gave way, and bare cliffs rose along the river's edge. Near noontime we could see ahead a sharp horseshoe bend in the river. The big motors of the ship began running at full power. The boat vibrated as the propellers strained against the current. The pilot headed the ship straight for the curve of the shore. It looked as if we would go dashing right into the cliff. Suddenly we felt the big ship swing around with the current, and we were safely around the

"Devil's Whirlpool" and headed into the inland port of Matadi.

On the steep, grassy hills, nestled among moss-covered rocks, stood the city. Tall cranes outlined the shore, and streets led abruptly up past stores to colorful homes on the hillside. One tall building towered above the others.

"That's the Métropole Hotel where you'll be staying," the captain told us.

It seemed ages before we were docked alongside the river warehouse. Another age passed while we were being checked and declared ready to disembark. It was almost five in the afternoon when we checked into the hotel. We were given two big rooms opening onto a small terrace. From there, we could look far down over the ships in port.

We watched the Africans passing nearby in the street. Some women in colorful dress carried on their heads huge flat baskets loaded with produce. Others walked along with a single bottle or a bucket on their heads. Babies rode contentedly, strapped to their mothers' backs. In all the noise I heard not one baby cry. The voices were a jumble of sound.

Suddenly it came to me, "I can't talk to these people!" I knew nothing of the vernacular. And I had not had the usual special study of French, the official language. "It scares me. Listen to all that talk. Do you think I can really learn a dialect?"

"Don't worry, Sweetheart," Burleigh said. "You couldn't keep quiet in any language."

While Burleigh took care of the long customs inspection, the children and I spent a few days taking walks about the streets or sitting in the cool court of the hotel. There we found other children whose families were staying in the hotel. David and Paul joined them in play. Besides my two Americans, there were three children who spoke French, two who spoke Flemish, and two little Africans who spoke some dialect. They were obviously having a good time.

"What language did you use?" I asked the boys at lunch.

"Oh, laughin', gigglin', and kids' talk," said David.

Finally, our luggage was cleared and checked for the train to Léopoldville. Taking our lunch and drinking water with us, as we had been warned to do, we left for the station. Our first-class tickets simply meant we had a seat, as the train coaches were the same in every class. The train was off, jerking and jolting over the rough track, showering us with cinders through the open windows.

When the train stopped at a station, people came running and gathered about the train. Many of our passengers climbed off to greet friends. We heard music, a loud brassy blasting. Burleigh leaned out the window to look back.

"There's a band in the car behind us," he reported.

People began to dance on the platform. Each person chose the beat he liked best, so there were as many rhythms as there were people. A long toot came from the engine. With much shouting and calling, passengers ran back onto the train, some handing their babies through the windows to fellow travelers while they ran for a door. We were on our way, but every window was filled with passengers leaning out as far as possible, waving and shouting. Soon we reached another station, and our dancing scene was repeated.

Slowly the engine pulled its load up one hill after another, each higher than the one before, moving from sea level to 2500 feet and then descending gradually. More than twelve hours after leaving Matadi, we pulled into the flatlands of the Congo River at Léopoldville, a distance of two hundred miles.

Léopoldville was a beautiful city, well laid out with wide streets, walks, parks, and towering buildings, all very modern. Yet along the streets we again saw barefoot women with loads on their heads. One carried a radio balanced up top. The Congo seemed to be a paradox.

After an overnight rest in Léopoldville we were off again, this time by plane for Luluabourg—and surrounded by dried fish. What a smell, all the way! But we were getting closer and closer to "our" part of the Congo. We put down at a dirt landing field with one small shelter.

A Presbyterian missionary was there to welcome us. On his radio he had picked up the word that we were coming and relayed it to our Methodist mission. He assured us that someone would come for us soon. The mission was only two days away. I noticed he measured the distance in days, not miles.

We went to a hotel to wait, and late that same afternoon, Dr. William Hughlett, a Florida friend, arrived from Minga, one of the stations on our Methodist mission. "I heard over the Presbyterian broadcast that you were coming," he said.

Early the next morning, after years of dreaming and

planning, months of preparing, and four weeks of traveling, we were with Dr. Hughlett in his four-year-old
Dodge on the last leg of the trip to our new "home."

The first Congo road we traveled on was a wide,
sandy one leading out across the grass-covered plains.
It was fairly smooth although two narrow ruts marked
the best route to follow. Occasionally we met another
vehicle, and one car had to climb up out of the tracks to
the side. Our car slid and swayed as we made our way.

Trees began to appear along the route, occasionally
shading the road. Before long we were in the forest
region where the tall mahogany trees and thick underbrush growing in a solid wall along the road made
traveling cooler than on the plains.

The sandy road gave way to clay. Instead of swinging
and swaying, the car jolted and banged. Hard rains had
washed down, leaving trenches in the clay. Heavily
loaded trucks driven over the wet, soft clay had made
deep tracks that the sun had dried into hard ridges. It
was very rough going.

A wide cleared space ahead gave signs that we were
approaching our first African village. About fifty feet
from each side of the road was a row of small, round
huts, each hardly tall enough for a man to stand up in.
The grass roofs came to a point at the top and were tied
into what appeared to be a short handle. The untrimmed
edges, giving the house a shaggy look, extended over
walls plastered in red clay, some of them decorated with
designs drawn in white clay.

The road was long. The sun became hotter and hotter. The first villages were interesting, but before long
every hut looked like its neighbor. The monotony was

broken only by an occasional chicken which suddenly darted out trying to cross the road. Would it make it or not? One could always secretly wager its chances.

"We'll take a rest stop at the top of this hill," Dr. Hughlett said. "There is no village nearby."

He stopped the car and we got out. True, there wasn't any village. There wasn't anything. He handed me a roll of toilet tissue without saying anything. He and Burleigh started on down the road ahead. David and Paul followed them. I looked back the way we had come.

"Oh, for a gas station!" I thought.

Once again we were on our way. The road went on interminably. Finally, as we came around a curve, a truck jolted toward us. "We're in good luck," said Dr. Hughlett. "The ferry to Lusambo where we'll spend the night will be on our side. That truck just drove off."

I'm not sure what I had expected. Surely I had more sense than to think of a ferry such as one in the States which carried dozens of cars. But I couldn't have imagined anything like this; four big hollowed-out logs supported a flat platform just large enough for one car. A motorboat was alongside the ferry.

It was leaving when we drove up, so Dr. Hughlett blew his car horn. The motor on the boat stopped. The ferry began to float back toward shore and was pulled up to the bank and secured. As we sat watching, under a blazing sun, the car was soon full of all kinds of flying creatures.

"Here. Rub some of this on your arms and legs," Dr. Hughlett said, handing me a bottle of insect repellent.

But it seemed as if the insects liked me even better with flavor rubbed on.

Taking their time, four of the ferrymen lifted two heavy beams from the ground and rested them on the ferry in a steep incline to make a track.

"Maybe you'd better get out while I drive on," Dr. Hughlett suggested.

He didn't have to make that suggestion a second time. We were quickly out. One of the men stood at the far end of the ferry and motioned to Dr. Hughlett to drive up. Slowly the car moved toward the beams and rolled against them. The beams moved, pushing the boat away.

"Stop!" the ferryman shouted in Flemish.

Another man ran over and picked up two big iron pins. The men pulled the ferry back into place and dropped these pins down through the beams and into the ferry floor to hold them. Someone had forgotten these the first time around.

Finally, we were on the ferry. There were no guard rails, just the flat platform. "What would happen if you didn't stop?" I asked Dr. Hughlett.

Chuckling he answered, "Maybe you'd better ask missionary Dot Rees that question."

Something told me I would be happier if I didn't pursue the subject.

Dr. Hughlett opened the car trunk and took out a loaf of bread and tins of cheese, corned beef, and pork and beans. There was drinking water for David and Paul and coffee for us. It was then past two o'clock.

As we ate, Dr. Hughlett said to me, "Lusambo will

be your last opportunity to shop. I suggest you stock up on what you'll need. The transport supply truck made its monthly trip last week, so it'll be three weeks more before you can get anything sent up. Maybe you'd better leave your order now for next month's groceries. A Mr. Moyes, who lives here at Lusambo, fills our orders when the truck comes down."

I felt a little overwhelmed at having to plan this far in advance.

"And, by the way," he added, "the dry season is beginning. That means the river barge won't make it upriver this far. You'd better stock up on flour and sugar to last through the dry season."

"How long will that be?"

"Just three months if we're lucky."

I thought to myself, "Three months if we're lucky. What would it be if we weren't lucky? Let me see. Buy now for the next three weeks of April and write my order for the grocery truck coming to haul up the orders for May. That means planning now for seven weeks, besides ordering flour and sugar for three extra months. How much flour does a family of four need for three months?"

I'd always prided myself on my ability to plan my menus and shop just once a week, and that was before the days of deep freezers, too. But this Congo planning completely stymied me. Grimly I sat in the car considering my shopping list as we swayed over the river. Making a list was impossible. I decided to wait until we got there and to shop by sight.

It was over an hour before we drove off the ferry at Lusambo and started toward the store.

I knew the stores would not be like the ones in the

United States. But I suppose we always imagine that the unknown will be like the known, so I pictured something like a country store in northern Florida.

We drove up before a mud building with a steep-sloping grass roof. Strung across the wide front porch were lines hung with rows and rows of carefully folded bright cloths measured into six-meter lengths. On the porch was an open sack of rice with an old soup can for measuring, a sack of peanuts, a box of dried fish, and a box of coarse gray salt. On the posts supporting the roof were beads, bright bracelets, and head scarves. A Congolese man sat at a sewing machine, busily turning the wheel with his right hand as he sewed a pair of trousers.

Burleigh walked over to the machine. "Look at this. Isn't it something? It doesn't have a belt. He just turns the wheel by this small handle. Direct drive." Smiling, Burleigh added, "It's a Singer, too. I see the Singer salesman beat us here."

Prospective African customers, standing or squatting on the porch, moved aside to make a passage for us. As we entered, the proprietor chased away a few chickens and dusted off the rough counter. Our eyes had to adjust to the dim light before we could see.

"Potatoes?" I asked.

"No, we don't carry any here."

"Lettuce? Carrots?"

"What's that?"

"Onions?"

"Ah, yes." With pride the proprietor brought out some onions about the size of large acorns. At least they had the onion smell. "How many?" he asked.

Dear me! How many onions of that size could I use?

On the shelves were some tins among which I spotted some Klim, which is *milk* spelled backwards. I had heard about it. When the appropriate measurement of water was added, the dried powder would once again be milk. I asked to see a tin, struggled to read the label with my limited knowledge of French, and tried to figure out how much milk one tin would make so I could divide the total by a day's supply. "Oh, for just one milkman even if he did bang the bottles at five in the morning," I thought.

Flour came twelve five-pound bags per drum. It wasn't safe, I was told, to buy it in an opened drum, so I took one drum although it looked like enough flour to start a bakery. It was. I just didn't know then that I would bake any bread my growing sons ate.

"Remember to order for the dry season," Dr. Hughlett reminded me. "Order on the heavy side. You'll use the supplies."

"But the flour won't be fresh after three months."

"Well, it really doesn't make too much difference. The flour that arrives just at the beginning of the rains is the flour that got stranded coming upriver," he said. "It'll be the same flour."

"Isn't it buggy by then?"

"Yes, but you can always sift it through a nylon stocking. That will catch the bugs your sifter misses."

He was right. You can do just that. And now I will add one word to this useful advice. Put the flour in the stocking to begin with, not in the sifter. The sifter just cuts up the worms. Then shake the stocking hard over a pan and empty the residue into the garbage pail without looking even once at the stocking. This will greatly enhance the flavor of the bread.

Shortening and salt were familiar even in this setting. Sugar came in forty-kilo bags. "Watch out for the sacks that are wet on the bottom. You'll have syrup by the time you eat down that far," Dr. Hughlett warned me.

There were tins of peas, beans, soups. I got some of everything available.

Just as we came out of the store, a Chevy carry-all drove up, its back end almost dragging on the ground. A young man got out, dressed in a white T-shirt, knee-length shorts, high white socks, and heavy brogan shoes. He came toward us, smiling as Dr. Hughlett greeted him cordially and introduced him as Dr. Deale, the dentist from Wembo Nyama.

"Just call me Hugh, Burleigh," the young doctor said, extending his hand and welcoming us all. Then to Dr. Hughlett he said, "I came down to get the new missionary family, but I see you beat me to them."

"Didn't you get the note I left at the Minga crossroads?" Dr. Hughlett asked.

Hugh shook his head. "I stopped to ask if there was any message, but the sentry wasn't there. We heard on the radio that the Laws had arrived, but didn't know if anyone from Minga would hear. When I got to the ferry down here, I saw that you had signed the passage book yesterday."

As they discussed this I thought, "Why didn't they just phone and arrange for someone to meet us?"

It hit me suddenly. There are no telephones in all this part of the Congo!

The next morning we divided our load between the two cars and were off toward Minga and then on to Wembo Nyama. Remembering yesterday's trip, I asked, "How's the road from here on?"

"You ain't seen nothing yet," answered Dr. Deale with a twinkle in his eye.

I wasn't sure just what he meant, but I soon learned.

We were riding "on bottom" to begin with. "These springs don't have much tension left," Burleigh remarked casually. "Have you tried adding extra main leaves?"

"Not me. I don't try adding anything unless it's in someone's mouth," the dentist answered. "I'm no mechanic."

Keeping on that road was something. Instead of hairpin curves these were bobby pin ones, with the slope out toward the ledge. I felt we needed a rope to attach ourselves to the cliff while swinging around.

The road surface was red clay mud washed into gullies. Speeding along at twenty-five miles an hour, we suddenly came upon a gully across the road. Wham! On with the brakes—which didn't hold—and bamm! Down we went into the hole.

"How're you coming?" Burleigh asked, turning around and looking back at David, Paul, and me.

"We're still here."

Without warning we met another hole in the road. This time the brakes suddenly took hold. The carry-all stopped, but the load in the rear didn't. Everything shifted forward, including three Laws.

At the suggestion of Dr. Deale, Paul and I rode with Dr. Hughlett for awhile, but that car wasn't really much better. The Dodge was "on bottom" too and the road the same. There was only one difference. I could at least hear what Dr. Hughlett said above the noise of the motor.

Kasongo Batetela, where Dr. Hughlett had to stop for a few minutes, was our first Otetela-speaking village. The villagers gathered around the car, pointing, laughing, and chattering. Our children laughed with them. I asked Dr. Hughlett what they were saying.

He chuckled. "They say you know how to give birth well."

That seemed a strange way of putting it, but I sensed that it was a compliment to the boys.

When we were ready to leave I asked, "How do you say good-bye?"

"When you are the one leaving, say, '*Utshikali la wulu*,' which means literally 'stay with strength.'"

I tried, but we were off before I could say it. Then I asked how to say hello.

"*Moyo* is the hello to one person in Otetela. To several persons it is *Moy'anyu*," Dr. Hughlett told me.

Practicing my first Otetela lesson kept me busy for many kilometers and was better than thinking about the roads.

We stopped in another village so that Dr. Hughlett could see the medicine man.

Behind us we could hear the carry-all sputtering as it pulled up the hill. As it drove up, Paul jumped out to go back to his daddy, and I followed. Burleigh had the hood of the car up. He took out his scout knife, opened the screwdriver blade, and began working on the carburetor. "Try the motor now," he called.

Hugh started it up. A few more turns of the screwdriver and even I could tell that the car was running much better. The Congolese standing around were greatly impressed. I could hear them saying one word, "*Utshudi*."

"What does *Utshudi* mean, Hugh?"

"It means in this case 'mechanic.' They are saying that Burleigh is a mechanic."

When Dr. Hughlett came back, we started on our way. "The medicine man is going to bring me some herbs for the hospital," Dr. Hughlett explained. "I have a young mother without enough milk for her baby, and he has an herb that helps produce milk."

I was surprised. "But isn't he a witch doctor?"

"Not exactly. He may practice some magic, but he's a regular medicine man. He calls me his fellow doctor, so he thinks he and I are the same."

I could tell that Dr. Hughlett got some pleasure out of such a relationship. "Can he actually cure illnesses?"

"Yes, some things. Unfortunately, not enough. The big problem is his dosage. One teaspoonful may vary from five percent of a potent drug to ninety-five percent. There is no control of standards. A little might cure, a lot kill; so there are real chances in taking drugs from him."

At the crossroads to Minga, we left Dr. Hughlett and traveled on to Wembo Nyama with Dr. Deale. Now the roads were somewhat better. Instead of being on crooked clay roads, we were again out on sandy plains. As we went around a curve, Dr. Deale began to blow his horn. He kept blowing. "For the ferrymen," he shouted above the motor.

Down a hill and around a curve and we reached the river. I wondered about the brakes as we stopped on a steep incline facing right into the water. "Throw one of those logs under the wheels," Hugh called. Burleigh jumped out and quickly placed two big logs under the wheels.

I mentioned that the trees along the curve in the road were marked as if they had been hit often.

"Yes," said Hugh, "some trucks just head for those trees to be sure they stop."

A crowd of Africans sat in the shade, with large, oval-shaped shallow baskets beside them. Some baskets were piled high with small pancakes about one inch thick and three inches long. Hugh told us they were banana cakes.

We waited while the ferry came over to our side of the river. It looked very much like the one at Lusambo, but there were two improvements. First, it had three big metal boats for a hull. They actually looked as if they would hold us up. And second, it was run by cable. On the beams placed for us, Hugh drove onto the ferry, with the usual starts and "Stop!"

Then the pedestrians filled up the platform around the car. The ferrymen changed the cable from the front to the back of the ferry, and the swift-flowing current swung us out across the river. It felt as if we were going downriver for sure, but the ferry quickly moved across and bumped the other shore. Burleigh was intrigued by the arrangement. We drove off and were on our way again. Hugh seemed to relax. "That's our last ferry."

We traveled over the rolling plains. From the hill-tops we could see for miles across brown, waist-high grass. "This is the grass they use to roof their homes," Hugh explained.

Scattered across the plains we could see clumps of trees making small forests. "Look for antelope near those trees," Hugh told us. "Lions, too."

A little later we passed a village. Instead of the small, round huts we had seen near Luluabourg, the tall houses of this village were about twenty-five feet square with thick, well-trimmed roofs. In front of the houses large, vivid red cannas bloomed, and bushes of bougain-villea bent over. Above, white clouds floated in a clear blue sky.

I had not dreamed the Congo would be so pretty, but Burleigh said he had always thought it would be.

Two hours beyond the ferry, Hugh turned to me. "Better get your hair combed. We're just about home."

I doubted that just combing my hair would do much good, but I made the effort.

Wembo Nyama was a large, beautiful station with ten missionary families, a church, a school with several departments, a hospital, and several resident Congolese families. It had been established in 1914 after Bishop Walter Lambuth made his way into this section of Central Africa, deep in the interior and remote from foreign influences. He decided that a mission should be built near the village of Wembo Nyama to serve the Batetela tribe.

Whether the welcome comes from Biblical example or not, I'll never know, but a visitor expected in a Bate-tela village enters through a palm-branch arch and proceeds down a street decorated with branches and flowers. So Wembo Nyama village greeted us.

Waving and smiling, a large group of Africans and missionaries came out to greet us. "*Yayo! Yayo!* Welcome! Welcome!" they called.

It was good to come to the end of our journey.

As we approached the station, I saw a row of stately palm trees leading from the main road to the station proper. To the left was the old hospital; to the right the brick primary school with its grass-roofed dormitories. Here the road became divided by a wide lawn between the two roads stretching more than a quarter mile. Then the roads joined again to make one that led to the girls' hostel at the end of the compound.

I was not surprised to see the beautiful tropical flowers, shrubs, and palm trees, but the lawns were a complete surprise. I hadn't expected such lovely grass. "Someone has done a lot of work to make such charming surroundings," Burleigh said. And we thought with gratitude of the pioneer missionaries who had opened the station a generation ago and all those who had worked here through the years.

To our right, as we drove on, stood the normal school for teachers, the Bible school for pastors' training, the tall bell tower above the Lambuth Memorial Church, the homes of the missionary families, and at the end of the street, a large house we learned had three nicknames: the "council house," for the many meetings held there; the "archway," for the architecture of the porch; and the "W-dears," for the single women, or, in Otetela, *Wamamas*, who lived there.

On our left, past the hospital, stood the graveyard where the early missionary babies who had died for lack of modern medical care and a few Portuguese traders were buried. A long lawn and more missionary residences rounded out the buildings up to the fork of the road.

Off at a right angle from the road in front of the church was a road leading to a network of streets lined with the homes of the Congolese preachers, teachers, married students, household helpers, nurses, and workmen who were part of the station. Their children became our children's playmates.

On our trip up, we had been somewhat prepared for our new house. There had been a recent increase in missionary personnel, causing a shortage of living quarters. Although the missionaries had been pushing hard to get a new house ready for us, the rainy season had lasted longer than usual the previous year, so the bricks didn't get burned. The workmen, sawing all the lumber by hand, had suffered delays, and there hadn't been enough boards to finish the windows and doors. They had hoped to install glass windows, an improvement over the wooden shutters used in other homes, but the glass hadn't arrived from Léopoldville.

After words of welcome, our new friends escorted us over to the house. It did eventually make a lovely home, but that morning it was only three-fourths finished. It was made of red brick with cement floors. The ceilings were of beautiful brown mahogany boards, which, I later learned, swelled and shrank with rainy and dry seasons, popping and cracking in the process. A few screens were in place, but no windows and no doors. The furnishings gave the house the look of an old-time parsonage. The people had donated reed chairs, odd tables, and dressers. I was surprised to see a light blanket across the foot of our bed. "Do you need a blanket here?"

"Most nights we do, before morning," a missionary told us. "We are on the plateau where we get a breeze. Usually when it gets really hot, it's just before a rain. Then the rain cools everything off. A hot night is rare. Maybe two or three a year."

"That's good news," Burleigh said. "It doesn't matter how hot it is in the daytime if it cools off at night so we can sleep."

I noticed mosquito nets carefully mended and hung from frames over the beds. "Do you have many mosquitoes here?"

"I'm afraid so," our guide said, "but by using nets and spraying, we control them pretty well."

Beside each bed a woven grass mat lay on the floor. On each dresser was a container—a quart jar, an aluminum pan, or a vase—each filled with bright flowers. I know now, as I could not realize then, that some missionaries had put hours into cleaning, furnishing, and arranging that home for us.

After a quick tour of the house and washing up from the trip, we sat down to visit with our new friends. Our conversation covered our stateside locations, our schooling, our training, and a list of "Do you know . . . ?" Then conversation about the station ran low. "Did you know the lions were at Dimandja Shinga yesterday?" one missionary said to another. "I don't think they attacked anyone, though. A man going to his garden early in the morning saw one. He climbed a tree, and near noon his friends found him still there.''

Of course our ears pricked up at such news. I spoke a bit uneasily. "Do lions ever come here?"

"Not very often," the missionary assured me. "The last time was around mid-February."

My heart missed a beat. Mid-February and this was only mid-April.

Then Burleigh and I heard in detail how the lion came upon the station, wandered around different homes, roared out back of one house, and ate two goats.

I looked around our house. No windows, no doors. I couldn't imagine those mended mosquito nets being much protection.

But lions or not, we were "home." Almost six years to the month from our resignation at Eglin Field we arrived at Wembo Nyama, deep in the Congo.

Friends back in the States tried to locate Wembo Nyama in an atlas and wrote, "You aren't even on a map. How far back in the bush can one get?"

It was true. We weren't on a map. I wrote, "Find Luluabourg, Stanleyville, and Kindu. Between these points on the map you'll see a great expanse. We live in the middle of that."

It wasn't an empty expanse, of course, just one with nothing map makers record, namely cities or towns. Yet we felt at home.

CHAPTER FIVE

Learning to Live in the Congo

WE MIGHT BE "HOME," BUT OUR HOUSE WAS FAR FROM being a home yet. Burleigh went right to work trying to finish it. He felt the need for screens, windows, and doors as much as I did. As he worked, I was busy trying to learn how to run a house in the Congo.

"You'll need help in the house," my missionary adviser told me.

I felt rather superior as I said, "I don't think so. I never did in America."

We had been making the rounds of our neighbors for meals each day. But now the time had come for me to take over for our family. With my supplies from Lusambo and items lent or given to us, I was equipped to begin.

A few more days passed.

"I know a cook who worked for a missionary before. Maybe you'd better hire him to help until you get accustomed to the wood stove," my adviser again suggested.

This time I felt less superior. "Maybe so," I admitted. I knew now that cooking in the Congo was a time-consuming business. It meant baking all bread and cookies, grinding all my meat, and so on, and using a wood stove which had to be stoked. And there were no modern conveniences for cleaning up. So I hired my first helper.

The major operation of even getting a meal planned took place every morning. First, I listed what I had that we could eat; then I went to my neighbor's to get her to translate my menu into Otetela. Next I took it back to the new cook and tried to read it to him, since he couldn't read. He didn't understand my pronunciation, so back we both went to have the neighbor give the orders. Then he prepared the food—and often we didn't recognize it when it came to the table.

"What are you going to do for water?" my adviser asked me a few days later. "My helper who's been bringing it to you is going to work in his garden next week."

That was the first time I had fully realized that someone had been carrying all the water to the drums placed about the house. "Where can we get it?" I asked.

"Down over the hill at the spring."

"Can I drive the car to the spring?"

"No, you'll have to bring the water up in buckets. The workman brings two buckets at a time, one on each end of a pole across his shoulder," she explained.

I could hardly see how I could bring water for the family, bucket by bucket. Certainly Burleigh couldn't take time out to do that job. We hired our second helper.

Then my cook came in very disturbed. He kept pointing out behind the house to the pile of stovewood which had dwindled. Somebody else had been supplying the wood that I had taken for granted went with the house!

Someone must go out to the forest to hunt for wood that would burn into coals, not just ashes, bring it in on his shoulders, and chop it into lengths for the stove. And enough had to be kept on hand so there would always be dry wood. Here was another job neither Burleigh nor I could handle if we were going to do any mission work. We hired our third helper.

Our dirty clothes began to pile up. "My laundryman can help you this week," a neighbor offered.

"Wonderful!" I accepted, thinking that I'd need help only for that week. Then I watched the laundryman. I saw him lift the water from the drums, bucket by bucket, heat it on a half drum in the yard, then rub the dirty clothes on a wooden rub board. The next day he ironed them with a heavy charcoal-heated iron that I could hardly lift. I hired my fourth helper.

Yes, we became one of those servant-loaded missionaries that you have read about. We even hired a fifth one, a gardener named Djamba. We needed vegetables. Our home was new and so was our garden plot behind the house. Djamba first had to clear away the brush and trees. It took him weeks because he had only an axe and a machete. Then more weeks were spent building a grass hut where he could protect from the heavy rains some seeds he planted. While these were growing, he dug a series of trenches. He filled these first with a layer of grass to keep the rains from packing down the dirt, and then with compost which he had brought from where the people threw their trash in the village. Only then was he ready to transplant. Over each trench he built a frame and covered it with palm branches to protect the crop. Gardening was a full-time job, and months later, cabbage and Kentucky Bibb lettuce had never tasted so good.

I loved to go out and watch Djamba work in the garden, for here I could see something that was clearly progressing. One afternoon while I was there, Djamba's spade struck something. He dug about a little and lifted a human skull.

"Good horror!" I shrieked, and rushed off to tell an experienced missionary.

She was calm. "Oh, yes. Wembo Nyama station was the 'plot of death' before the early missionaries came. The people staked their old or helpless ones out here to die."

It sounded gruesome. But as I looked at the growing plants, I could see that it was certainly no longer the plot of death.

It took us several weeks to hire our help, start our garden, unpack our bags, and settle in our Congo home. Burleigh was busy finishing our own house and helping with jobs on the station. During this time the intuitive Congolese, working with him, were looking us over and appraising us.

When we had been there some time, a large group of village Christians gathered at our front door, bearing gifts of rice, chickens, eggs, peanuts, bananas, and pineapples. They had come to receive us into their fellowship and to give to us our African names, the names we would be called in Batetela-land, names we came to love and cherish as an identification with the people.

Pastor John Wesley Shungu (now Bishop Shungu) was the spokesman for the group. With pride he said to

Burleigh, "After weeks of watching you work, we bestow upon you your Otetela name, *Uwandji Utshudi A Koi.* In Batetela-land a leopard is the king of the animals. Your name means Chief Leopard of the Artisans."

It was a name of real honor. Burleigh was recognized as the Leopard Chief of the blacksmiths, the carpenters, the masons, the sawyers. He was chief of all who work with their hands!

A Leopard Chief must kill a leopard and make a belt which he brings home. The villagers watch with great interest to see who among his wives gets it. When a wife appears wearing the *Uya Koi,* she is recognized wherever she goes as the "Chief's favorite wife." So, to me went the name *Uya Koi.* In the Congo, I was recognized as Burleigh's favorite wife! For David, just five, and Paul, three, the Congolese simply Otetelarized their American names. They became Davidi and Paulu.

There was gratitude in our hearts as we looked over the gifts spread before our door, all given in sacrifice to show their love and acceptance of us.

I looked up at Burleigh, the "Leopard Chief of the Artisans." I remembered how he had searched to find his place of service in the mission field. I could recall the shocked looks and the question, "Not going out to preach?" Burleigh's name, Leopard Chief of the Artisans, meant that these people understood he was here to serve with his hands.

Burleigh worked hard to make our home pleasant. To have an inside bathroom, we'd need running water. He followed the ingenious arrangement used in the other homes. On an elevated platform he built outside the bathroom wall, he placed empty gas drums connected at the bottom. From these he ran one pipe directly into the bathroom. This was our cold-water supply. Then he built a brick furnace and ran another pipe through a drum on top. A fire in the furnace provided our hot-water supply. Slowly he added doors, windows, and screens to the house. Then Burleigh had to get to other jobs.

There we sat with just odds and ends for furniture. "That will just have to be your realm," Burleigh said to me. "Decide what you need. Then I will work on it when I have time."

So with an old Sears catalog, I tried to plan what I wanted.

One night after supper Burleigh drew plans for what I wanted, designed so the furniture could be built at the station. The supervising of the job was mine. I went out to the carpenter shop many times during the day to see what the men were doing, for some of our sketches were completely revolutionary. I hadn't seen on the mission any dining room chairs that one person could lift gracefully. They were all too heavy.

My sketch called for a chair without two-by-four crossbars to support the structure. It also avoided the straight backs suitable only for a British judge. I wanted a nice curved back to fit my shoulders. The carpenters took a piece of mahogany, ten inches thick, and chiseled out the curve. They did a grand job. Gradually we added beds, dressers, and a hutch cabinet. By October, all our boxes of supplies and household goods from America had come by barge to Lusambo and then up to Wembo Nyama by truck. Finally, we were really settled.

In the meantime Burleigh was hard at work planning for the big, new job on the station, that of constructing the Lambuth Memorial Hospital. The first phase took place in Lusambo where tons of wonderful, revolutionary, new machines stood waiting. Nothing like them had ever been seen in this part of the Congo.

The machinery had been packed in cases and shipped from New York by men accustomed to dock cranes for loading and unloading. But in the Congo the great cases had been dumped off the river barges by manual labor. There they had lain for months, close to shore. Now it was the rainy season. The river was swelling and beginning to flood over the banks. It was essential to move these cases to dry ground.

Burleigh and a group of Congolese men started the job, using sign language as their common language. They put down boards for skids, tied ropes and chains on the cases, then hooked on the winch cable of the new Caterpillar tractor. Slowly the huge cases moved, riding on the skids. The ropes broke, the chains slipped, the boards slid, but the cases were finally all on dry ground.

Next, there was the almost impossible job of loading those heavy cases onto the truck without any cranes. It was amazing what the Congolese workmen could lift, chanting and pulling in unison. Some of the cases weighed tons. Burleigh dug a deep ditch sloping on one side so the truck could back down into it, bringing the truck bed level with the ground. Again with a cable, the "Cat" winch pulled while the workmen pushed, and a case groaned onto the truck. When the truck was loaded, the cable was attached to the "Cat," and slowly the truck was brought up out of the ditch and back onto the road.

The next phase was to transport the cases from Lusambo up to Wembo Nyama over 165 miles of the worst road in the Congo. One trip sometimes took many days. For part of the way through the red clay hills, the road was only a slick, narrow ledge with a sheer drop-off on one side. It then rushed steeply down into the valley, around a sharp curve, and onto a narrow bridge wide enough for only one vehicle. Beyond this bridge was yet another hill, rising just as steeply, so a truck had to go fast downhill toward the bridge for momentum to get up the opposite side. This was only one of many similar situations along the route.

One hill in particular became famous. On several different trips the workmen spent hours trying to get to the top of a two-mile stretch. Often, in pouring rain, they dug soft mud from under the truck and placed grass, sticks, leaves, palm branches, anything they could find under the wheels. Then with a rope tied to the front bumper they pulled the truck forward inch by inch. Often, though, it would just start to move only to bury itself again in the mud. Then the process would start all over again. Many times, when Burleigh and the workmen finally reached the top, they were too exhausted to cheer. But when the truck groaned up the hill under its own power, the workmen, straining with every turn of the wheels, would let out a cheer that rang through the countryside.

These bridges they crossed were made of logs tied together with forest vines and topped by boards often loosened with use. Two parallel heavy planks served as the car track. There were no side railings for protection.

The heavy rains washed out one pole underpinning after another. Often a bridge developed a deep sway in the middle. A heavy truck would creep onto a bridge built to hold half that load.

When a bridge had to be replaced, a government man would supervise the work. Sometimes the mission truck would come around a curve and find a barricade across the road, and beyond it no bridge across the river. Burleigh and the workmen at times sat waiting for days until the new bridge was finished.

When the dry season came in mid-May, new problems arose. Out on the plains between the stretches of forest and hills were sand beds. Soon the dry sand ruts were deeper than the truck clearance. The road workmen threw the loose sand out to the side of the road, building it into high mounds. Burleigh tried to ride these ridges alongside the ruts and sometimes succeeded. But at other times the heavily loaded truck would skid, swing about, and bury itself in the loose sand. Then came the job of jacking up the wheels, cutting armloads of tall grass from the plains, and building a grass ramp over which the truck could ride out over the sand.

So the hard work of moving the heavy machinery went on, trip after trip, week after week.

When Burleigh was on a trip to Lusambo, I had no way of hearing from him. Sometimes many days passed while I waited anxiously, not knowing what was happening. But fortunately I had now started regular work in the mission. This kept my days full and busy.

I had been asked to take the woman's school on the

station. Each afternoon the wives of the students in the school and a few village women came to learn the three "R's," plus sewing and cooking. I enjoyed teaching them.

But they had no place to practice. One day I mentioned this to Burleigh.

"Why don't you build a regular stick-and-mud practice house?" Burleigh said. "Like the ones they have in their villages? If you will draw up what you want, I'll try to plan for workmen to build it."

That's how Burleigh became involved in the woman's school. After the nice, big practice house was built, he collected some hard, black anthills that reminded one of bowling balls. Using these as bricks, he placed them around an emptied gas drum with one end hinged for a door. Now we had an oven. We could cook. And whenever Burleigh came by to check on our progress, the women would cheer. He was our sponsor.

The last items we had added to our own furniture were two living room chairs of Danish Modern design, without arms. I upholstered the cushions with materials that came with our household goods. One I did in a deep maroon, and the other in a lovely gold brocade. The work was finished just in time for my meeting of our village Ladies' Circle.

As the women arrived, they sat timidly around the room in all the chairs in a very formal, orderly fashion. But the gold chair remained vacant. A late arrival was an old woman with many years in God's service. I offered her my new gold chair. She hesitated, so I repeated, "You sit here, Mama."

Looking at me with an expression which said, "You asked for it," she climbed up and sat in the traditional African squatting position used by those unaccustomed to chairs. There were half-concealed smiles on the faces of my other guests, more accustomed to the strange ways of the white people. But this was her way of sitting, and there she sat all evening.

When the last guest had gone, I turned back into my living room. "Good horrors! Could it be that the children who had come with their mothers were not house-broken!"

All over the floor were puddles. They were small ones, but puddles they were. What a mess! The next morning the whole floor was scrubbed with Lysol.

When I told a senior missionary, she smiled. "It's not at all what you think. When drinking tea or coffee in your home, the Africans pour out the last few drops to show how much they hate to see their cups become empty. It is their way of being polite."

That was fine on their hard dirt floors, but on my cement one it was a problem. At our next social I provided a big potted fern and announced, "Here is the place to pour your last drop."

The women and I learned together at the school. It was the ideal place for me to practice Otetela. Listening to them chatting away, especially on sewing day, I learned both words and customs. And we became friends.

One afternoon the conversation was about the beauty of missionaries. One really attractive girl, with a figure all the missionaries admired, was considered too skinny.

Another was ruled out because her legs were too thin.

Finally my name was mentioned. Before I got the once-over, I spoke up, "I'm too fat."

They laughed with glee that I had understood their conversation. Then one girl spoke up. "Oh, Mama *Uya Koi*, we think you are pretty." Seeing the doubt in my eyes she added, "because you start big at the ground and go all the way up." I learned it was true that they liked plump women. A Congolese wishing to compliment you might remark, "Eh, you look well fed."

My days were more than full. But after class, with Burleigh away, night soon came, and I was lonely. After the two boys had gone to bed, I often sat by a kerosene lamp trying to read. Then in the quietness of the Congo night above the chirp of the crickets, I would hear the the sound I was listening for: a Brockway truck shifting gears, coming home.

All of us were striving to learn both to speak and to live in the Congo. We seemed to be making progress.

David and Paul appeared to be wonderfully healthy. Then one morning David came in with a disturbed frown on his face. "My ears are sick," he complained.

Oh dear! Some horrible African disease! I reached for my book, *How to Keep Healthy in Hot Climates.*

"Where do they hurt?"

"Oh, they don't hurt, they're just sick."

"How do you know they are sick if they don't hurt?" I asked.

"These Africans just talk, talk, talk, and I don't hear 'em. It just rumbles in my ears."

I laughed. It didn't take an ear specialist to understand that "sickness." Their talk rumbled in my ears, too.

I was home alone one afternoon when a soldier came to the door bringing a dirty piece of yellow paper. He handed it to me. I tried to read the very poorly spelled English words. Finally I deciphered the message. Two weeks before, Burleigh's dad had died suddenly from a heart attack.

I wondered how I could tell Burleigh. His dad was very important to him. He talked more about "my dad" than about any other person. I waited until both boys were in pajamas, ready for bed. We all went into our living room for our evening prayers. There, as we waited for Burleigh to read the Bible, I told him. He sat very still. Then, quietly he said, "He seems closer to me now than when he was in the States."

Turning the pages of the Bible, Burleigh read with a voice filled with confidence, "In my Father's house are many mansions: If it were not so, would I have told you that I go to prepare a place for you? And when I go and prepare a place for you, I will come again and will take you to myself, that where I am, you may be also."

We now counted our residence in the Congo by months rather than weeks. It took many months and more trips than we ever counted, but eventually some sixty-five tons of machinery—well driller, brick press, sawmill, light motors, and power tools—were hauled from Lusambo to Wembo Nyama.

As the cases arrived at the station and workmen began to open them, Burleigh was faced with another

problem—rust. Rains had filled the cases with mois-
ture, and rust had had almost a year to work on the
machines. It took hours for the workmen to clean it
away and to oil the exterior parts. Burleigh had to dis-
mantle the moving parts, bearings, and gears, clean
away the rust, then reassemble them. For this work he
needed trained mechanics. There were none, so he
chose the four most likely prospects to begin "on-the-
job training." There were other willing, ready watchers,
always under Burleigh's feet. David and Paul were two
of them. And a cook in one of the missionary homes was
another. Talasua would rush through his work and
appear, still wearing his bright red plastic cook apron,
wherever Burleigh was working. Finally, the missionary
gave up and asked Burleigh to take Talasua as his first
full-time student in mechanics.

Talasua's interest increased as he was on the job. He
seemed to drink up everything Burleigh said and was
always the last one to leave. One afternoon I heard the
truck coming up through the station, running irregular-
ly, starting and stopping. Talasua was learning to drive.

Teaching and turning over responsibility for machinery had its hazards, however. Burleigh felt that he
should not take time to make every trip to Lusambo for
supplies once he had someone who could drive well
enough. So one day he sent Talasua down for a load.
Returning home at night, Talasua went around a curve,
met a car—and our radiator was smashed beyond use.
Wembo Nyama was seven thousand miles from a
Brockway dealer. With luck it took six months to get
repair parts.

Burleigh *had* to have a truck. First, he built a small

platform on the front of the truck. On this he sat an empty fifty-gallon gas drum. He attached the radiator hose and filled the drum with water. On every trip the truck made, the warm water would be drained periodically and replaced with cold at a river crossing. For over six months the truck was kept running by this method.

CHAPTER SIX

Trees, Schools, and Idols

SETTING UP THE SAWMILL WAS THE FIRST ORDER OF BUSINESS, but even before this could be done, a simple shelter had to be built where the parts would be protected from the rain. For it was not a quick and easy job to put the sawmill in operating condition. No instructions had been sent, but Burleigh knew it was essential that the mill be level so the logs would feed into the saw exactly right. Dozens of heavy, straight and true boards were needed as a platform for the mill.

He was dependent for such lumber on the hand sawyers. Their method was to fell a big mahogany tree, dig a pit underneath it, and then, with one man in the pit and another above, saw the tree into boards. Burleigh discovered that of the available lumber, every piece varied in length as much as two inches.

He called the sawyers to the station and showed them the new sawmill, laid in pieces under the shed. He explained to them how it would work, how it would help build the hospital, and how important the hospital was. He appealed to them to bring him some straight boards. They did their best and finally produced some usable lumber. Burleigh then figured out how the parts of the sawmill went together. The Congolese marveled that he could make every piece fit without a guide.

At last the sawmill stood completed, and the day came for its first trial. People gathered from all the surrounding villages and watched in amazement as the huge circular saw bit its way through the logs, sending up a stream of fine sawdust and making a screaming noise such as they had never heard. Fulton with his steamboat created no more excitement than did Uwandji Utshudi A Koi with his sawmill. Without reservation it was declared a *Dikambu dia mamba*—a marvelous feat.

Up to this time, we had purchased all our lumber from the African pit sawyers. They chose the trees, sawed the boards, and then carried them on their shoulders to the road where a truck could pick them up. It was a different matter to get enough logs for a sawmill. Burleigh needed to fell trees in an area where the tractor could snake them out to a road for the truck.

Finally he found just the area. Then came the job of getting rights to the timber. One afternoon we all drove to the village of Chief Ona Lua. The chief and his village elders were sitting under the low, grass-roofed palaver shed. When they saw us, they all rose and came out toward the jeep.

Ona Lua was a young man, a chief for only a few months since the death of his father. He was dressed in Western pants and shirt, whereas many of his elders wore only a piece of cloth printed in vivid shades of deep blue and green wrapped around their hips and rolled into a knot at the waist to hold it up.

Burleigh went forward to meet the Chief, extending his right hand and supporting his right arm with his left hand in the African gesture of respect as they shook hands. The Chief came to greet me and then turned to the boys. He smiled with amusement as David and Paul each extended his right hand supporting it with his left in imitation of their daddy. The Chief lifted both boys down, and the two ran off with some village children to chase goats.

As Burleigh leaned on the jeep and chatted with Chief Ona Lua, the elders gathered around and other villagers also pushed in to hear. The two men talked about the harvest, the rains coming too soon, the taxes to be collected. Only then did they get around to discussing the sawmill. The Chief had seen it working and was struck with wonder at such a machine. "Did you build sawmills in America?" he asked Burleigh.

"No, but I've seen some operate."

"*Dikambu dia mamba.*"

The conversation then turned to the discussion of the new hospital.

"It will be a big hospital," Burleigh explained. "We want one building just for the mothers. They can give birth there. Fifty can stay at one time. Then there will be another big building where the doctors can operate, some X-ray rooms where they can take pictures of a person's insides to see what's wrong, rooms for drugs so we can always have everything our doctors need. Besides all this, there'll be rooms for sick people to come and stay until they are well—room for 250 people at the same time."

"Mete, that *is* going to be a big hospital," Chief Ona Lua said, shaking his head in amazement.

Burleigh said, "Have you ever looked up inside the mission church?"

"*Elu.*"

"Did you notice how much lumber you can see?"

"*Heyama Mvuta,*" (more than you can say) answered the Chief.

"Think of ten times that much building." Burleigh waited for the image to register. Then he added, "That's how much lumber we will need for your hospital."

The chief stood quietly, his face drawn as if in deep thought. Burleigh waited again. Then he spoke.

"Do you know of any place we can get lumber except trees?"

The chief shook his head. "No, it takes trees to make lumber."

"Then we will need trees, hundreds of them. For weeks we've been looking for a plot where we could get these trees. We've found such a plot behind the village of Okunda. We'll have to build a road back from this main road across the crest of the hill so the truck can get in to haul the logs. You are the head landowning chief of that area. We want to borrow this land long enough to cut some timber for the hospital."

The chief understood. "Will it still be my land?"

"Yes. All we want is permission to cut some trees for the sawmill. I'll build the road. You can haul the cotton from your gardens over it."

The Chief turned to his elders. Now they chatted together, and so did all the villagers crowding around.

Finally, one old elder shouted, "Quiet! Our chief speaks!"

Calling a young boy, the chief said, "Run, bring me a white chicken."

Quickly the boy was back. Handing the chicken to Burleigh as a binder, the chief said, "I agree."

Burleigh's closing the timber concession deal with Chief Ona Lua was only the beginning. Our mission legal representative made a formal application to the Belgian government, and a state agent came to check the plot. Sometime later this agent called together Chief Ona Lua and his subchiefs, who sealed the contract with their thumbprints.

Work in the forest then progressed without further hitches. A road was built, a path for the tractor was cleared, the pit sawyers felled the trees, and Burleigh's men loaded the logs onto the truck which hauled them to the sawmill. The men had good supervision from *Kapita* (foreman) Wembo Lua. Though not so young and strong as he had been when he came to work on the mission years ago, he was still a real leader among the workmen. He was dependable and trustworthy, a quiet man who never raised his voice or shouted, but who didn't need to speak loudly to be heard.

Others on the station needed the jeep, so Burleigh got a motorcycle for quick trips to check on work in the forest and for running about the station. David and Paul liked it even better than the jeep. One would ride sitting on the gas tank in front, the other on the rack over the rear wheel.

One afternoon all three of them had gone to the forest. As they were speeding back, the motorcycle slipped slightly in a sand bed but straightened up and rushed on. When they reached the station, Paul looked back. "Daddy, where's David?" he shouted.

They discovered they had left David sitting in a sand bed about two miles down the road. He had gotten up, dusted off his pants, and started walking up the road. He knew his daddy would be back.

Never in the Congo can one tackle jobs one at a time. While Burleigh was facing the problem of trees and lumber, he also faced the need for bricks. Since the early days of the mission, bricks had been used for building. But these had been hand pressed, with a workman tamping the wet clay into molds, then turning them onto boards to dry. They were fragile, and a good workman could make only about two hundred bricks a day. The hospital would need a million bricks before it was completed. Burleigh had hauled the brick press up to Wembo Nyama, but it was another complicated machine that had to be set up. How would the bricks be handled? It was simple for a workman to walk over and lay his one freshly molded brick on a board, but when the press started operating, sixteen thousand bricks a day would come rolling out.

There had to be sheds for drying, with racks on which to stack the bricks. Carts were needed to transfer the bricks to the sheds, as well as tracks on which those carts could run. The bricks had always been fired during the dry season, but it would take more than ten years to fire all the bricks needed for the hospital if the drying season was only three months. There had to be a permanent kiln so the bricks could be fired as fast as they were ready.

For three years now Burleigh had been trying simply to get all the wonderful machinery into action. For three years he had trained truck drivers, cat skinners, and mechanics. Many missionaries had helped, yet Lambuth Memorial Hospital still existed only on an architect's blueprint, and the Belgian government had not yet approved the American-drawn plans.

Our doctors were laboring in an old metal-roofed dispensary, using grass-roofed, mud-walled huts for wards. Babies were dying from tetanus. Our nurses feared that the mud flooring in the delivery room was causing the infection. "Clean dirt" dug from a deep hole, unexposed to surface contamination, was brought in. But this was only temporary relief. Burleigh felt he *had* to make progress on the hospital.

Burleigh wanted to spend all of his time on this project, but he couldn't. There was always something calling him away, some other pressing job.

While sitting on our porch sewing one morning, I heard a commotion and saw several African nurses, still in surgical gowns, racing on their bikes down the road. One came directly to our house.

"Where's Uwandji?" he screamed.

Our water carrier shouted back, "Out in the shop!"

The shop was behind our house. Hearing the question, Burleigh came running out, jumped into the jeep, and sped down to the hospital.

Another nurse rushed up to my door crying, "Give me your flashlight, quick."

I found Burleigh's big hunting light and thrust it at the nurse who raced toward the hospital.

The story soon came back. In the middle of an operation our doctor's light motor suddenly stopped. There he stood with no light, no fan, no pump. He couldn't leave the patient to see about the motor. He could only do what he could for the patient while his nurses rushed to get Utshudi A Koi.

Burleigh tried to crank the motor. It fired but died again. Quickly he pulled off the carburetor. Sure enough, someone hadn't strained the gas through the old felt hat kept for that purpose, and dirt and water got in. Burleigh cleaned it out, replaced the carburetor, pulled the crank wheel once more, and the motor started. The operation could begin again.

Besides the constant emergencies at Wembo Nyama, our own station, there were frequent pleas for help from other stations. Each had light motors, cars, trucks, and various equipment which had to be kept in repair. The Congolese had no training for this work, nor often did the missionaries themselves. They called for Burleigh to come for a few days to help them out.

Being isolated, we needed a way of keeping in touch with outside areas. Shortwave radio sets operating on the forty-meter band were our answer. These had to be installed, aerials had to be raised, and someone had to teach an operator. The Conference appointed Burleigh to that job. The missionary responsible for hauling supplies from Lusambo to five other stations of the mission went on furlough. Burleigh was appointed to that job. These were jobs that had to be done, too.

One day Burleigh got a frantic call from the Katako Kombe Station, about seventy-five miles from Wembo Nyama, to repair a light motor.

This time the boys and I went with him. At the end of

the day we were waiting for dinner while the children played on the porch. Suddenly the door opened and a seven-year-old girl came rushing into the room headed for the kitchen. In midflight she stopped, turned. We could see in her eyes that she had a new idea. She headed toward her room and returned with a doll in one hand and a dismembered arm in the other. Holding them out to Burleigh she said, "Uncle Buree, my doll's been waitin' for you."

Burleigh fixed the doll as she knew he would. But there were just too many odd jobs that required his attention. His major work at the hospital was interrupted again and again.

Into all this frustration came engineer Al Burlbaugh, appointed by the Board of Missions to Wembo Nyama. What a joy it was to have him! Each morning Burleigh and Al planned to divide their responsibilities; Al would go to the brick press, Burleigh to the sawmill. But it always worked out that they would go together to the brick press and then both go to work at the sawmill. When the day's work was over and the workmen gone, they would talk with their foremen, then stand for hours looking over the whole project and making plans. The Africans nicknamed them the *wasa* (twins). Now the "twins" began to make headway on the hospital project.

While Burleigh had his problems with timber concessions, bricks, and mechanical emergencies, I had mine at woman's school. One morning a student appeared at my school office with sad countenance asking for permission to go home. "My mother has died," she said.

With my pass and my condolence, off she went to her home village.

The next week she again appeared with the same sad countenance and story of her mother's death. After several deaths of her mother I learned that before offering my sympathies, I must always ask, "Is this the mother who gave you birth?"

It wasn't. In fact that mother was hale and hearty, harvesting her rice crop. Within the village life, everyone is related to everyone else, so a mother to them could be simply that woman at the end of the street. Once I understood this custom, I felt I knew how to control the absences.

The next time a student asked for leave because her mother had died, I inquired, "The mother who gave you birth?"

"*Elu*, yes."

Off she went. She returned to us and a few days later came to me with the same request.

"Didn't I give you a pass just last week for the funeral of the mother who gave you birth?"

"Not her funeral, Mama; just her death. She was dead, but she hasn't yet finished dying."

"Has she finished dying now?"

"I'm not sure, but my family sent word they thought so."

Complicated and strange, I thought. Then I remembered: in the Congo when a patient sinks into a deep coma, there are no scientific instruments to determine whether life has ended. I was slowly learning the ways of the Atetela.

Burleigh and I weren't the only ones who were learning. Seated one afternoon on our front porch were two little boys. One was our son, Paul, with light, straight hair, fair skin, bright brown eyes. The other was Utuka, with black, short, curly hair, dark skin, shiny black eyes, the son of foreman Wembo Lua, on Burleigh's workline. Both boys had been scrubbed until their skin shone. They had put on their best short pants and colorful shirts. They were waiting for the arrival of Dr. Ralph Dodge (now Bishop Dodge), then the Executive Secretary for Africa from our Board of Missions.

Utuka began teaching Paul a greeting for this important visitor. Twice he said it, and Paul repeated it. Then in disgust Utuka turned to Paul and said, "You're gonna talk just like a white man."

"Going to talk like a white man." Didn't he realize Paul was a white boy? No, he didn't. Paul was his playmate, his friend.

Going to my class one afternoon, I noticed four nurses with a stretcher, running across the station toward the schools. Then I heard the distant sound of weeping and moaning.

I quickened my pace and arrived at the school just as the nurses started back to the hospital with someone on the stretcher. The students were milling about, wringing their hands. When they saw me, some came crying, "Mama leee, Mama leeee," and told me what had happened.

During their noon hour a primary-school teacher had sent one of his older students up a very tall palm tree to gather palm nuts. Somehow, this agile student had lost his footing. He slipped down through the vine belt he had tied around the tree and fell some twenty-five feet to the ground.

We spent that afternoon waiting for doctors' reports, none of which sounded good. All the next day we lived under the aura of hovering death. That night, sitting on our front porch waiting for Burleigh to come for supper, I heard a terrible wailing down at the hospital.

My cook came in looking shocked and bewildered. "His family has arrived," he told me.

This could explain the wailing but not the obvious emotional disturbance of my cook.

Then he added, "If the boy dies, his family is going to place his corpse in the teacher's doorway."

"Oh," I shuddered. "Why do that?"

"It is an old, old custom of our tribe. I've never seen it myself, but I've heard my grandmother tell about a time when it happened. Our forefathers thought this would prove who was guilty. Anyone who moved the decaying corpse would be guilty of the death."

"What did the people of the village do the time this happened?"

"They just moved their village. The village of Shungu Koi was once down by the swamp. It was moved because of a corpse left at a door."

We looked at one another, each with his own thoughts. "But that wouldn't prove anything," I said.

"I know it and you know it. They don't know it."

That night the student died. The teacher was secretly taken away from the station for safety.

Obviously we were all very concerned. What *would* we do if they did place the corpse at our teacher's house? Could we, as missionaries, move the body without bringing condemnation upon ourselves and the mission for breaking an ancient tribal custom?

Several persons tried to talk with the family. Since it was the custom among them for children to serve adults, someone asked, "Would you have objected to his climbing the tree if you had been here?"

No one said anything for a long time. Then an older man said, "No, not likely."

The leaders suggested, "Let's take this to the chief and let him cut the palaver."

This gave some gleam of hope but no real assurance that the custom would not be carried out.

That night the cool air vibrated with the beating of the funeral drum and the wailing of relatives. No one was sleepy. Every movement on the station brought us to our window.

Finally I went to bed, but I couldn't sleep. That horrible wailing sounded to me like the crying of the doomed. Burleigh couldn't sleep either. He gave up trying. "I'm going down to the hospital," he said.

He walked over to the grieving family, gathered about a small fire in the hospital yard, and sat on a stump near them for a long time, saying nothing. Occasionally, he added a log to their fire, stirred up the coals. He just let them know that he grieved with them.

Next day we watched while the family prepared the body. Then with relief we saw them turn and, chanting their grief, go toward their home village. They were not going to leave the corpse.

As the work on the hospital project grew, Burleigh and Al hired more and more workmen until over one hundred reported each morning in front of the carpenter's shop for roll call. Many of the men left home long before daylight, walking as far as ten miles to work. Those from villages where there was an African pastor had to miss customary morning prayers, while many came from villages without pastors. Burleigh and Al were concerned about this. They felt that not only were the workmen missing something, but they too, as missionaries, were missing an opportunity for worship with the men.

They talked this over with Wembo Lua and his assistant.

The foremen agreed that in pushing to get the job done there was danger that the job would become more important than the men doing it. "Let's have our own early morning service here," Wembo Lua suggested. "We can have it just after roll call when all the men are here."

Burleigh shook his head. "If we have worship after roll call the men may feel they have to attend. They may think of it as something we force them to do."

Wembo Lua nodded thoughtfully.

"Then let's begin our service at seven o'clock. At seven-fifteen we will have the roll call. No one has to be present until the call. But those who want to come for the service will not need to leave home any earlier than they have been leaving."

It was decided that Burleigh and Al would each lead the services one morning a week, and Wembo Lua and his assistant would each provide someone for other mornings. On Fridays, they would teach the men hymns, Bible verses, and prayers.

Studying and preparing for their devotionals, Burleigh and Al began to understand the needs of the workmen, and this opened to them many unrealized opportunities. As they listened to the Africans speak of their experiences, they began to see things they had missed in their American culture, and they felt a closer fellowship with the workmen. The workmen, in turn, felt closer to their missionaries who now became approachable.

One morning Talasua, the truck driver, came to work terribly upset. Burleigh had planned to send him on a trip, but he could tell immediately that such a job was out for that day. He smiled at Talasua and said, "I don't think you're up to driving the truck this morning."

"No," said Talasua. He stood for a long while alone, and then walked over to the toolroom where Burleigh was. Pulling up his trouser leg, he pointed to a wound still oozing a little blood.

"My wife bite me," he said.

After closing the door for privacy, Burleigh spent almost an hour talking with him. It was a long story. Finally Talasua admitted that it hadn't all been his wife's fault.

"But if she only loved me like Mama Uya Koi loves you," Talasua said.

"Do you think you treat your wife as I treat Mama Uya Koi?" Burleigh asked.

Talasua thought and said, "No."

"Why don't you begin to change the way you treat her? Then maybe she'll change in her treatment of you," Burleigh advised. So counseling became a part of his day's work.

Chanting and singing their newly learned hymns, the workmen labored day after day. The truck coming from the forest with workmen riding aloft the load of logs sounded like a moving revival meeting as the great old hymns rang out across the mission.

As Burleigh and Al spoke with the workmen of personal problems and listened to their talk, they realized that the message of Christ's love was not really reaching the men. "Why not have a workmen's revival?" Al asked.

Wembo Lua and Burleigh agreed that this was a good idea. "Who could we get to lead the services?" Wembo Lua asked.

"Who would you like to have?" Burleigh countered.

They discussed the different pastors. Some were pastors of a station church, better educated than most. Others were pastors of churches in out-villages but were graduates of our mission Bible school.

Wembo Lua suggested Pastor Kikumba Paul from the Katako Kombe district. Although most of his work had been among the small village churches, he had always had an effective ministry. He was more the workmen's equal in background, but was capable of leading them in a spiritual search.

They consulted other foremen, and Pastor Kikumba was their choice.

Burleigh promised to invite him. "Where will we meet?" he asked. "In the church?"

"No," answered the foremen almost in unison. "Here in the carpenter shop."

Pastor Kikumba came. Each morning at seven o'clock he conducted an hour's service, the men sitting around on the carpenter's benches. At three o'clock they met for another service. Pastor Kikumba knew how to speak directly to the hearts of these workmen. Following the services, Burleigh and Al helped the pastor counsel any who asked for help.

Several days after the services began, a workman came running in late one morning. He rushed to the front and flung down several machetes and a pick axe. "Here they are," he announced. "I stole them. God knows this is now all I have left to confess."

Turning toward the door, the man took from his wife a witch doctor gourd and laid this beside the tools. "I gave three goats and four months' salary for this gourd. It was supposed to protect us from harm and bring peace to our home. We know now it is no good. My wife and I want to become Christians. We are giving this up. In its place we are buying a Bible."

He reached for the Bible his wife was holding and lifted it high, peace shining from his once disturbed eyes.

Burleigh came home with a joyous heart. He had come to the Congo to build the Lambuth Memorial Hospital, but his real service was symbolized by that surrendered witch doctor gourd.

CHAPTER SEVEN

─────────────────────────────────────

How Boring?

V IRGINIA, WHAT DO YOU DO OUT THERE TO KEEP FROM
being bored?" a friend wrote.

"Bored?" What a question! Life on a mission station
was anything but boring. Before we left for the Congo,
another friend greatly concerned for our children had
asked Burleigh while two little Laws listened, "What
will your children do in the Congo?"

Patting both boys on the head, Burleigh had replied,
"They'll just put down their roots and start growing."

David and Paul had no trouble getting their roots put
down and their reaction was "How else would you want
to live?" They loved all those "Uncles" and "Aunts"
they suddenly acquired. Around the world children on
mission stations have sought a title for senior missionaries and have arrived at Uncle and Aunt. "Mr." or
"Mrs." sounds too formal, and first names too familiar;
Uncle and Aunt are just right.

One of these aunts once reported that she heard two
young voices at her back door, those of our Paul and
another boy, both four years old. Paul was leading the
way.

"Come on, Ricky, let's get a cookie."

Peeping through the screen door Paul pointed. "See that box, the red one, right there?"

"But this isn't your house, Paul. You don't have any cookies here."

"But this is our Aunt Lippe's. You know an aunt would want us to have a cookie."

Fortunately the aunt was there to welcome her callers. She gave them each a cookie and advised them always to ask before taking cookies out of the red box.

Wembo Nyama was the biggest mission station in Central Congo. There were always other children for Paul and David to play with, and when their daddy let his two little mechanics go along, there were rides in the jeep and trucks. Birthdays came just as they did in the States. The preparation began days in advance for often the gift had to be built or made. Whispering and closing of doors were expected. No one would dare peep "'cause that spoils the fun, doesn't it, Mommie?"

The birthday cake was always a very special one decorated for that person on that day. No two could ever be alike. One was in the shape of a rabbit, another a bike, another an African hut all covered in brown coconut with orange frosting on the sides.

Surprise gifts always seemed to appear. When packages arrived from grandparents or friends, only one or two gifts were opened. The rest were carefully stored for just such a day. All missionaries had their trunks in the attic which usually yielded something as a gift for the party. Sometimes it was a very simple gift, but when one is seven thousand miles from a shopping center, it is amazing how much joy even the smallest gift brings.

Birthday parties weren't just for the children. The adults had their parties, too, and everyone joined in the celebration. We had lots and lots of birthdays.

My first year in the Congo I faced Christmas with dread. Then the first of December we were invited to a neighbor's house for tea. A bright Christmas wreath greeted us at the door. Inside she already had a few decorations up. "I always begin Christmas on the first day of December," she explained, "and each week I add something more until Christmas day. It helps the Christmas spirit to grow."

I went home to start my own preparation and soon realized why she started early. Without stores, bakeries, or toy shops, one had so much more to do. I made fruit cake, candying the fruit myself: orange peel, green papaya for citron, pineapple preserves, dried banana slices, grated and dried coconut. Add some borrowed nuts, and I had fruit cake.

We had a nice, big duck ready for Christmas dinner. Corn was ground for dressing, and sweet potatoes were bought from the villagers. Mango sauce, cooked thick and tinted red, or, better still, a native timwimbi berry which didn't have to be tinted became our cranberry sauce. Aunt Dot Rees made perfect pink, green, and white mints, so she made them for all of us. Fudge, peanut brittle, and popcorn balls were my job.

But what would Christmas be without a tree? There were no real Christmas trees about, but a few very big, old cedars were growing on the station. "We couldn't cut them down," I lamented to Burleigh, "and besides they're too big even if we could."

"Ask if we may have a few branches," Burleigh suggested.

I asked and reported back that we could.

A few days before Christmas, Burleigh came home from the carpenter shop carrying a strange-looking pole. It was about four feet tall, three inches in diameter and was attached to a base to hold it upright. All around were holes drilled at an angle down into the pole. "Let's go get our cedar," Burleigh called to the boys.

They came home with the pungent-smelling branches. They began at the bottom of the pole, breaking off branches and sticking them into the holes. Up the pole they worked, shortening the lengths as they came toward the top. At the very top Burleigh put a stick to hold the star. Then they decorated it. Burleigh's ingenious tree became the model for our Congo Christmas trees.

Sometimes our Christmas boxes from home arrived on time, but more often not until March or April. Starting months ahead, Burleigh built block sets, seesaws, tables and chairs, picture frames, fruit bowls, meat pounders, bread boards, and doll furniture.

Other missionary fathers joined him at the shop as Christmas drew nearer. Even the mothers were forbidden to visit the shop during that season, but we really didn't have time. Sewing machines were humming, making shirts, dresses, doll outfits, and stuffed toys.

So we had gifts for our family, gifts for our missionary children, and gifts for our African friends. And from these friends we received eggs, chickens, bananas—gifts that expressed the spirit of Christmas.

Another important occasion of the year was the Central Congo Annual Conference of the Methodist Church. Missionary and African delegates gathered from each of our seven stations and districts scattered throughout an area the size of the state of Ohio. It covered the northeastern part of the Kasai Province and the western part of the Kivu Province. Bishop Booth presided. For ten days the work of the stations was discussed. Policies were made, rules set up, reports received, advice and encouragement offered, and elections held. It was also a time for visiting. Groups sat about laughing and talking. Some missionaries were famous for their stories, and these were repeated from year to year by request.

One of these was about the missionary who could roar like a lion. One night he was visiting in a village, and the village people came to call on him in the yard of the guest house. It became late. He was weary. He waited until he almost fell asleep, knowing it would be impolite to leave them and go to bed. Then he slipped out behind the guest house and roared a loud and long mating call. The people quickly dispersed, running to their houses. The missionary had just started into his house, relieved at having started the crowd home, when from just behind him a lion answered his call.

Conference was also the one time of the year for dressing up. There was always some missionary just back from a furlough, and as she unpacked, we would gather around to get a look at the latest fashions.

We could usually tell the year of a woman's term by the condition of the clothing she wore. The first year the clothes were bright and pretty. The second year the light shades were very light, almost white, the dark shades dimming. By the third year, the blues were purple, reds became pink, and browns, rust. The fourth year there were patches; colors became unimportant, and any blouse might have three kinds of buttons.

Hoping to avoid this state, I sent for my Sears catalog. When it arrived and I had sent back my order, I learned that the time taken to receive the book and return my order was too long. The book was out-of-date. But Blackburn, our beloved purchasing agent in New York, looked up the old catalog, figured out what I wanted, and airmailed the appropriate pages of the new book to me. Now the question was, "When the order comes six months later, will I still want what I have so carefully ordered in my attempt to avoid being out-of-date?"

Hair styles definitely dated you even if clothing did not. Heaven help some poor soul who let it be known that she could cut hair! Her back porch became the station beauty parlor. When I laughed one day at my inexpert new Toni wave, a veteran missionary replied, "You should have lived out here when we didn't have Toni waves."

On Saturday afternoon, usually at least one man would be seated in the backyard in the highest chair available, a cloth draped about his shoulders, while his wife attacked with a pair of hair clippers. It always took time and patience to get started. The clippers must be adjusted correctly so strictly by feel the husband could tell his wife how to proceed. One missionary commented, "We are never nearer to a divorce than at hair-cutting time."

Another husband, after looking at the finished job,

turned to his barber and asked, "Tell me just one thing, Dot. How *did* you do it?"

I had taken my "Ten Easy Lessons for Haircutters" at Kennedy School of Missions, but all that did was to place me in the category of those who should know better. Burleigh had wavy hair, and I couldn't notch it. It just waved at another place. But when a visiting bishop arrived and requested a haircut, that presented another problem. I could write a stirring article on "Haircuts Given to Bishops Sitting on a Box under a Palm Tree."

We took some interesting trips in the Congo. Burleigh often received an urgent call to another station for some repair work. Whenever it was possible, he asked me and the boys to go with him. Traveling between two stations at night, we kept our eyes on the road looking for animals. We expected to see one around each curve, were scared to death we would, and disappointed when we didn't. Burleigh always took his guns as protection against dangerous animals.

Along the Congo roads are high banks which the road builders, working only with hand shovels, have thrown up as they cleared the roadbed. At regular intervals there are trenches through this bank so the heavy rains can run off without washing gullies in the car tracks. Each one of these trenches is a possible hiding place for a big animal like a lion, leopard, or antelope.

One night, just when we were becoming weary of looking, I suddenly saw the flash of light I was watching for. "Stop quick, stop quick!" I called out. "I saw the flash from some big animal's eyes. It must be three feet high."

Burleigh stopped, reached for his gun, slipped in a shell, then slowly backed up until the spotlight could shine down the trench. At the end of the trench the bank was three feet high. The grass moved slightly. "Look!" I whispered.

The tall grass swayed, and off the bank into the trench jumped a small, domestic kitten! This poor kitten was afterward referred to by the boys as "Mother's great big wild animal."

Burleigh could never take time from the hospital project to go to another station to help in a leisurely fashion. We had to rush over and then rush back. Sometimes we would spend weeks on our station without leaving it.

One Sunday afternoon after just such a long period, we were walking home from our five o'clock English vesper service.

"Couldn't we go for a ride?" David asked.

Burleigh agreed, and we took off.

It is surprising what pictures one can find in the colorful clouds late in a Congo afternoon. We rode along, watching and commenting upon these interesting cloud formations. As the light dimmed the clouds changed, and it became harder to find pictures in them.

Suddenly Burleigh shouted, "Look, there's a leopard!"

"Where?" We searched the heavens thinking he meant a cloud picture.

"There in the road! See it?"

The sleek yellow and black spotted leopard was looking directly at us. Burleigh slowed down, tooted his horn, and turned on the spotlight for a better view. The leopard sprang from the road up on the bank. As we passed, he snarled showing his sharp teeth. Our spines tingled with safe excitement.

About a half-mile on, we met a man pushing his loaded bicycle and two women carrying overfilled baskets on their heads.

"Do they know that the leopard is there?" David asked.

We knew that the Congolese fear the leopard even more than the lion. For them the leopard is king of the forest. It comes at night, without roaring, and attacks from behind.

Soon afterward, Burleigh turned around and headed toward home. We passed the travelers again. Only a short way beyond them our leopard stood in the road.

"Goodness, those folks are gonna get hurt," Paul said.

Burleigh stopped and backed up. "We'd better warn them."

In his best Otetela, he told them of the fierce leopard. "Wouldn't you like to ride your bicycle in our headlights and let the women ride with us to the village?"

The man turned to the women. They discussed this offer at length, then replied, "No, thanks."

This puzzled us. Maybe the women were afraid to get into the car. Burleigh had a better idea. "Would you like to put your bike in the back of the station wagon? We can open the tailgate. Then all three of you can ride with us."

There was another long discussion, but it was obvious that the women liked this idea even less.

Really puzzled now, we wondered if the man understood Burleigh. I tried to communicate. I explained carefully that there was a leopard which could be dangerous just down the road.

"Yes, we understand about the fierce leopard."

"Aren't you afraid?" I asked.

"Oh, yes, we have great fear."

"Why won't you ride with us?"

"The women are more afraid of you than of the leopard," he answered.

To them, we were those strange white people, and the leopard was that familiar leopard they had learned to live with. So finally, at Burleigh's suggestion, the three of them walked in the beam of our headlights.

Burleigh went down before seven o'clock each morning to open the shops, check over the job sheet, and be ready to assign the daily jobs. One morning he found only a few workmen waiting. "Where are the others?" he asked.

"They're afraid to come this early," a workman answered.

"Afraid to come?" Burleigh said. "Why, they've been coming this early for months."

"Yes, but now there are lions in this area. Over at Dimandja Shinga a lion ate an old woman who didn't have doors on her house. Then yesterday he ate a man going to his forest garden near Shilu."

Burleigh began the day's work with his small crew. Much later in the morning, the other workmen and some students arrived together, carrying spears, machetes, and clubs.

"You are late," Burleigh said to Djamba, our gardener, when he arrived around noon.

"Yes. We usually leave home when the second chicken crows, but now we wait until it is good light and we can see."

We didn't blame him. Looking around the house, I was thankful we had our windows and doors in.

Each day when the workmen arrived, we got news about the lion. He had visited one village after another, and although he had attacked no more people, he had eaten chickens, ducks, and goats. Nearer and nearer he came to our Wembo Nyama station to get his evening meals. One morning an excited group from the village of Vili, about five miles away, came with the workmen.

"Uwandji Utshudi A Koi, you *must* come out and kill that lion," the elder said. "Last night he came to our village and ate two goats and ten ducks. Besides, he tried to get into a house, and the people had to stand against the door to keep him from pushing it down."

"But if I do come to Vili, how do you know the lion will come back there?"

"Oh, if you'll come, we'll fix it so he'll come back. We'll build a pen and put a small baby goat in it. When the goat cries, the lion will hear it and that will call him. All you have to do is come with your guns."

I was in the house and didn't know anything about this until some missionaries rushed in saying, "Burleigh's going to Vili tonight on a lion hunt. Are you going with him?"

"Well, I just might."

"Could you talk him into letting us go, too?" they asked.

Burleigh came home very much excited over the lion hunt. "Let's have supper early. We need to be off to Vili before dark."

"Who is going?" I asked.

"Chuck and I, and Ngandjo, one of the mechanics."

"The station wagon will hold more. Can some sight-seers go along?"

"Well, I don't see why not, if you can keep quiet and sit maybe half the night waiting. We have no idea when, or if, the lion will come."

Just before dark, Burleigh, Chuck and Ngandjo, with five women as spectators, were off on the lion hunt.

When we arrived in Vili, we found that the villagers had built a strong pen at the end of the village. There they had tethered a young kid with a long vine tied to its leg. The vine led out about fifty feet from the pen toward the village. "Here you will park your car," they told us.

Burleigh parked the car with the driver's side toward the pen. He instructed me exactly how to turn on the spotlight to shine on the kid. He sat in the driver's seat with his 30-0-6 aimed on the pen. Chuck sat in the middle seat behind Burleigh, his shotgun loaded with buck-shot, and on the very back seat sat Ngandjo, who would pull the vine to make the young kid cry. Handing me the revolver, Burleigh said, "Here, you hold this in case we need it for close range."

We settled down. There was not a sound except our heavy breathing. We waited. It grew darker. Then darker.

"Ssssss," Ngandjo said, very softly. He pointed up the road toward the village, away from the pen. "I hear him," he whispered.

Suddenly there was a flash of light from two eyes. Dimly in the starlight we could see a big body creeping in the grass at the edge of the road. It drew nearer. A cat the size of a young cow stalked toward its prey.

The lion stopped about ten feet from the car. He stood looking, then came closer until he was about three feet away. Just the closed glass separated me from him. He looked up at the car, and I sat frozen, looking at him. Then he turned and started around the back of the car toward the pen. A moment later Ngandjo whispered, "He's there."

I turned the switch. The spotlight flooded the darkness, picking out the lion in front of the pen. BANG! One 30-0-6 shot missed. The lion whirled to run. BANG! A perfect buckshot aimed at his rear. He reared up and roared. Burleigh fired another 30-0-6 shell right into the base of his brain. He fell over dead. We waited to be sure and then cautiously approached.

When we measured, he was forty-six inches from the top of his shoulder to his feet, and six feet long not counting his tail. We had our lion. He would terrorize no more villages.

The village people came dancing out to rejoice in the street. The drummer beat his message across the plains and through the jungles, "The lion is dead. Uwandji Utshudi A Koi killed the lion. Uwandji Kana Yimba shot the lion. Brave men!" After we moved the carcass back to the station, villagers came from all over to see it. Strangely enough, many of them had never seen a lion. Pregnant mothers came to eat a piece of the meat, thought to make their babies brave. We sat around recounting to anyone who would listen the detailed story of how "we got him."

Pressing jobs filled up the days. Week followed week,

and only Sunday and mail day broke the pattern. On Sunday we went to the Otetela church service in the morning, ate dinner, and took a rest in the afternoon. Then at five o'clock we had a vesper service in English with different missionaries taking turns preaching. Like people everywhere, the missionaries needed this, for all people worship best in their own language.

Mail day always gave a lift to the week. On that morning we awoke with the feeling that something interesting would happen. Then we waited for the big truck to come. The time of arrival was never certain. In fact, even the day of arrival wasn't certain. Sometimes the truck came before breakfast. Other times it might arrive after we had gone to bed at night. It might come loaded with letters and packages, or with only a few three-month-old magazines. But this once a week mail service was a line of contact for the missionaries with their friends, families, and their native country.

Then the routine was broken by another adventure, this one at home. One week our family got a basketful of mail. After supper I rushed through my bath and curled up in bed for a nice evening of reading my newly arrived magazines. Burleigh and the boys had a new *Popular Mechanics*, and they settled down in the living room with it. As I lowered my magazine to turn the page, I caught a glimpse of movement near my foot. Not twelve inches away was a black mamba, its head flattened out and raised high above the floor, its long tongue swinging in a circular motion as he charmed my foot. I screamed, "Burleigh!" and froze. One glance and he, too, froze. What should he do? If he shot over me, he might hit me. If he didn't shoot, the snake might strike. He pushed the children away and backed out of the room to get his gun.

I lay perfectly still, watching the snake. Slowly it swung around, its head still more than two feet from the floor. But as it moved, the head turned away from me. In that split second of safety I jumped up and ran into the living room and climbed onto the back of the couch.

Burleigh returned with his shotgun. Standing in the door of our bedroom, he watched the snake moving around the floor. At the corner of the room, it crawled over a table. Then as it sped toward the door, Burleigh fired.

Still sitting on top of the couch, I heard the blast echoing through the house.

A few minutes later David came in dragging across the broom handle the eight feet of snake that was left after Burleigh had shot off its head. Paul danced behind, shouting, "We got him, we got him."

Now we had our snake tale to tell! "Weren't you afraid?" someone asked me.

"Why should she be?" Burleigh teased. "She sat on top of the couch while I killed it."

We had another animal encounter at the station— this time a near-tragedy. At the close of a Sunday afternoon vesper service, a nurse rushed up to call Dr. Hughlett to the hospital. As we walked home, we could see people milling around the front of the hospital. Burleigh walked up to a group. "What's the trouble?"

"They just brought in a man who's been gored clear through his middle by an elephant," someone said.

"Where's he from?" Burleigh asked.

"A village down on the river. He went out hunting

kodi vine to fix his house and met a mother elephant with her baby. She grabbed him with her trunk, threw him up in the air, and he came down on her upraised tusk. His family carried him to Samangua and then hired a truck to bring him here to the hospital."

"It's a wonder she didn't kill him," Burleigh said.

"She tossed him off to trample him, but just then her baby cried. She turned and he was able to climb through the underbrush and get away. He climbed a tree. His friends found him there."

Dr. Hughlett came out. "He's had a pretty rough time," he said. "It took a couple of days for his friends to bring him in. I can't operate now. He's too weak. We're giving him a transfusion and glucose. He'll get some relief from pain, and then tomorrow we'll see what to do."

The next day we heard that they had operated. Then Dr. Hughlett reported. "It's unbelievable. That tusk went in at an angle and missed every vital organ. Except for a couple of broken ribs and punctured peritoneum, he seems to be in pretty good shape."

Daily we watched for the health bulletin on our elephant man. He improved steadily and left the hospital. One day months later he called at our house. "I've come for my gift for escaping death," he told Burleigh. "I'm changing my name."

"What is your new name?"

"Panda Ndjovu" (salvation from an elephant).

Burleigh gave him two milk cans with nice tight lids. He thanked us and walked on. We thought he had gone out of our lives.

The bringing of the wounded man from so far to the

hospital reminded us that there were distant and almost unreachable villages in our area and so many places we had not been.

Almost as if he knew our feeling, the next time we saw Dr. Alex Reid, Chairman of the Field Committee for the Mission, he asked, "Why don't you plan to join me on my next safari to the pygmies? There are several young first-term single missionaries who want to go. I'd like to have a married couple along."

Burleigh sighed. "I wish we could, but we can't stop the workline at the hospital for that long."

"You're going to have to give the workmen time off to cut and burn their own gardens. Why not plan to go then?" Alex proposed.

Burleigh looked pleased. "That might work. They usually want about two weeks in May."

"That's the beginning of the dry season and the best time to go anyway. So let's plan it for that time," Alex decided.

We began to get ready for the trip. There would be eleven missionaries in the party. We would need cots, bedding, and food. Then, there would be two missionary nurses and several African nurses who would hold clinics along the way. They would need drugs and supplies. "Take only the basic personal essentials," we were warned.

Just what are basic personal needs? Well, I found that one leaves behind face cream, hair rollers, and powder boxes. And the men don't take shaving kits.

Basic clothing includes two pairs of good walking shoes, heavy socks, a skirt, a change of blouses, two changes of underwear, and a sun helmet.

Only the bare essentials in tinned food were taken—milk, salt, instant coffee, and oatmeal. Our main diet would consist of rice with whatever game we could find along the way. Dried soups would be the appetizer; cassava leaves, the vegetables; fruits, our desserts; and candy, the energizer.

Forty porters would carry everything. We planned to walk, and there is always the danger that a sprained ankle, a sudden illness, or some other emergency might require that someone be carried. So in addition, we needed sixteen "kipoi men." Eight men can carry a kipoi or hammock on their shoulders, and our group was provided with two teams.

We looked like a small army as we assembled at the village where we would leave the cars, over one hundred miles from our nearest mission station. Here all the boxes and duffle bags were weighed one by one on a scale hanging from a tree branch, and loads apportioned out. Twenty-five pounds per porter was considered the norm.

From the edge of the village, we started walking single file through the deep forest, among the beautiful mahogany trees that spread their massive branches in a solid green canopy above us. It was dark and cool. Occasional shafts of sunlight pierced the cover, revealing the brilliant color of the tropical flowers. From time to time we would stop to listen as brightly colored birds called overhead. Occasionally a limb would sway, and we could see the fleeting form of a monkey jumping from tree to tree along the path.

I looked up at Burleigh. "Imagine us, here in the heart of the Congo!"

Not all the path was smooth. It led down slick hills where we had to test each step. In some places trees lay across the path. There were streams we had to cross.

Across a small stream there was only a large felled tree for a bridge. The bark had long ago fallen off, and the wood was worn smooth by passing feet. Vines attached to trees at either side made a swinging bridge over the deep, swirling waters of larger streams. Across the vines were laid small poles placed close together but not so close that a foot could not fall through. Turning and twisting to be sure each foot was placed squarely on a pole, we swayed back and forth as we crossed.

I clung to the sides for dear life. "Just turn loose and walk," Burleigh advised. "You won't ever get across holding on to the sides like that."

"Are there crocodiles in that stream?" I asked.

"I don't know, but they can't reach you up here."

"But suppose I fall through?"

"Well, you aren't likely to fall through those small holes, unless you stay here until you starve so you're thinner than you are now."

"You go on. I'll come by myself when you get off."

Burleigh walked across, doing acrobatics to show me just how simple it was. I stood still, holding fast until he was on the other side and the bridge stopped swaying. Then slowly, so not a pole would move, I maneuvered my way over. How nice it was to walk again on solid earth!

Our kipoi men had been engaged to carry people, and their hammocks must not be vacant. Their honor was at stake. At first we asked for volunteers to ride; then came conscriptions. "Virginia, it's your turn now."

So instead of walking on solid earth, I now jostled through the forest in a hammock. "Huh, HUH, huh, huh" rang in the deep forest as the carriers chanted in rhythm. Then they began a different song. The leader cried out a phrase in a high pitch and the seven repeated it in a lower tone, sounding as if it came echoing from deep in the forest.

"*Wutshu wa Ndjovu, wutshu wa Ndjovu,*" they chanted. It began to sound familiar. I could understand it.

"Weight of an elephant, weight of an elephant," resounded through the forest, first in high tones, then in low.

I felt a hundred pounds heavier.

"If I'm so heavy, I'll just get out and walk," I told the men.

"Oh no, Mama, we weren't chanting about you but about that other mama."

Which one they didn't say, and I knew better than to ask.

And their chanting suddenly changed to "*Lusaka le Nzambi, wutshu ambutsho.*" (Thanks to God, the heavy one's gone.)

We felt unusually secure on our safari, and I learned it was because each missionary had been assigned, without his knowledge, an African guide to "keep his eye on him." If one faltered even for a moment, he appeared to check. If one stopped to take a picture, he stood waiting, sometimes just around a slight curve, but he was there. In fact, it proved difficult to get the privacy one occasionally needed. They really looked after us.

It seemed farther and farther between overnight stops

each day out. One day Burleigh asked a man we met on the path how far it was to Shamba, where we would spend that night.

He stood thinking for a moment. "It's two streams," he said and walked on.

Now, that's real road information for you. I wondered what the man would have told us if there hadn't been any streams. The following day I found out. We had finally reached Shamba, held services and a clinic, and spent the night. Now in the afternoon of the next day's trek my feet were again dragging. When we met two hunters, Burleigh asked, "How far from here to Otepa?"

"From where have you come today?" one responded.

"From Shamba."

"Where was the sun when you left?" the man asked.

Burleigh made a guess, holding his hand up toward the horizon at the angle he thought the sun would have been at seven o'clock.

"If you keep walking like you have been, you'll reach Otepa when the sun reaches there," the hunter said, pointing to a place on the western horizon.

When we entered a village, our kipoi men had no trouble getting volunteers to ride the hammock. Hearing their chant, the village drummers sent the news ahead. The villagers were prepared to greet us. And such a greeting!

Chanting and clapping, they surrounded us, and joined the kipoi men in a ceremonial dance. Forward, backward, feet stomping, forward again, always in perfect rhythm. There was no doubt that we were received with joy.

The farther into the forest we went, the more questions the villagers had about just who we were. They had heard of our missionary leader, Dr. Alex Reid, and our welcome was based on his reputation which had been carried from village to village. But the reasons for our coming they didn't understand.

At one interior village, the only contact they had had with white people, other than a government official, was with a Catholic priest who had called there months before. Unaccustomed to consonant endings for a word and not having the "r" sound in Otetela, "Mon Pere" had become "Mon Peli." This was the greeting they knew.

This particular day all our missionaries, men and women, just happened to be wearing jeans, except me. For no special reason I had worn my full skirt. In front of the house they had prepared for us was an arched canopy of palm branches with flowers tied in it. People were standing along both sides, smiling and greeting each traveler with "*Moyo Mon Peli.*"

Burleigh and I were the last to arrive. They quickly greeted him, but they looked at me with a perplexed expression. I was dressed differently. Everyone stared, trying to decide just what my greeting should be.

Then one bright little boy in the front smiled, his eyes alight with a sudden inspiration. Bowing his head reverently he said, "*Moyo Mama Mariya*" (Greeting Mother Mary). To him I was the Virgin Mary.

At the selected spot our nurses set up a clinic to treat the sick and wounded. To me with only my "Healthy In Hot Climates" training, the wounds looked terrible. I had never seen such tropical ulcers, open and draining, such itch-covered children, such human suffering as I saw in these isolated villages, deep in the beautiful African forest.

Four o'clock in the afternoon is supper hour in most Batetela villages. Then the people have their one real meal of the day with huge pans of rice, and meat if the hunters have been successful. At the village where we were staying that day, the hunters returned from their day's hunt just at the crucial time. Over their shoulders were the huge nets they used for hunting. They hang their nets from one tree to another. Then spreading out through the forest with their dogs and gongs, they try to chase a fleeing antelope toward their net. Today they brought back an antelope, hanging by its hoofs from a pole supported on two carriers' shoulders. There was meat for supper.

Seeing Burleigh with his gun, the men wanted him to go hunting with them, and the next morning he did. Not long after they had left, we heard a shot, and the men returned with a water buck. Burleigh had hit him with a perfect shot just between the eyes. With admiration the hunters called him *shaba* (deadeye). But they boasted of the skill of the pygmies who hunt elephant with neither nets nor guns. Their technique is to creep up close and spear the animal in the side with a poison-tipped spear.

We were hoping to see the pygmies, and at each village we asked where they were. But no one could tell us, for they do not stay in one place. Wherever they kill an elephant, they build temporary huts and live there until the meat is eaten. Then they kill another elephant someplace else and move again.

Eventually, however, we heard that the pygmies

weren't far away, and a village elder offered to send word and ask the chief to come in.

"How far away are they?" we asked.

"Not near. They don't ever live near our village. They don't want their people getting mixed up with other peoples."

"Do they intermarry with Batetela?" we asked.

"Hardly ever. They marry only one wife or husband and don't remarry. They are monogamous until death."

We could understand why the pygmies would stay away from the polygamous Batetela villages.

That evening we gathered for our usual evening worship service. There were no churches in the villages, so we chose an elevated spot. At this service a high anthill served for the pulpit. Most of our audience came directly from the first-aid station, wearing their first clean bandages, feeling their first relief of pain from an aspirin. Then we saw a new group approaching. The pygmies had come!

They didn't seem afraid as they sat down among the Batetela. I had expected short people but not as short as these. One woman came just to Burleigh's belt, and her baby was smaller than a doll. We learned she had borne nineteen children.

The audience heard Dr. Reid preach, "I came that you may have life, and have it abundantly."

What is the abundant life, I wondered? Would it be the same for these people as for me? Surely Christ's purpose in coming to men included them as well as me. But what does His coming mean for them in terms of everyday life, manners, customs, culture?

After the service we talked with the villagers around

the campfire. Sitting across from us on two-legged stools, a feat in itself, were the *Kuma Kundas* or Lords of the Forest—the rulers, judges, and spokesmen for the people. They wore loin cloths of homespun raffia and small leopard skins. Around their ankles were bracelets of polished copper. Leopard-tooth necklaces were testimony to their bravery.

They asked intelligent and interesting questions. They had heard from some relative, trader, or passing tribesman about the mission and were glad we had come to visit them. They marveled that white "mamas" walked so well. "But are you blind?" they asked. "Don't you see that we need churches, schools, dispensaries?"

"Yes, we can see your need," Dr. Reid told them, "but where will we get preachers and teachers and nurses? Send us your youth to go to our schools. They will become your preachers, teachers, nurses."

"But we need a preacher to get our youth to want to go to school," they countered.

"Where is a home for a preacher? Where is a school for a teacher?"

There followed a long discussion of why it would be difficult to acquire such things by volunteer labor.

"It is hard," Dr. Reid agreed, "but we never send a pastor unless the villagers want him enough to build a home for him. A teacher goes only where there is a church. A nurse waits for the beginning of a school."

"So we have to get ready for them?" they asked.

"Yes, nkusha koko, ndu kanga lodi?" (Do you expect us to give you the chicken and also the medicine to kill the hawk?)

They laughed. They understood from their own prov-
erb the thinking of the white man. "We help those who
help themselves."

It grew late. We told them good-night, and they went
home, leaving us still around the fireside. We sat talking
about the day. Each of us was filled with the adventure
and excitement of this trip. Each had some special experience to share. We sang together and prayed that
our visit among these people might be helpful.

For nine days we trekked from village to village and
to pygmy huts deep in the forest, covering from ten to
fifteen miles a day. Each day beside the hammock
trotted a young African boy, maybe twelve years old,
who had joined our caravan on his own and who beat
the kipoi rhythm on his hollowed-out bamboo drum.
We were fascinated by his faithfulness and interest in
this strange party. Each evening as we sang our evening
devotional songs in English, he stood or sat in the
shadows, listening.

It was the last night of our trip. The next day we expected to reach the car road and rejoin our cars and
truck. In the bright moonlight Burleigh and I decided to
take a final walk down through the village. It would be
good to get home to hot baths and beds, and to the
children. Yet we hated to leave these people who had
welcomed us so warmly. As we strolled, hearing the
Otetela chatter coming from behind the enclosed fences
around the homes, suddenly we heard a strange sound.
"That sounds like English," I said.

We stopped to listen. We could barely make it out as
a high voice sang over and over, "E'vebody ough te
know, e'vebody ough te know." It was the boy who had

attached himself to us. We had sung just that much of
the chorus for nine evenings around our campfire,
"Everybody ought to know who Jesus is."

Burleigh smiled. "That's why we are here."

Walking on I remembered the question in my friend's
letter, "What do you do out there to keep from being
bored?"

CHAPTER EIGHT

Getting a Big Project Under Way

BURLEIGH, BURLEIGH! COME QUICK!" SOMEONE SCREAMED through our bedroom window.

Burleigh bolted upright in bed. It was still dark, but the moon dimly lighted the room.

"Come quick! It's Max Ritter! Doctor needs you."

Burleigh jumped out of bed and rushed to the Ritter home, pulling his trousers over his pajamas as he ran. I followed close behind in my housecoat. Anita Ritter, a beautiful young missionary, sat alone on the porch steps.

"What is it?" I asked her.

"Max woke me just a few minutes ago. He was having trouble breathing. I ran for Dr. Bitsch-Larsen. He and a nurse are giving Max artificial respiration now. They asked me to wait out here."

I didn't know what to say. "Maybe he'll be all right," I mumbled.

"No," she said quietly.

I couldn't believe he was seriously ill. Max hadn't been well for a few days, but we thought it was only the usual malaria.

Now other missionaries and Africans gathered in the front yard, standing uncertainly in groups.

In the house Burleigh joined in giving artificial respiration. For hours they worked—the doctor, missionary, and African nurses—to keep Max alive.

Since there was nothing I could do, I went home to see about the children. Finally Burleigh came back for breakfast. Exhausted and white, he sat down at the table, his head in his hands. Nothing was said for a long time, and then he sighed, "Nothing to work with."

I knew how he felt. Suddenly he faced what our doctors faced every day—trying to save lives without the equipment they needed.

After eating, Burleigh said, "I'm going over to the radio to see if I can get an emergency call out. Maybe someone could fly in an iron lung. It looks like polio."

For several hours Burleigh called but got no answer. Finally, a Presbyterian doctor heard his call. He didn't have an iron lung, but he did have an airplane. If Burleigh could find a lung, he could pick it up and fly it to Wembo Nyama. "Could I land?" he asked.

"There's no field here, but there's a wide, straight road. We could get the grass cleared and the shoulders knocked down for you."

Then a Belgian railroad agent, operating his radio station far south of us, heard Burleigh's call. His railroad station had a phone connection to the Luluabourg station, and in Luluabourg there was local telephone service to the hospital. The hospital agreed to get their mobile iron lung out to the airport for the doctor to pick up.

Just as all the details were worked out, someone ran up. "Hold it, Burleigh!" he called. "It's too late. Max just died."

Again Burleigh cried, "We didn't have anything to work with!"

After a few minutes he went to the carpenter shop. Soon we could hear the planer moaning as it worked the wide mahogany boards which Burleigh polished and waxed and made into a casket. For this he had something to work with.

The next afternoon African and missionary friends gathered with Anita while she saw her husband buried on the Wembo Nyama station under the green palm trees. A few days later we helped pack Anita's cases to ship stateside. Burleigh drove her and her two-year-old son Mark to the plane at Luluabourg.

This experience deeply disturbed Burleigh. Never had he felt so keenly the need for the hospital he was trying to build. He went back to work with renewed energy. "Our doctors must have a hospital," he said.

Still on Burleigh's desk, however, were the elaborate hospital plans that he had gone to Philadelphia to study. All the present buildings had been erected from plans drawn up on some missionary's dining room table after supper. These professional architects' plans looked wonderful, but there was a serious problem: the Belgian government wouldn't accept them. The mission needed approved plans to receive the subsidy grant the government would make for a hospital.

No one seemed to know exactly how we had come to such an impasse. All we knew was we had $20,000 worth of beautiful plans we couldn't use.

Al Burlbaugh had been construction engineer on many big projects in the States. He also had a head full of good "horse sense." Then Dr. Jim Mathews (now

Bishop Mathews) came from the Board of Missions to visit the Congo. Al and Burleigh sat down with him and went over the plans, pointing out all that was wrong about them for Central Congo.

"Oddly enough," Al said, "there's too much ventilation. We'd never keep our patients warm in such airy wards."

He pointed to the plans. "These inside corridors would be a problem here. Whole families come with the patients. They would congregate in corridors and make them impassable."

Burleigh's finger touched another place. "Look, here's a salad room! We won't need a salad room for two more generations."

On and on went the list of problems. "Besides all this," Al told Dr. Mathews, "we understand that the copies we submitted to the Belgian government are filed away. They won't even consider the plans."

"We know the Board has put money into these plans, but wouldn't it be better to junk them now than to put more money into revisions and still not be able to use them?" Burleigh asked.

Dr. Mathews heard them out, asked questions, discussed the problems. Then he suggested, "Why don't you and the legal representative of the station go to Luluabourg with me. We'll talk to the government officials there about the plans and see just what can be done."

No sooner had they gone than I discovered that I was completely out of vanilla flavoring. "If only I'd thought about it, maybe Burleigh could have found some in Luluabourg," I complained to my neighbors.

I then discovered that everyone else was out too.

"Why don't you send Burleigh word on our noon-day broadcast?" someone suggested. "Surely he'll hear you."

So every noon for several days the radio operator sent the message, "Burleigh Law, Virginia sends an SOS for a carton of vanilla flavoring."

Burleigh returned about a week later much excited over the hospital, but he hadn't been able to find any vanilla.

Two weeks later in our weekly mail came a small package addressed to me. I opened it and found a note: "We have heard on the radio here in Elisabethville your pitiful plea for vanilla. We feel that cooking without vanilla is one sacrifice no missionary should make. (signed) Charlotte and Jane"

Missionary friends of mine in Southern Congo, more than a thousand miles away, had supplied our station with flavoring!

But the important news was that Burleigh and Al had some workable plans for a hospital. As we had heard, the officials in Luluabourg were not even considering our American plans. But they had some excellent plans already drawn up for a hospital at Louisa. They would be delighted for us to use those for a beginning. And they would consider any changes we felt were necessary.

The medical personnel from the entire mission met at Wembo Nyama station to consider the hospital. For several days they went over the Louisa plans in detail, discussing each section, making suggestions. Everyone liked what Burleigh and Al finally worked out. So once more, mission plans were drawn on the dining room table, but this time under the supervision of Al Burlbaugh who really knew how to make them.

The first plan to be completed and sent to the medical office for official approval was for the maternity building. It was to be separate from the main hospital. "We've got to get our patients out of that dirt-floored ward," insisted the nurse.

While waiting for the report on those plans, Burleigh and Al went to work making bricks. Even the new, more simple plans called for a million bricks to complete the hospital. The big brick machine, all set up but never used, was in a valley where there was a vein of good red brick clay. Two long, narrow drying sheds stretched down to the firing kiln.

"Maybe we'd better clear the jungle back from the sheds," Al said to Burleigh. "Snakes are bad this time of year."

"We'll send men down in the morning with machetes," Burleigh agreed.

The men had been working only a few minutes when one came running back, shouting to Burleigh, "Come, Uwandji! We've just killed a big python."

It measured eighteen feet without the head.

Burleigh whistled. "It *was* a good idea to cut back the jungle from around the sheds."

The time had come for a trial run of the brick press. Al and Burleigh were really "green" brickmakers.

"Burleigh's the specialist," Al teased. "He saw a brick press once in America."

After the first few bricks were set up to dry, it was discovered that the vein of clay was too pure. The bricks were too heavy, and as they began to dry, they cracked. It took eight weeks to make them ready for the kiln and ten days to fire them once they were in it.

"At this rate, we'll be making bricks the rest of our lives," Burleigh said to Al.

"Wonder if we couldn't mix something with the clay to make it lighter and easier to dry and fire. We could use sand, but where would we find enough sand of the same consistency for all the bricks?"

"What about sawdust? We'll sure have enough of that from the sawmill," Burleigh suggested.

So Al and Burleigh started mixing sawdust with the clay. At first, just a little, but after experimenting, they used as much as forty percent. As a safety factor, they coded on inside walls the ones to be used.

The bricks were light now, but they still took too long to fire.

"Somehow we must core those bricks to give them more drying surface," Burleigh said. He thought out a plan. "If we weld three one-inch iron bars onto a knife-edged plate, we could fasten this across the extrusion head so that it reaches into the extrusion die."

Al was pleased with the idea. "Let's try it. If it works, we'd have three holes in the bricks."

This made a nice after-work project. Al's wife, Mary Ann, and I rode our bikes down each afternoon to watch the men inventing a coring device for bricks. And it worked.

Bricks began to run off the press, fifteen thousand per day. Workmen shoveled the clay into wheelbarrows and pushed them up inclines to dump it into the press. Burleigh or Al had to stay with the job when it was in operation. The workmen had not yet learned to detect motor trouble in time to prevent a breakdown.

We watched with great excitement while the sheds filled with bricks, then waited impatiently for them to dry.

"We'll start stacking the kiln tomorrow," Burleigh told us one evening.

"Do you know how to stack a kiln?" David asked his dad.

"No, but I don't need to know yet. Foreman Wembo Lua will teach me. He knows how."

"Wembo Lua's son Kasongo is gonna teach me and David to catch *dikalilis*," Paul announced. "That is, if we can have a flashlight."

"How can you catch a big cricket with a flashlight?" I asked.

"He comes up out of his hole to chirp at night," Paul explained. "You can listen and hear where he is chirping, but you have to see which way the hole goes in the ground. Kasongo knows how to slip up and stomp his hole shut behind him. Then all we have to do is pick the *dikalili* up."

"What are you going to do with *dikalilis*?" I asked.

"Eat 'em," said Paul simply. "They're good, like white ants."

I smiled, for I remembered one night when I was sitting reading by our kerosene lamp. Burleigh sat on the other side of the lamp studying the hospital plans. The two boys were tucked in bed. Everything was quiet, and I was lost in my story until something touched my lip. I looked up. The room was full of fluttering insects. We began to search for the source of this air force and discovered they were pouring in at the door and window.

"I'll get the spray gun," I said as I dashed out to the kitchen and back with the DDT spray.

Burleigh pumped away. Slowly the flying bugs began to fall in showers.

The next morning our living room looked as if it had rained bugs. We were proud of our effective DDT spray. But Shinga, our household helper, shook his head. "What a waste of good flying ants. You can't eat 'em with all that medicine on them."

"Where did they come from?" Burleigh asked.

"Out of the anthill, there in the yard," Shinga said.

"What can we do about them?"

"You'll have to dig up the queen ant. That's the only way to kill the nest."

After breakfast Burleigh returned from the workshop with two workmen armed with shovels. From time to time I looked out my window to watch them. The hole grew deeper and deeper in the side of the six-foot-high anthill.

Then at my door I heard, "Mama Uya Koi!"

"*Elu.*"

"Do you want to see the queen ant?" a workman called.

I hurried out to see a white gelatin-looking mass lying on one half of a clay shell.

"You can't kill a nest no matter how long you try unless you dig her out first," I was told. "The ants are swarming now, but when they do go back home, they'll die. The worker ants won't work without their queen."

Looking over at the hole in the anthill, I saw sticking up the dirty seats of two pairs of jeans. Paul and Utuku were busy stuffing ants into their mouths, the discarded wings fluttering out at the sides.

Paul looked up at me and grinned, wrinkling up his nose. "They're so good, Mommie."

I took his word for it. Now he had to find out how good crickets were.

At last it was time to fire the brick kiln. With Wembo Lua as chief of this operation, the workmen began a slow fire. They cut and trucked in tons of firewood. "That should be enough wood for the whole hospital," I remarked to Burleigh.

"We'll be lucky if it'll fire this one kiln," he replied.

Each day they forced in more and more wood, working round the clock. Paul, David, and I rode down with Burleigh to watch the fire getting hotter. We brought the workmen rice, sardines, coffee and sugar. Later we took wieners down to roast in their hot fire and ate with them picnic style.

Each day the excitement mounted. When would the kiln be ready to close down?

"How long, Wembo Lua?" Burleigh asked late one afternoon.

"Not quite ready yet. Maybe by two in the morning."

"Can we come back then?" David and Paul asked.

"Yes, if you jump up the minute I call you."

When the alarm rang at two, a little voice called, "Daddy, you up?"

As we came to the top of the hill above the kiln, we

could look down upon a valley aglow with a bright red light. We stood still in wonder. We could hear the clear hum of the kiln above the voices of the men.

As we drove down the hill and around to the kiln, Wembo Lua was barking orders to the men. "Mix the mud! It's ready to close up."

Quickly the men began to pour water on the clay in the large wooden troughs, mixing up a nice, soupy mud. Other men, with shields before their faces, started stacking broken bricks before the kiln openings. They had to work fast. Burleigh jumped in to help them. David and Paul carried buckets of mud to the workmen. I took a hand, helping mix up the mud. Back and forth we dashed with buckets of mud or arms filled with bricks. One by one the firing holes were closed tight. At last the kiln stood silent, drawing air no longer. We would have bricks.

We climbed in the jeep and rode home, dead tired.

A few days later, the government approval of the plans for the maternity building came through. After all the preparation—moving the machinery; getting timber right; setting up the sawmill, the brick press, the kiln— at last construction could actually begin!

Digging the foundation came first. It was satisfying to trace the outline of the future walls. I rode my bike down late one afternoon to join Burleigh as he looked over the project.

"I think you'd better stay off your bike," Burleigh warned me. "You just might slip in the sand. David and Paul would hate to lose their baby sister after praying for her so long."

Months before, David and Paul had decided our

family was not complete. We needed a baby girl. They pushed the buggies of the baby girls in other station families and decided to put a sister as top priority on their prayer list. Fortunately Mother and Daddy were wanting one, too, so now the Law family was awaiting its fifth member.

We had followed the development of "our baby" with the aid of a life-size birth atlas. But Burleigh and I realized that the expectation was centered too much on a "baby sister." We explained again and again that we could not choose and should be happy with either a baby girl or boy.

"But," replied our little boys, "God knows we want a sister. We didn't ask Him for a brother."

One afternoon we heard a commotion coming from the old stick-and-mud maternity wing. Not far from us people were milling about and talking in high-pitched, excited voices.

"What's the excitement?" I asked Wembo Lua.

"Oh, a woman has given birth to a duck. They have just brought her from her village with the dead baby."

"How old is the baby?" I knew that they count the age of babies from conception.

"It's three months old. It was all bloody, but it has a duck's bill and web feet," the foreman explained.

Burleigh looked skeptical. "Does she have any other children?"

"No, this is her first pregnancy, and she's getting old—maybe thirty-five."

Burleigh probed further. "Does her husband have any children?"

"Yes, he took a young wife last year, and she gave

birth to a baby a few weeks ago," Wembo Lua answered.
Then he added, "Now, this older wife has given birth so
they are even."

"Have you ever seen this before?" Burleigh asked.

"No, but I've heard of it happening when a wife gets
too old to have a child but gets pregnant anyway. It's
better to give birth to a duck than not to give birth at
all," he declared as he walked toward his home.

Burleigh sighed. "How tragic for the woman."

A Congolese wife has no real value until she can give
birth, even if the birth is premature. The poor woman
must have skinned a duck and passed it off as an embryo.

"Well, being good Congolese by now, I suppose the
boys will agree that it would be better for me to give
birth to a baby brother than not to give birth at all," I
teased.

After four years of planning, the maternity building
actually began to go up. But something more than just
the building was involved. Piles of reports had to be
sent to the government specifying the amount of lumber
being cut, the tons of gravel being used. I think that on
every mission station there is an unsung saint who does
the paper work. At Wembo Nyama Marshall Lovell,
our legal representative, had the privilege of earning his
crown. He was a tall, large, blustering kind of fellow
with a voice to match. When he preached, you didn't
need to enter the church to hear; you could just as well
sit at home on your porch.

I was assigned to help him fill out all those forms. I
added the numbers twice by machine and twice by head
for fear one or the other would be off, before I took them

over to him. Otherwise, through my door would come a loud call, "Virginia, girl, this isn't right."

When he laughed from across the station, we could hear his loud "haw, haw, haw." Sometimes we would hear him saying to some African, "Haleyi, ongenyi." (I don't know, my friend.) It sounded a little brusk, with the "my friend" added as if to soften the blow. His manner disturbed me as a new missionary. Was he too impatient? In Otetela it sounded harsher than in English.

At one meeting of missionary and Congolese delegates from all over the mission, we planned an orientation program for new, young missionaries. We began to list on the blackboard those personality traits that would contribute to more effective service. Our list looked like the "Attributes of the Saints." Then a very wise African teacher, Emambulu, spoke up.

"This isn't really worthwhile," he said. "I'm not sure we'd want a missionary with all these traits. Look at Uwandji Ukito Kunda (Marshall Lovell). You'll see him walking across the station, talking in what sounds like a terribly harsh voice. You think he is blessing someone out. Yet alongside him will be trotting some workman, trying to keep up just to hear what he has to say."

There were chuckles in the group and a loud "haw, haw" from the corner.

"So long as a missionary comes out here to serve," Emambulu continued, "and wants to love us, we can accept him even if he lacks every trait on the board."

The committee agreed, dropped the list, and turned

to the more constructive planning of ways to help a new missionary come to know and understand the people among whom he would serve. If he could accomplish that, he'd love them. I went home feeling grateful to Emambulu, for I knew I lacked most of the "Attributes of the Saints," but I did love the people.

I couldn't ride my bicycle any longer, but every afternoon I walked down to meet Burleigh and come home with him. There were always so many things happening around the workshop, for Burleigh and Al never had just what they needed and were always having to improvise. I enjoyed seeing them work out these inventions, and I needed something to keep me interested at this point.

I was to have the baby on the Wembo Nyama station delivered by our mission doctor and a well-trained nurse. I felt in good hands, but I did want to get the show on the road; and it was late.

"Maybe instead of a duck, this is to be an elephant," Burleigh suggested.

Everything was ready at the hospital. Sterile packages stood waiting in a sterile cabinet. Before bedtime each night either the doctor or nurse dropped by to check on how things were going. And finally, as is often the way, I called Burleigh at one in the morning.

"Go get Dr. Bitsch-Larsen in a hurry."

The doctor had been in bed for only a few minutes, following an emergency at the hospital. He called Dottie Gilbert, the mid-wife nurse. Then he came over to see about me. No doubt about it, he decided, but there was still no great rush.

Burleigh went down to start the station light motor, Dottie went home to get her white uniform, and Dr. Bitsch-Larsen sat down in a chair in the corner to snooze.

A few minutes later I called out, "Doctor!"

He jumped up, made a quick examination, and yelled, "Nurse!"

Dottie was just coming in, followed by Burleigh.

And Margaret Ann arrived at our house with the aid of just one sterile glove.

David and Paul heard all the commotion and raced into my room before anyone knew they were up. Dottie marched them right back to the living room. As soon as all was clear, they were allowed in. Pulling the pink blanket back, they both nuzzled their faces right down on the baby. Then they lifted their heads a little, looked at each other, and asked in unison, "Is it a sister?"

I nodded. In a flash they were both showering me with kisses.

Burleigh wore a broad smile as he went to the work-line that morning. The workmen were excited to hear that Uwandji had a new baby girl. Girls bring dowries into a family, so they are always an added blessing.

"You can have any palm nuts you want in the village today," a workman told Burleigh. "The father of a new baby girl can select the biggest, ripest bunch. The owner will cut it for him, and the village children will carry it home," the workman explained.

"I'll remember that," Burleigh responded.

During the next few weeks, the walls of the maternity

building rose high. The frames went up, and it was ready for roofing.

"It looks as if I had my baby just a few weeks too early," I told Burleigh one day when Margaret Ann and I went down to visit the project.

"Oh, no, you didn't," Burleigh said, lifting the baby buggy into the doorway. "This may look nearly finished, but we still have months of work."

Burleigh and Wembo Lua discussed work assignments for the next day. The masons were about finished until it was time to pour the concrete floors. In the meantime, they could begin digging and building the septic tank for the sanitary installations. The next day's work was pretty well planned when Wembo Lua stopped at the buggy.

"Has the baby dropped her navel cord yet?" he asked.

"No, she hasn't," I said, rather surprised at such a question.

This question was asked almost daily by any workman I happened to meet. It was a relief to me when finally I could say, "Yes, she has."

The next afternoon after work, Burleigh and I were sitting on our screened porch, enjoying the cool breeze. We saw a group of workmen coming up the station, and they turned into our yard.

"Dear me," I thought. "Just when I have Burleigh for a few minutes all to myself, here comes a discussion of the work."

Then I saw that the men were carrying two chickens, some fruit, and a pan of rice.

Smiling, they came up to the door. Burleigh stood up to greet them.

"We hear the baby has dropped her navel cord," they said.

It hadn't occurred to Burleigh to wonder about such a matter. He turned to me. "Has she?"

I nodded.

Wembo Lua spoke for the group. "It is our custom to cook a feast in the village at such a time and give the child its name. We have brought the food here for your cook to make a feast for you."

They came onto the screened porch and put their gifts around Margaret Ann's carriage. Burleigh pulled the blanket back so they could see how long and strong she was.

They "ohhhed" and "ahhhhed" over her. Then Wembo Lua spoke again. "We have named her Amena, for truly she is the beautiful one."

We were pleased with the Congolese name they had chosen for our daughter.

But Burleigh also learned that he had to pay a fine. I had failed to make it to the hospital, and when a baby is born elsewhere, the father has to pay a fine to cover the cost of penicillin shots.

"A hundred francs isn't too much to pay for being able to be right on hand myself," Burleigh told them.

Only a few days later we came in from a stroll to find David standing on the porch looking pretty grim. He began, "You know my turtle?"

We *did* know his turtle. We were forever sending David out of the house to a pen in the yard with the huge turtle a workman had found and brought to him.

"Well," David went on, "it's kinda like Mother with Margaret Ann. She didn't get to her pen to give birth."

We opened the door, and there on the living room rug were four big smashed turtle eggs.

Burleigh kept a solemn face. "You'll have to pay the fine. Get a pan of water and some soap."

Relieved, David ran to get the water. He could think of stiffer fines.

The finish work on the maternity building went slowly, for using the power tools required skills the workmen had not yet learned. So Al and Burleigh worked from early in the morning until late in the evening. It would be dark before we would see them riding home on their bikes for supper. Meals had no time schedule.

After several weeks of this irregular life, I spoke out. "Something has to be done. The children can't eat at such erratic hours. Besides our cook needs to know when he can go home."

"Well, I can't leave forty men standing at the shop waiting for a door frame while I go eat eggs," Burleigh said. "You and the children go ahead and eat when the time comes and keep my food on the stove."

"But that isn't any family pleasure," I protested.

We discussed the problem at length. Finally Burleigh said, "Set a definite hour for breakfast and lunch. I'll try to make it, but if I don't, you go ahead and eat. Supper will be our family meal. Send me a reminder, and I'll make every effort to come on time."

I accepted this arrangement, for I knew that work on the hospital had to go on.

At last bright aluminum roofing flashed back the hot sunlight. The next big project was pouring the concrete for the floor. For years all the cement floors on the station had been a thin layer of cement spread over a brick floor. It was neither pretty nor any protection from white ants, an eternal problem in the Congo. Often we went to sleep at night, our shoes by the bed, only to find no shoestrings the next morning. They had become a white ant meal overnight.

For a really good concrete floor, tons of gravel were needed, but no one knew where to find such a supply. Weeks later Burleigh was in a village some distance from our station, sitting under the Utshudi shed and visiting with the village artisans. He always enjoyed watching them, never ceasing to marvel at the way they could use what was available.

The blacksmith's bellows was an example. A native clay pot was firmly bedded down in hard clay. The top was covered over with banana leaves attached to a long handle. When the leaves were lifted, the pot filled with air; when lowered, air was forced into a long clay tunnel and out over a bed of charcoal nuggets, fanning them white hot.

With homemade tongs, the workmen lifted pieces of crude iron out of this forge and placed them on a smooth, round rock to pound into spears, knives, or hair shavers. Burleigh, fascinated with the work, noticed the rock and asked where it came from.

"Down behind our village in the stream," the blacksmith replied.

"Are there many rocks like it?" Burleigh asked.

"Elu, more than you could count. Come and see."

Burleigh went with the blacksmith and found a fair supply of rocks and gravel in the stream. He thought it likely that there would be a supply of gravel somewhere close by, so he and Al returned later to look further.

They found exactly what they wanted about halfway between the village and our station, but a long way from the road.

"The cotton company had a road back there once, but the bridge washed out," Burleigh reported. "Now the chief of one of the forest villages says his people will fix the road if we'll take care of the bridge. It looks like our only hope if we're going to have concrete floors. And all the equipment in the hospital needs good concrete floors for protection." Thus, bridge construction became the next project.

The stream ran through a swamp area and fill was essential on each side, so dirt was trucked in and unloaded. When Burleigh went to check how the work was progressing, David and Paul went along. Both boys loved to work on the job. Getting shovels, they climbed in the truck to help spread the dirt as it was thrown up from below.

The work went rapidly that day. When it was time to go home, David, imitating the workmen, lifted his shovel high and plunged it into the sand. One of the workmen screamed and lifted his foot, spurting blood, out of the sand. Burleigh came running. Quickly he picked up the workman and lowered him to two men standing on the ground. "Put him in the jeep," he ordered.

Seeing David's colorless face, Burleigh realized that he was somehow involved. "Hurry and get in the jeep, boys," he said to them. "David, you sit in the back and hold this tourniquet on the man's leg." Off they rushed to the hospital.

I didn't know what had happened, but I saw a very

dejected little nine-year-old boy coming home. When he came up on the porch and I saw his face, I didn't ask any questions. He went to his room and fell on his bed. Only later when Burleigh came did I find out just what had taken place.

He called David out on the porch, and pulling him close, spoke quietly. "Son, you made a serious mistake this afternoon. I know you realize it. I won't ever need to tell you again that when you use any tool, you must watch carefully where you put it."

Burleigh waited a moment, then patted David's arm. "I know you didn't mean to do it, but the workman might not know it. Go into the kitchen and ask Ngandu for some tea and sugar. We'll go down to the hospital, and you can tell him how sorry you are. Hot tea will make him feel better. Then tomorrow you can wash the jeep to get the blood out of it."

Later I saw them walking home from the hospital and could tell even from a distance that David felt better.

The next afternoon they were off again to the bridge. "Put in a couple of shovels," Burleigh called to David and Paul. "They'll be needing some help out there."

Such trips as these were sometimes conditional on the boys' getting their morning schoolwork done. Neither boy could go until every arithmetic problem was worked, every page read in the day's lesson. This helped me, for I was their teacher. School for them and for another missionary child was in our dining room.

Every morning with as much seriousness as we could muster, we settled down for studies. Keeping from being interrupted was a problem. Someone was always calling, "Mama eko?"

"Yes, I'm here, but I'm in school. Come back later," I'd call out. But rarely did the caller go away immediately.

Another distraction was Paul's parrot, a lovely gray one with bright tail feathers of many colors, which we had bought from an African.

"Mama eko?" a voice would call out.

With my mind still on the lesson, I'd answer, "Elu."

Then I would suddenly come to when the same voice called out shrilly, "Ah, shucks."

"Paul! Get that parrot out to the wash shed!"

It requires continual alertness to keep a hundred men going on a workline. As the maternity building progressed, there was a demand for more and more carpenters and fewer masons and workmen. Al and Burleigh decided to use these men to start digging the foundations for the main hospital. What deep trenches they were! "There'll be almost as many bricks below the ground as above," Burleigh explained to me one afternoon when I had ridden my bike down to join him.

Then we walked over to the construction. It was beginning really to look like a hospital.

Burleigh pointed out the new cement floors. "Aren't they pretty? Al and I put red oxide dust in the finish coat to give them a color other than cement gray."

They did look good. At the doorway I could see that the slab of concrete was more than two inches thick. Then Burleigh smiled. "All education isn't in the book. I read up on pouring concrete floors until I thought I knew just how. Then Wembo Lua asked me whether I wasn't going to sprinkle the tamped dirt with kerosene before pouring the concrete. I told him we didn't need to because this would be a thick concrete floor, not a thin cement slab. Well, I just didn't know. We poured our first trial room. Fortunately it was the small entrance room. The next morning there were little mounds of dirt all over it where the white ants had pushed up through the wet cement for air. That left fine holes for the ants to use in the future."

"Too bad," I said.

"Yes, but a good lesson to remember. This is Wembo Lua's home territory. He knew we should have killed the ants before pouring the concrete. He got a charge out of my asking him whether he wanted a whole drum of kerosene for the other rooms."

During these days Burleigh and Al seemed to live at a running pace. The "Cat" was needed for work in the forest. The logs needed sawing. The bricks needed pressing, stacking, firing. The windows and doors of the maternity building had to be made. The gravel had to be hauled in. The nearer the hospital became to reality, the harder they pushed.

CHAPTER NINE

Problems and Satisfactions

IN THE MIDST OF THIS ACTIVE LIFE AND WITHOUT ANY APPAR-
ent cause, I began to feel peculiar. I couldn't sleep at
night and would lie and toss until early morning hours.
I had never had such trouble before. In the mornings I
could hardly wake up. I had to push myself to class and
was just half awake when I did get there. I could hardly
wait for lunch to be over so it would be time for a nap.
When two o'clock came, I simply couldn't wake up.
The women of the sewing class would come and call me.
Distantly at times I could hear Margaret Ann crying.
Finally I would barely manage to drag myself out of
bed.

"I'm just not going to bed for rest hour," I said to
Burleigh one day. "If I can break this vicious cycle and
once stay awake all day so I will be sleepy at night, then
I'll be all right."

So I went into the living room to sit it out. The next
thing I heard were dim voices calling, and I found I had
fallen asleep and slumped over in my chair. I was getting more and more disturbed, but Burleigh was so
busy, I hated to bother him about it. Besides, I thought
it must be temporary.

Then I woke up one morning with a terrible headache. "Dear me," I sighed, "surely I'm not starting migraines." I had friends on the station who suffered with them.

Finally I called Dr. Akerburg who gave me a shot. I felt better, but by late afternoon I was right back where I had been. This continued for several days. A shot in the morning, another in the afternoon. I began to sink into a real depression.

One evening our doctor came over to talk with Burleigh and me. "Virginia is on entirely too much dope," he said. Kindly he probed to see if he could find some hidden psychological reason for my headaches. No, I loved Burleigh; there was no marital discord in our home. He seemed convinced that I was being honest with him.

Burleigh now became disturbed. He had been so busy that this was the first time he realized just how sick I was, and he felt terribly guilty. On top of everything else, I had to try to convince him that I didn't feel neglected or left out by the time-consuming hospital project.

The next morning a nurse came from the hospital to take a blood sample. "Dr. Ake is going to run you through the lab," she said.

She took one from me and one from each member of our family. At the lab, one of the slides made her shriek with dismay. "Come quick! Do you see what I see?"

Another trained eye looked through the microscope. No doubt about it, there were thirteen perfect trypanosomes in that slide. I had sleeping sickness. I was the first missionary in our mission-field to contract what everyone called the "dreaded African disease." The cause of my headaches, my sleepiness in the daytime, my depressions was now known. But what were we to do?

We reported my illness to the Board of Missions in New York.

They answered immediately, "Whatever Virginia feels is the best cure for her the Board stands ready to finance."

Bless them! But what did I think best? Go to some famous medical center? London? Antwerp? Tulane?

Burleigh and I talked it over. We had to face the dangers. We had seen African patients sitting hopelessly in a stupor waiting for death, and we knew that any brain damage would be permanent.

"What do *you* really want to do?" Burleigh asked me.

"I don't know. I don't see how you could possibly leave now to go home."

Finally Burleigh said, "Would you consider going home without me? Your family could meet you in New York and take the children. Then you could go to Tulane for treatment."

I sat for a moment, not being able to bear the thought of leaving Burleigh. I remembered how much it had helped to have him holding my hand while those terrible spinal punctures were made during the lab tests. We decided to let the subject rest for a day. I noticed that Burleigh prayed longer than usual in his early morning devotions.

Dr. Ake brought me a book on sleeping sickness. In it I noted a statement that the author of a particular section was a specialist, for he had studied extensively and had treated thirty-five patients.

When Dr. Ake came again that afternoon, I asked

him how many sleeping sickness patients he had treated.

"I don't have any idea. I think we have about 134 cases in the mission now," he said.

"Ake, could I stay here in the Congo and be treated by you?"

He knew it was a serious decision, but he spoke with quiet confidence. "Yes, I think so, if that's what you want."

After he had gone, I lay praying and thinking. I longed for my family in the States. But I did not want to go without Burleigh, and I couldn't take him away from the hospital project. It was moving along well now. We had hopes of seeing the new maternity building completed and occupied within the next year, before our regular furlough. Burleigh was desperately needed on the job, and I knew that for his morale it was important for him to see something actually accomplished after years of frustration.

When Burleigh came home that evening, I simply announced, "I'm staying here. Dr. Ake is going to treat me. He is willing, and the Board said I could do what I wanted to do. This is what I want."

A look of relief flooded Burleigh's face. I wondered if maybe the Lord and Burleigh hadn't already worked out that solution!

The treatment was rough. I reacted badly to many of the drugs and had further reactions to the drugs taken to counteract the drugs. But I was with Burleigh, he was continuing work on the hospital, and I had a doctor in whom I had the utmost confidence. It was the best solution.

One afternoon shortly after the news had spread that

"Mama Uya Koi has sleeping sickness," Wembo Lua came over to visit.

"I just don't understand," he said with a tremble in his voice. "In almost thirty-five years of having missionaries here in the Congo, not one has ever had sleeping sickness."

He wiped a tear from his cheek. "What will this do to our work? Missionaries will surely be afraid to come here now. I just don't understand why God let this happen to you."

We sat quietly for a long moment, and finally Burleigh spoke. "I've asked the same question for several days now. Mama Uya Koi has taken the preventive shots every time except when she was pregnant, and they aren't safe then. We don't know why." He waited and then continued, "Often we don't know why, Wembo Lua. Then we have to trust God."

Wembo Lua's eyes were steady. "Truly, that is so."

It was a long, slow process back to good health. I was completely incapacitated for three months, spent six months under treatment, and many months passed before I was completely well. Yet I had to take care of my family. David must finish his third-grade work because he was going to Central School for missionary children in August.

Listening to the Presbyterian radio broadcast on a Saturday noon, I heard the children of Central School sending their weekly greetings home. One childish voice came on, "Hello Mother and Dad and Dud! This is Alice. Everything is fine here. Hope everything's fine there. Be sure to feed my kitty."

Just the thought of Alice, one of our own mission children, being at least four hundred miles away from home, sent me, weak as I was, into sobs. I saw just ahead of me my own son going away to school.

I think that separation from one's children is almost the greatest problem for missionary families. In any isolated mission such as ours, there is no way to provide adequate education beyond the primary grades. If they are to be prepared for college, they have to begin by going to boarding school while they are young.

During the period I had been "holding school" in the dining room, I had observed other children from our station pack up in early August and go off to "C.S." At Christmas, they came home joyfully. But by mid-January, when they again left us, they were eager to get back to school. Burleigh and I compared these children with a few we had seen whose parents had tried to teach them at home because they felt the separation was too hard. We were convinced separation was hard indeed, not on the children, but on the parents. So our minds were made up. When he was ready for fourth grade, David would go to C.S.

Gradually, I began feeling better and was able to resume my responsibilities. The day in August came when David would leave us. When the station wagon was packed and we were ready to be off, our cook, Ngandu, appeared with a box of cookies, a loaf of bread, some jam, and a jar of freshly ground peanut butter for his little missionary ward.

When the weekly mail truck arrived the first week David was away, we were interested only in that crumpled little envelope that looked as if it had spent days in a little boy's hip pocket.

Every Saturday we listened for that special voice on the radio broadcast from C.S. Somehow Burleigh always managed to make it home for dinner in time to hear, "Hello Mother and Daddy and Paul and Margaret Ann. Everything's fine here. . . ."

Everything was fine at the station, too. Paul was in the second grade, Margaret Ann was learning to sit up, and the main hospital had begun to rise above the ground. It had taken months to get the foundations poured and the brick walls laid to that level.

One afternoon, as we were inspecting the work, we chatted with Ulungu Albert, who was studying to become our first really qualified Congolese nurse. He was the elder son of a very important chief near Wembo Nyama, the only Christian in his village. He had given up his chance of inheriting his father's position to come to the station to study. In our nursing course he had done outstanding work. Some missionaries had been tutoring him for months, and the next week he would take the exam to enter the advanced nursing course at Kimpese.

Later, Burleigh said to me, "When I see someone like him and know that the hospital is a place for him to serve his people, I'm really proud to have a part in building it."

The next morning Burleigh spoke to the workmen at their early morning worship.

"There were once three workmen who went to work on a building. Each of them was laying bricks. A traveler passed by. He stopped the first man. 'What are you doing?' he asked.

"The first man looked up. 'Can't you see? I'm taking this brick, putting mortar on it, and placing it on the other.'

"The traveler stopped the second man. Again he asked the question, 'What are you doing?'

" 'I'm building this wall,' said the man with a grumble.

"Then the traveler asked the same question of the third man. This man raised himself straight, pulled back his shoulders, and said with pride, 'I'm building a church.' "

Burleigh went on. "We aren't just sawing lumber, digging gravel, laying bricks. We are building a hospital. This hospital isn't just to treat illnesses. It will be a place to show God's love. You and I are workers together with God."

Then Burleigh spoke of something he and Al had often discussed. The workmen were interested in their own worship service, and the attendance had stayed amazingly good. But shouldn't there be a ministry for these laymen to carry on in their own villages?

Thus began the layman's witnessing program in the villages. Volunteers gathered each Friday afternoon after work and planned their Sunday services. Burleigh and Al helped them when they needed it and went with them to lend support. One Sunday they would go on their bikes to neighboring villages; the next Sunday by truck to more distant areas, dropping the workmen off in one village after another as they went out and picking them up as they returned late in the afternoon. The effectiveness of the simple witnessing, "This is what God has done for me," proved to be amazing.

I looked forward to Burleigh's return from these trips because he was always so enthusiastic. "When the Christian message is carried by the Congolese themselves from the mission station out into the villages, then we are really building a church here," he said.

One afternoon he came in especially excited. "We had a wonderful day in Lutula's village," he reported.

Lutula was one of the workmen whose previous life had been so obviously evil that we were all astonished to see what changes took place when he became a Christian. His home village was some distance from the station, and Lutula had not been back there between his conversion and this trip with Burleigh in the truck.

"There's no church in the village, so we met out under the palm tree," Burleigh told me. "A good crowd came. Lutula spoke last. What he said wasn't profound, but the villagers who had known him knew that God had really changed his life. At the end of the service several persons came forward for prayer. One of them was an older woman. She said she wanted a new heart like Lutula had.

"'Do you believe that God can give you a new heart?' I asked her.

"'Oh, yes, if he can give Lutula a new heart, he can give anyone a new heart.'

"'Why do you feel you need a new heart?'

"'I practice witchcraft,' she said."

Witchcraft is so feared by the Congolese that it is a legal offense even to call anyone a *Doka* or practicer of witchcraft. Yet this woman had openly confessed that she engaged in that practice for her livelihood. Burleigh said that the group prayed and she accepted God's forgiveness and grace.

Then she went to her house, returning with a large bowl of unshelled peanuts which she placed before the group. Each man looked at the other, wondering. This woman had just confessed to witchcraft. Could there be poison in those peanuts?

"What did you do?" I asked Burleigh.

"I took some peanuts and ate them. Then Wembo Lua did, then Lutula, and finally all the men."

The weeks raced by. Now the time of our furlough was near. Knowing that Burleigh would be pushing until the last minute, I started sorting what would go into storage for the year we would be gone. I had a little too much help at this job. Every day or two something more would disappear. "Paul, where is that white shirt I put right here on the dresser?" I asked one day.

"I sold it to Kasongo for some bananas," he said.

"You mustn't do that. You don't know what is to be taken stateside and what is not. Let me decide."

Knowing that I was getting rid of things, a nurse stopped by one afternoon. "Do you have any good men's clothing?" she asked. "We'd like anything you can spare for Ulungu Albert. He passed the entrance exam for the Kimpese Nursing School and will be going there in the fall."

Only a few days later one look at Burleigh's face told me he brought home bad news.

"Ulungu Albert has been killed by lightning. He was sitting by his new radio with an aerial and no ground when lightning hit."

We rode our bikes down to his home. His widow had just arrived from her garden where she had been told the news. She sat in a chair, weeping.

"Has someone gone to his village?" I asked.

"Yes, Mama Ongenyi (missionary Barbara Hartman) went in the station wagon," a nurse said.

Burleigh went to the shop to build his second casket. Much later in the afternoon, I went back to Ulungu's home. His relatives had arrived. They were wailing and screaming, and some of the women rolled on the dirt in front of the house. They had taken Ulungu's corpse, set it upright in a swing-type lawn chair, and painted his face with white chalk markings. One woman sat holding his feet in her lap, hugging his legs; two others held his arms.

His widow sat on the dirt floor, stripped to her waist. Her head had been shaven clean and her body marked with soot. She was exhausted from wailing loud enough to satisfy his relatives.

There was a discussion going on in the yard between the station pastor and Ulungu's elder brothers. The pastor wanted a service in the church with a Christian burial in our station cemetery. The brothers were emphatic that he be taken to his home village.

"I think they're not going to use that casket," Burleigh said when he came home. "I think they're going to take him home wrapped in a grass mat and bury him that way. But it doesn't really matter. A mat or a box, it's all the same to him."

"It's not Ulungu that I'm concerned about now," I said. "It's his widow. She really will suffer if they hold the funeral in his village. They will follow all the old customs. No doubt she'll be beaten. Someone has to be held responsible for that lightning. She'll be the one."

Ulungu was taken to his village to be buried. I gave vent to all the frustration I felt. "As if superstition and ignorance weren't enough! If we have to fight lightning, too, I don't see any hope."

During the days that followed, our grief slipped beneath the surface. But from time to time the grief returned in a wave. Each time we had a sense of failure. Didn't God know how badly we needed Ulungu?

Some weeks later we had a visitor from the States. He was making a survey on missions, and for a day, missionaries and Congolese sat answering questions. His last one was "What is the most significant event showing progress for the Christian church in your area during the past year?"

The question was translated for the Congolese, and almost in unison several of them answered, "Ulungu Albert's funeral."

"Ulungu's funeral?" I couldn't believe my ears. That had been a bitter defeat.

Then we heard the rest of the story. When the family reached home, they began following the ancient customs. The widow had gone to the spring and climbed the hill on her knees, carrying a bucket of water on her head. She had pounded rice and cooked for the relatives. She had been abused. Then suddenly in the midst of all this, Ulungu's oldest brother had stood up.

"We can't do this. We can't bury Ulungu in our old

way. He was a Christian. We can't treat his wife in our old way, either. She too is a Christian. He loved her in the Christian way." The brother spoke with all the authority of his position. Finally the family listened.

They sent across the hills to a village nearby for a pastor. And Ulungu had the first Christian funeral ever conducted in an out-village. Our sense of defeat was eased.

Preparation for the dedication of the maternity building gave a further lift to our spirits and kept us busy every minute. The newly placed glass windowpanes had to be cleaned and polished. The floors had to be scrubbed. The carpenters worked hard to get tables and cabinets finished and moved into place. Then we rubbed them with a polish made of motor oil and candle wax until they were shining. Metal beds with springs had come for the wards. We bought woven mats to serve as mattresses. By the time Bishop Booth arrived for the dedication, we were ready.

Burleigh and I stood beside Al and Mary Ann Burlbaugh for the dedication service in May, 1955. As we looked out over the crowd, we could see the nurse's aides dressed in white aprons over blue uniforms and wearing white caps. The male nurses wore new khaki uniforms with red crosses embroidered on the pockets. Near us stood a group of male student nurses proudly wearing bright blue shirts and shorts. At the close of the service Bishop Booth, Burleigh, and Al shook hands with each student.

As we walked away, after hundreds of expressions of thanks and appreciation, Burleigh said, "Well, there stands the building. God will have to raise up other Ulungus as nurses to man the wards and operating rooms."

It was then only days before we would leave on a furlough. The closing exercise for the primary school was in progress, and the time had come for graduates to receive their certificates. Each one went forward dressed in clothes newly acquired for this great occasion. Each carried an elaborately embroidered handkerchief by which to hold his certificate. It was much too precious to be touched by even slightly soiled hands.

As I glanced over the group, my attention rested on one boy wearing a nylon shirt. My mother had recently sent our boys such shirts for travel. The student looked familiar, and I realized it was Pastor Dendi's son, Ahoka, from Usamba. The boy was one of Paul's best friends. Then I knew that Paul's furlough travel shirt was appearing at this primary school graduation.

As soon as the program was over, I found Paul.

"Was Ahoka wearing your shirt this morning?" I asked.

"Yes, Ma'am," he said lowering his head.

"Did you sell it to him?"

"No, Ma'am. He just borrowed it for the program. You know, Mommie, he had to have a new shirt to get his certificate, and he didn't have one. That was the only new one I had. He'll bring it back."

Late in the afternoon, up our path a proud graduate came skipping, carrying something wrapped in a paper.

"Mama Uya Koi, will you give Paul this shirt and tell him '*Lusaka Heyama Mvuta, mete*' (truly, more thanks than one can express)."

After storing all our belongings in various attics around the station, we were ready to go to Kindu to catch a plane for Cairo, Athens, Rome, and then America. As we drove from the station, friends stood waving. We drove past the completed maternity building, and then past the hospital rising half-finished out of the ground. There was a smile on Burleigh's face, but I noticed how terribly tired he was. The work had taken his strength for more than five years.

As we drove through Usumba, we passed a small boy —one of many—waving with all his might. It was Ahoka, telling Paul good-bye.

In my heart I wondered, "Which is the bigger accomplishment? The maternity building completed or the friendships built?"

CHAPTER TEN

Through Another's Eyes

MOMMIE!" PAUL CALLED OUT IN DISTRESS. "DAVID DRANK some water out of that faucet."

In the Congo all the water for drinking or brushing teeth had to be carefully boiled, cooled, and placed in bottles in the bathroom. Drinking water out of a faucet was only one of the many changes for the children as they returned to the United States.

"What do you want for supper?" I asked the family our first night back in the States.

"Hamburgers, milkshakes, and icecream, icecream, icecream!" Burleigh responded promptly. We ate just that.

Then we walked past the shops of New York, stopping in front of every window to marvel at what one could buy. Before going to the Mission Board Headquarters to be greeted, interviewed, and given our physical examinations, we wanted to go shopping. We were determined not to look like returning missionaries! But afterward a friend said, "We can always tell a missionary family when they come from the field because they always arrive dressed in new outfits."

From office to office we went, reporting on the Congo, bringing special messages from missionaries, and working out furlough plans. We found out that a furlough did not mean rest. Burleigh would be busy speaking for most of our year in the States.

From New York we went to visit Burleigh's friends in Weirton, West Virginia. Burleigh's home church held a big reception in our honor. At the close of the evening, the chairman of the official board spoke. "It is hard for us to tell you just how proud we are of you and how happy we are to see you back home," he said to Burleigh. "We know that if you had chosen to stay here and work in the steel mill, you'd have gone to the top. But you've chosen instead to be a missionary. Accept this check from your church and buy with it anything you'd like."

There was no adequate way for Burleigh to express what he felt.

We decided to locate for the year in Tallahassee where my parents still lived. Once settled, we began the big job of the furlough—making speeches about the work of the mission.

Before leaving the Congo, I received my first invitation. The camp that I had attended during my high school days had invited me back as the missionary speaker. I remembered how much the speeches had meant to the campers. I worked hard on my message. For an illustration, Burleigh suggested Ulungu Albert's death and Christian funeral. This seemed just right. So at the close of my message, I recounted the death of the promising young Congolese nurse and the burial in his village. I emphasized that after forty years of missionary work among the Batetela, in Ulungu Albert's village was held the first out-village Christian funeral in all that part of the Congo.

Following the service people gathered around with the usual comments of appreciation, but an old man came up to me. "Weell," he said in a trembling voice, "I've been supportin' them missions for nigh onto forty year. I've given regularly. But if in all that time you've only had one convert, and he's got killed by lightnin', I ain't givin' no more."

Fall came, and it was time to put David and Paul in school. It was, of course, their first experience in an American school. David's year at Central School in the Congo gave him some preparation for larger classes, but Paul came from one classmate to a class of thirty-five. New experiences for him came all at once.

He did not know how to put a dime in the slot of the milk dispenser. He did not know how to go through a cafeteria line or how to open a carton of milk once he did get through. He did not know he was supposed to join a line and tiptoe while going down the hall to the rest room. He did not know what "pass your papers forward" meant. The little boy just in front of him was a "slow learner." Paul did his best to read just like his classmate did, thinking that was the way his teacher wanted him to read. Each time the teacher had asked Paul, "Where did you go to school?" he would answer, "In the dining room." This sounded unbelievable.

An hour or so in a mother-teacher conference, and we had many of Paul's problems solved. Thereafter he liked American schools and did well in them.

David joined the Scouts, eager to make "Eagle" as Burleigh had done. Margaret Ann was finding the States full of icecream cones and candy, for Granddaddy always had dimes ready for the bell-ringing icecream man.

Looking after the children and helping them to adjust kept me pretty much at home, but Burleigh traveled all over the States. He had gone to the Congo to build, to work, to witness as a layman. This message appealed to the men in the congregation.

Sometimes the audience made useful gifts. One Sunday morning the owner of a Ford dealership was at the service. He felt deeply moved by Burleigh's message. Following the service they talked together. "I can't go myself. I'm not even sure I could see a child of mine go. But I can give you some help." And he presented us with a sturdy new Ford Ranch Wagon for our work in the Congo.

For young people Burleigh's special appeal was in his tales of hunting experiences. And he used the story of the man who had been gored by an elephant to illustrate the work of mission doctors and the need for the new hospital.

The furlough year passed quickly for us. We were to return to the Congo in August, 1956, by way of Belgium for our postponed year of French study. We both wanted to learn French, the official language in the Congo. Now, two weeks before time to sail, we were all packed when we received word from the Board of Missions, "Would you consider going direct to the Congo?"

Again, it was the hospital project. Al Burlbaugh felt he must have Burleigh to help. "I don't see how I can refuse," Burleigh said. "I remember all too well what it's like to be there alone on that job."

So he replied, "We'll do whatever the Board feels is best."

Three days before we were to sail came the message, "Laws proceed Congo."

My first question to Al who met us in Luluabourg was "What house are we going to live in?"

"Well," he said, "when the committee met during Conference, they discussed the houses on Wembo Nyama station. They decided that the old DeRuiter house was the worst. We voted to put you in it so Burleigh would make it over." After a moment, he added, "They did vote a thousand dollars for Burleigh to use on repairs. I went ahead and poured some good concrete floors because the white ants are terrible in that house. I also took out the partition between the living and dining rooms. Mary Ann said you told her you'd do that if you ever lived in that house. Before we get Burleigh tied up on the hospital, he can take time to make the house livable."

When we got to Wembo Nyama, the house looked just as bad as I had remembered, and I was dejected. But Burleigh began work immediately. He built a beautiful thirteen-foot mahogany mantel and under it made a fireplace of old bricks. He built cornices so the irregular windows appeared the same height. He turned the side porch into a glassed-in dining room. He screened in the front porch to make a pleasant outdoor living room and play porch for Margaret Ann. He transformed the old house. I honestly hadn't thought it possible.

Both David and Paul were now at boarding school and another mother with young children arranged to take care of Margaret Ann. This left me free to teach in the primary school where they were very short on personnel.

The hospital required all of Burleigh's and Al's time. There was wiring to be done as the walls went up, plumbing to be installed. It seemed the job would never get done with only two trained workers. Then the Board sent out an electrical engineer. "What Larry doesn't know about electricity hasn't been found out," Burleigh said to me enthusiastically. Now the building moved forward much more steadily.

One day a letter came from Iowa. "I heard you speak when you were on furlough," Burleigh read. "I was greatly impressed by your story of the man who was gored by an elephant. I am planning a trip through Africa and would like to visit your area. I'm doing a series of educational slides for schools and an illustrated lecture for churches, and I want them to show the on-going work of the station as accurately as possible. I would especially like some pictures of this man and an interview with him, if possible."

We wrote back inviting the writer, Skip Westphal, to come, telling him we hadn't seen the elephant man since returning from furlough, but we would try to find him.

Burleigh asked at the hospital whether they knew the man's home village. They checked and reported that it was on the river about a day's walk from the village of Samangua. The next morning Burleigh sent a man with a note to the chief of that village, asking him to send the elephant man to the mission. It was several days before the courier returned with a message from the chief: "The man left this village months ago. He went to another village. Our church is finished. When can you send us a pastor?"

To the next village Burleigh sent a messenger who returned with a similar message. The elephant man had moved on. The village people now had a church. When could they have a pastor?

Burleigh sent yet another messenger. "Hurry back," he told him. "It's only three days before we go to meet the visitor."

Late in the afternoon on the day before we were to leave, the messenger returned. "They say he left Lodja to go toward Katako Kombe."

It was at the new airport at Lodja that we were to meet our guest.

When we met the plane, Burleigh explained to Skip that we would try to locate the elephant man on the way back.

On the dirt road between Lodja and Katako Kombe, we came to a small sign with the village name LoKombe printed in uneven letters. On a hunch, Burleigh turned out across a grassy plain, following a very rough path. In the distance we could see the peaks of houses. As we drew nearer, we noticed a man working on the roof of one of the buildings. Passing a villager Burleigh called out, "We are looking for a man named Kotambulu; he was gored by an elephant a few years ago."

"Oh, yes, you mean Panda Ndjovu." Turning, he pointed toward the man on top of the building. "There he is. He's roofing our new church. That's the eighth village church he has built since he was saved from the elephant."

It was indeed our elephant man, and he was pleased to see us. "Could you come with us to Wembo Nyama?" Burleigh asked, "Our visitor wants some pictures of you with Dr. Hughlett, who save your life."

"How long will I need to be gone?"

"Only about two weeks."

"All right," he agreed. "Just so I can get back to finish this church before the rains begin."

We started for Wembo Nyama with Skip and our elephant man. Farther along the road, we saw a truck being pushed by a crowd of people, mostly women. Burleigh stopped and got out. "Moyo," he greeted one of the men. "You are Chief Kokolomami?"

"Yes," the chief said, stepping forward.

"Are you on a trip?" Burleigh asked politely.

"Yes, I am going to Lodja."

Turning to our visitor, I said, "That's an important chief who lives near here. Those women are probably his wives. I've heard he has forty of them. His brother died last year, and he inherited about fifteen wives from him."

Thinking something was wrong with the motor, Burleigh walked over and lifted the hood of the chief's truck. Immediately he put it down again. Then he shook hands with the chief, and we started on our way.

"Why didn't you work on the motor?" I asked.

Burleigh chuckled. "It didn't have one." He grinned at Skip. "With forty wives a chief doesn't need to have a motor to make his truck go."

For days at Wembo Nyama, Skip climbed over the hospital, taking pictures and asking questions. "Do you know that a woman at the hospital walked two hundred miles to get to the mission doctor?" he asked us.

"We often have people come that far," I said, unimpressed.

"But she passed up two state hospitals. She said it

was because they give love along with their drugs here at the mission hospital."

Suddenly I saw the work of our hospital as I had seen it when I was a new missionary, and I realized I had come to take it for granted.

"I asked them to call me if anyone comes in by hammock," Skip was saying. "I want to get a picture of that."

Two nights later a nurse called him. "They are bringing a man in."

Burleigh went along to translate for him. When they returned, Skip was very excited. "This man came forty kilometers. Porters took him first to the dispensary at a village nearby his, but the nurse couldn't treat him. She came along because the porters were afraid to bring the sick man out of his home area lest he die on the way. Then his spirit would roam forever without a home to return to."

"I told Skip that we would go out to Shilu one weekend to see a village dispensary," Burleigh said. "We'll plan to take a group of the laymen out there."

We packed our camping equipment and drove out one afternoon. The dispensary was a simple mud-and-stick building with grass roof, but was spotlessly clean and orderly. Skip was very much impressed with the nurse whose name was Wembi. "How long have you been on the mission?" he asked.

"I was brought to the Wembo Nyama station by my father when I was just a baby."

"What about your mother?" Skip asked.

"My mother died in our village. There was no way to

feed an orphaned baby. It had to die of starvation. So to save me from that terrible death, when they buried my mother, they dug the grave deeper to bury me with her. My father went with the villagers to the graveside. My mother's mother held me, ready to pitch me into the grave. Just before it was time to throw me in, my father grabbed me and ran away with me to Wembo Nyama. It took several days for him to get here. Crossing the plains, he was afraid my hungry cry would attract the lions. When we finally got here, I was almost dead. The missionaries didn't have dried milk as they have now, but they knew how to make peanut milk and fed me that. For months I lived in a missionary's home, and she cared for me day and night. Then I grew stronger and was taken to live with a Congolese widow on the station."

That night we sat in front of the village guest house. It was a clear, starry night. In the distance we could hear the village people talking and calling from hut to hut. "What's that whistling?" Skip asked.

We listened. We could hear a multitoned whistle, then a response in the distance. "That's just two boys talking back and forth," Burleigh said. Here was another African skill we had come to accept as the usual.

"Can they send any message they want to?"

"That's what people say. I have never tested them," Burleigh said, "but I've heard them call to each other in the forest that way."

He called the boy who was nearer to us; he in turn whistled, and soon the other boy came running, too.

"Show me how you whistle," Skip said.

With his fists, the boy formed a whistle, then by lifting his fingers he made the different sounds. Skip still wasn't convinced that they could actually send messages. "Take one of these youngsters down to the second house," he said to Burleigh. "I'll give Virginia a message for this boy. When he sends it, let your boy tell you what it said."

Burleigh went with the younger whistler. Soon Skip's message began to come through. Burleigh called back, "He says the message is 'I've lost my pencil in the garden.'"

Skip quickly became convinced. Back and forth he and Burleigh sent messages testing the boys' skill. Burleigh even tried to whistle as they did, but no sounds came out.

The next afternoon we were hurrying to get home for supper. When we came to the big village near the edge of the Wembo Nyama station, someone called out to Burleigh, "Python!"

We all got out to see. Stretched out on the ground was a huge python with a big hump right in his middle.

"He swallowed a pregnant nanny goat," the man explained.

It was hard to believe even after we saw the snake cut open and the goat taken out whole.

"If things get any more exciting around here," Burleigh commented that night, "we won't get any work done. Skip seems to make things happen."

Our visitor had only a few days left. One afternoon he came into our house very much excited. "Have you heard the new story about a python?"

He gave us the details. Two little girls were going to the spring for water when a python grabbed the younger one. A python's bite isn't poisonous, but he swings around his victim and crushes him. The older girl grabbed her sister so the python couldn't swing around. Finally its teeth pulled a plug out of the girl's leg. They ran fast, calling their father to kill the snake.

The next morning Skip visited the school. When we entered a third-grade classroom, the teacher was giving a lesson on "What to do when a python grabs you."

We stood listening. I wondered what I *would* do if a python got me. "Lie down quickly, flat on the ground," the teacher told his class. "He can't hurt you if he can't swing around to crush you."

"That's a great deal more useful for these children than reading about how to cross the street with the green light," Skip observed. "That's one thing I've noticed here. Your program is so practical."

Maybe that was one result of our coming to accept everything as normal.

The next day Skip was off to America, and we went back to our neglected work.

CHAPTER ELEVEN

Aluminum Haven

"THE REPORTS FROM THE CHURCHES AROUND LODJA SOUND
wonderful," Burleigh said to me one day. "I'd
like to take two or three of the laymen from the workline
up there. Would you like to go?"

I always wanted to go.

The revival around Lodja had started two years before and was largely the work of Pastor Ngondjolo
Moise, the district superintendent. We had heard reports of entire villages being transformed through
response to this Billy Graham of the Congo. Services
were currently being held in Diwoko, a large village
west of Lodja. In the village was a house we could oc-
cupy if we carried our own foods and sleeping equipment. Burleigh chose three laymen who had been active
in the Wembo Nyama lay-witness program to go with
us.

We arrived about mid-afternoon. Small square houses
with grass roofs lined the crowded village streets. News
of our coming had gone out. Some people had walked
more than fifty miles. Most had brought their food with
them, but the people of the village provided sleeping
accommodations.

We were directed to a small house at the end of the

177

village. Welcoming palm branches with flowers stood on each side of the path leading up to the front door. Inside, the dirt floor, a hard covering of broken-up ant-hills, had been dampened and swept clean. We set up our cots and table and unfolded our chairs.

Burleigh had just finished unloading the station wagon when Pastor Ngondjolo came to greet us. In the middle of his welcoming remarks, a young preacher rushed up. "The Esongo Mena are coming!" he announced.

The pastor looked startled. "The Esongo Mena? How do you know?"

"The chief sent a messenger, an Esongo Mena warrior."

Pastor Ngondjolo turned to Burleigh. "I must see about this. It will be hard to find sleeping places for these people."

We had long heard about the Esongo Mena. They were a clan of the Batetela tribe, but they lived in an area where there were no Christian missions. We had heard many hair-raising stories about them. Rumor had it that even the Belgian officials no longer bothered them, for after years of effort, the Esonga Mena still didn't pay taxes, work roads, or raise cotton unless they wanted to, and usually they did not. They lived deep in the forest, raised their own food, wove their cloth from raffia, made clay pots and carved wooden spoons, avoided other clans, and left the white man and his civilization strictly alone.

They arrived at Diwoko just about time for the five o'clock service. We watched them moving in a group down the road. Their highly oiled bodies reflected the late afternoon sun. Instead of the usual shaven heads or short hair, they had long hair, slick with black tar and worn in a big heavy braid down the back.

As they came nearer, I could see that their faces were covered with small raised bumps, forming designs and giving them a hobnailed appearance. "How did they get those marks on their faces?" I asked a village man.

"They make cuts in a child's skin when he is about eight. Then they put tiny pieces of crude rubber underneath the skin. The cut heals over and leaves those permanent markings," he explained.

The Esongo Mena had very sober faces as they marched by, three in a row. But one small boy looked at me and smiled. His front teeth had been filed into sharp points. His hobnails looked tender, obviously just healing over.

"Do they all file their teeth, too?"

"Yes, at the same time that they mark their faces."

On the bare breasts and stomachs of the women, who wore only raffia skirts, I saw still more hobnail designs. But I noticed that the bodies of the younger girls were untouched although their faces were marked. Our guide told us their bodies are not marked until they're ready to bear children. Marking assures that a woman will be fertile.

Some of the men carried spears. "Those men must be the warriors," Burleigh said. "I wouldn't care to tangle with one of them."

The village men nodded. "They are fierce warriors, and none of us would tangle with them either. They know it."

For the service, the village people had built a large

palm-branch arbor. Under it were rows upon rows of logs for seats. At the front was a raised dirt platform, and running the length of the platform was a long altar built of small sticks. As guests from another mission station, we were ushered to the front and given chairs on the platform.

Crowded together as close as they could possibly sit, the people filled the log benches.

"It is an amazing crowd. I wonder how many are here," Burleigh said. "Count those on this side, and I'll count my side."

We got the incredible total of 3140! Burleigh exclaimed, "Think of a gathering of this size at a Christian meeting in the heart of the Congo!"

There was still one vacant space which we decided was for the Esongo Mena. Then we saw them entering the arbor, still flanked by their warriors. They crowded the space reserved for them while the warriors stood at the edge, their long-handled spears in one hand, their bows in the other. Over each warrior's left shoulder hung a skin sheath filled with poison-tipped arrows.

The service began with lusty singing. When the singing stopped, Pastor Ngondjolo stood up. "We are at the time to talk with God. We will all bow our heads and close our eyes while Pastor Luhaka talks to God."

A rumble was heard among the Esongo Mena. It grew louder. Some voices sounded angry. All looked in that direction, some shifting uneasily in their seats.

Pastor Ngondjolo walked down from the platform and went to the Esongo Mena chief. "What's the trouble?" he asked.

"Are you asking us to close our eyes here among these people?" asked the chief.

"We always close our eyes when we speak to God," Pastor Ngondjolo explained.

"Not us. We don't shut our eyes among strangers," the chief retorted.

The pastor thought a moment. "Would the rest of you shut your eyes if your warriors kept their eyes open?"

The chief spoke with his elders and agreed that that would be all right. The crisis was over.

When Pastor Ngondjolo preached, the Esongo Mena sat with their eyes fastened on him. "'I am come that you might have life and have it more abundantly,'" Ngondjolo quoted. Then he asked, "What is the one thing we strive hardest to keep?"

He answered his own question. "Life! But what is life if you are a slave?"

He waited a moment. "You will know the truth, and the truth will set you free."

I had never experienced bondage and so had never known that deep longing for freedom or felt the burden of a life without hope. But that afternoon, listening to Pastor Ngondjolo describe slavery, I came closer to understanding what it all meant.

At the close of the sermon, a group knelt at the altar, including one of the Esongo Mena men. He wept, and Burleigh went over, knelt beside him, and quietly talked and prayed with him. Finally the man looked up at Burleigh, his face radiant. "Peace is in my heart."

Then he stood and turned to the congregation.

"Within the past three years I have killed and eaten five people. But—I was in darkness. I did not know."

I turned to Burleigh. There were tears on his face, too. It was a scene I shall never forget.

At the pastors' meeting later that same afternoon, Pastor Ngondjolo spoke of the need among the Esongo Mena. The entire Lomela district to the north of Lodja had no mission station and only a few isolated Congolese pastors, who had few opportunities to get together. The mission had been wanting to open a station there for a long time, and recently, a large gift had been received for such a purpose.

Moved with concern for these people, Pastor Ngondjolo pleaded for pastors who would be willing to leave their own tribal group and their established churches to go to these clans unreached by the Gospel.

"Is there anyone here who feels he could serve there?" Pastor Ngondjolo asked.

Burleigh stood up. "I feel that God may be calling *me* to Lomela."

There was a long moment of silence. Pastor Ngondjolo stared at Burleigh in wonder. He had been speaking to Congolese pastors, but a missionary had responded. Such a thought had not occurred to me and yet, somehow, as Burleigh spoke, I had a strange feeling that our future lay among these people.

The next day we returned to Wembo Nyama. We talked again and again about Lomela, about Burleigh's sense of call to that district.

There were many obstacles. Though the basic work was done, the hospital at Wembo Nyama was still not completed. Then, too, Burleigh was a lay missionary, not a minister. Our mission stations all had been opened by ordained ministers. It seemed unlikely that a layman would be appointed this time. Were we really the persons to pioneer a new work?

"We'll just pray and see what develops," Burleigh said.

I could tell that Burleigh felt a real call to Lomela, but I was concerned. We had just settled into our remodeled home at Wembo Nyama; I knew there was no place to live at Lomela. We had a mission doctor on our station; there was none there, and Margaret Ann was only five years old. We had many missionary friends on our station; at Lomela we would be the only missionaries. At Wembo Nyama we had made many Congolese friends, while at Lomela, we would be with people of different clans. In Wembo Nyama, the church had been working for over forty years; in Lomela we would be opening an area almost untouched by the church.

Then I remembered the words of the Esongo Mena man. "I was in darkness. I did not know." I could understand why Burleigh felt such a sense of call. And I remembered a promise I had made years before: "I'll never stand in the way of what Burleigh feels is God's Call for him."

Three months later a message came to Burleigh over the noon-day broadcast. "Bishop Booth's cabinet voted last night to ask you to open work in Lomela."

"Did you know you were going?" our surprised Wembo Nyama friends asked.

"Yes and no," Burleigh said. "Yes, I knew God was leading me there. No, no one had said anything to me about it."

Burleigh was very happy over the appointment, but he did hate to leave Al and the unfinished hospital. However, a new missionary would replace him on the project.

It took us months to get ready. Burleigh had to order building supplies which he had shipped direct by river barge to the Lomela port. We had to pack our personal things, selecting the bare necessities to take with us. Burleigh needed to finish some essential jobs at Wembo Nyama.

Finally the day came to tell our friends good-bye. I had very mixed emotions as we drove off the Wembo Nyama station. Tears were just under the surface. Burleigh saw me fighting to keep a happy face. He took my hand. "It's pretty hard to follow a husband all over the world, isn't it? God knew I'd need someone who could take it."

Somehow the tears dried, and I could smile. I was going with Burleigh to Lomela.

North of Lodja, we entered the tropical rain forest, and for miles tall trees towered over the road. As we neared Lomela, large rubber plantations lined the road. We crossed a river on a cable-drawn ferry, and a few miles beyond we came to the Lomela State Post where the Belgian administrator, police officer, agriculturist, health officer, and various clerical personnel lived. A little further along was a trading center with a few families. None spoke English. How we needed those French lessons! On the top of a hill, we found our mission concession. The location had been chosen months before. There would be good circulation of air and good drainage. And there was a good spring in the valley nearby. All these things were important, but on that first afternoon, all I could see was heavy forest.

Burleigh looked at the thick underbrush. "We won't have any trouble getting grass to grow."

. Growing grass did not seem to me to be our first problem! We had to have some place to live, some place just to be out of the rain and sun, with some privacy. Since it was two weeks until school started, Burleigh decided we could live in the school building at the village of Shutsha while he put up a temporary shed with our building supplies.

We drove the twelve kilometers to Shutsha and found a stick-and-mud school building with huge holes standing open for windows.

Before night, Burleigh had the windows covered with palm branches and our cots unloaded and set up, and we moved into our new home.

The next day Burleigh set up a workshop at Lomela and began building a shed. Margaret Ann and I made daily inspections. First, Burleigh had workmen clear away the underbrush, fell trees, and clear the plot. Other workmen cut long timbers six inches in diameter. With the big truck we had for the new station, Burleigh hauled in these poles, which were set into the ground with other poles tied across on top to support a sloping aluminum roof. Sheets of aluminum were also used for the walls, leaving only a continuous high window (with shutters, in time) and spaces for doors. Timbers, tied with native vines and covered with planks, made the floor.

Ceiling boards divided the long house into rooms—a combination living-dining-kitchen, two bedrooms, and at the far end, the bathroom.

And quite a bathroom it was, too. With a long hose, Burleigh siphoned the water into the room from a drum outside. The sink and tub drained onto the ground. Directly under the white toilet that had been sent with the supplies, he dug a deep pit, covering it with large poles and a tight web of small sticks. Over this he packed wet clay, molding it around a four inch pole in the center. Daily he moved this pole slightly to keep the clay from drying too fast. Before the clay was dry, the pole was removed, leaving a pipe into the pit. A weak cement mixture sealed the toilet in place over the pipe. We had our "American bathroom."

Long, wide planks made the window shutters which we could open and prop up with a stick. Our front door was the side of the crate that had carried the refrigerator. We could read on it the words "THIS END UP."

I arranged the few pictures we had brought, hung some ivy on a pole, and placed curtains at the shutter openings and around crates used for furniture. We were settled.

We named Burleigh's ingenious creation "Aluminum Haven," but when David and Paul came home for Christmas vacation, they took one walk over the floor and renamed the place "Rickity-Rackity Rendezvous." But to all of us it was home.

The first time the usual Congo windstorm came blowing our way late one night, every piece of roofing rattled. Burleigh sat up on the edge of his cot, then began to dress. "I think I'd better check the roof."

He was none too soon. One by one, sheets of roofing began to lift, shift about, and slide down. While Burleigh coped with holding the roofing down, I gathered up Margaret Ann and dashed to our station wagon whose roof seemed more likely to withstand the storm.

There was not much privacy in this new home of ours. Burleigh's shutter openings were not for ventilation, for we had plenty of that. They were windows to let in light and for us to look out. But just as we could see out, so others could see in, especially our newly acquired sentry, Kasongo.

While I found this fishbowl existence a little hard to take, Kasongo enjoyed observing all the peculiar ways of the white man. Most of all, he liked to hang over the shutter opening and listen to our conversation when we had visitors, often joining in.

He wasn't as interested in some other visitors we had. Walking up from the workshop one day, we saw our front yard covered with what looked like a moving blanket.

"Driver ants!" we shouted in unison.

Millions of them, though not yet in the house. It's good advice just to move out and let them have the house, providing you have some place to move. We didn't.

Burleigh rushed to get gasoline, and for three hours we fought driver ants by throwing out cups of gasoline and lighting it. One rank of ants after another was annihilated. Just at nightfall, the ants turned and started their march over the hill away from our unprotected "Haven."

The few workmen required to build "Aluminum

Haven" had each come to us recommended by some village pastor as "a fine Christian character." This they may well have been, but they also were all of the same clan. Now we needed more men for the other buildings on the station. Each morning in the chilly tropical mist, a line of men seeking work formed before our Haven. Much to our experienced workmen's dismay, Burleigh hired them, on trial, without restriction as to clan or religion.

There were frequent reactions of concern and disapproval when some stranger entered the work group. One morning the reaction turned into rebellion when an Esongo Mena with tatooed face and filed teeth sought work. Burleigh stopped to talk with him.

"But, Uwandji, you can't hire him," the foreman protested. "He's an Esongo Mena."

"I know that, but you are Basambala, Etume is Bakutshu, and Peli is Bahamba. We are not all of one clan," Burleigh pointed out.

"But we don't cut each other up. Why, an Esongo Mena would as soon cut you up as look at you," declared the foreman.

Burleigh stood wondering what to do. Then he decided to give the work assignments, and when the men went to their jobs, he returned to the Esongo Mena. The man, Simoni, was eager to work. "Uwandji, you don't have to pay me. I'm not asking for money. I just want a book for my pay, and your wife, Mama Uya Koi, to teach me to read. Not one person in my village can read."

Burleigh hired Simoni to help load fill-dirt onto the truck. He was a hard worker. But one day he almost cut another workman with his shovel, whether by accident or from agitation, we couldn't tell.

The screaming of the other workman brought Burleigh running, just in time to grab the shovel from Simoni. Who could tell where the fault lay? Most likely it lay in generations past where the fear and hatred for the Esongo Mena had grown. Clearly it was dangerous for him to be on the workline. But it was also impossible to send him home with his first book, purchased out of his first pay, until he had learned to read.

So Simoni became Burleigh's personal aide. He held the boards to be sawed, he ran and got the hammer, he rolled the gas drums to the truck. When he was not working, he sat in the shade of a tree, unwrapped his precious reader from a soiled cloth, and studied the words.

The permanent buildings must be built of either bricks or blocks. Burleigh tramped through the forest looking for brick clay or gravel. He could find neither, but Papa Penta, an old hunter who loved nothing better than to be with Burleigh, said he knew the perfect spot.

"But it's a long ways downriver. Best way to get there is to float down by dugout, then wait for the regular river barge to bring us back." Papa Penta's face lighted up. "While we wait, we could hunt," he said, remembering Burleigh's guns.

Burleigh arranged to make the trip when the boys were home for Christmas. They thought they took as little with them as they could conceivably get by with: sleeping bags, camp kits, lantern, knives, guns, first-aid kit, drinking water, box of food. All Papa Penta needed, however, was a blanket, machete, some matches, and a gun. He roasted his food on the fire and used a large strong leaf for a plate. For drinking, he folded the same kind of leaf around his fist, forming a cup.

The trip was a great success, and everyone found what they hoped to find: for Papa Penta, good hunting; for the boys, plenty of excitement; and for Burleigh, gravel, good, clean gravel. Since the supply was miles down the Lomela River and he needed tons of it, he sent a crew of workmen to work the gravel beds and arranged with the bargemen to haul it up on their regular trips. It was then trucked the five miles to the station on the hill. All went well for a time, and soon cement blocks began to fill the drying shed. But then the truck-driver problem struck again.

Drivers in the Congo all seemed to have a weakness for palm wine; Burleigh continually had trouble keeping them sober. This time a driver named Welo had overturned the truck when it was loaded with our Youth Fellowship group out on a preaching mission. Fortunately no one was seriously hurt. As much as Burleigh hated to, he had to fire Welo.

The gravel piled up at the river. David and Paul were both back in school. Burleigh could not leave the job on the hill to do the driving, but he declared, "I'm just not going to hire another drinking driver."

Rarely had I seen Burleigh so completely disgusted with anyone or anything. Then he said one morning, "Virginia, could you take the truck down for a load of gravel? The men must have it for the blocks. They're almost out."

I became the new truck driver. The Congolese found

this amusing as well as strange. But, at least, Burleigh knew his new recruit wouldn't be drinking.

A few weeks later, a strange man, obviously unsteady on his feet, appeared at our door asking for Burleigh. When he was gone, Burleigh said indignantly, "Of all the nerve! That fellow comes here so drunk he can hardly find the path and wants a job as driver."

I smiled. "Maybe he's heard that's the only kind you hire. He may have spent his last franc getting in shape for the job."

When Burleigh began to grin, I added, "Driving that truck may soon drive me to drink."

The situation was becoming serious. There was more and more hauling to be done, and I had other work to do. Each morning at our prayers Burleigh reminded God that we needed a *good* driver! Then one morning a most unimpressive-looking young man showed up. Burleigh talked with him but did not commit himself. The next day, and the day after, the young man came again. "I don't understand why, but somehow I feel strongly I should take this man Elonge for a driver," Burleigh told me.

This strong feeling was one of the greatest blessings of our stay at Lomela, for Elonge proved to be the best driver Burleigh had ever had.

Opening a new station meant much more than putting up buildings. We were responsible for encouraging and helping the Congolese pastors and teachers who had been working for some time in a few areas. They had really opened the work in the district, but most of them had inadequate training.

There were also some outstanding Christian laymen.

In the southern part of our district was Mama Dundja. Years before, she had walked all the way to Wembo Nyama to the mission hospital where she had undergone surgery. She stayed for over six months, regaining strength to walk home. For the first time, she heard the Christian message from the hospital chaplain, and she returned to her village as the first baptized Christian. When she gave a word of witness, she often displayed the scar from her incision as evidence of her hospital experience.

Mama Dundja could not read or write. She could only tell what she remembered. Every Sunday, beating her *ekuli* drum, she called the people to worship and preached to them.

Some young people from her area attended the mission school at Lodja. Around vacation time Mama Dundja would sit beside the road, and when she saw a young boy passing with a pencil in his pocket, she would assume that if he could write, he could read. She would ask him to read to her out of her Bible, and slowly, through hearing the same passages over and over, she committed great portions to memory.

Whenever we drove into her village, even if we were just passing through, she would come running, clapping her hands and laughing, "Oh, Uwandji—Oh, Mama —I love Jesus. Do you love Jesus?"

On one occasion, we were pushed for time. There were other villages to visit. "We'd better not stop today to see Mama Dundja," I said to Burleigh.

As we came around the curve at the edge of her village, we saw her sitting by the roadside. Clapping her hands in greeting she said, "Oh, I was down in my garden. God said to me, 'Hurry home! Uwandji and Mama are coming by.' I got here just in time."

I wondered if God talked so directly to this Congolese woman. I asked her pastor about it.

"Oh, yes," he said, "none of us doubts that God talks with Mama Dundja."

"Is she always so happy?" I asked.

"I never saw her otherwise. Let me tell you what happened last New Year. You know New Year's is the time when every husband must give his wife a new cloth. Last year Mama Dundja gave her new cloth to the New Year's offering for the poor. All this year she has been wearing her old one. It is now in shreds."

I wasn't sure that I had anything to teach Mama Dundja about Christian faith or living, but I knew she had much to teach me.

Only one school in the Lomela district had regular teachers and more than one grade, although each pastor conducted a class for first-graders in his own village. At the school in Shutsha, classes were held in an open stick-and-mud building. Students came from all over the district, each with his own supply of food, and they lived in a big, crude one-room hut.

We were disturbed to find such living conditions and concerned to find the classes so crowded and the rooms so poorly equipped. Twelve-inch logs, split in half, served as desks and seats. There were no paper, no pencils, no slates. Students wrote with black charcoal on soft white boards made from the umbrella tree. When the lesson was over, they took a rough leaf, which we called the "sandpaper leaf," and rubbed out the writing. But this was too complicated for the younger children.

In most of the pastor's schools, the first-grade pupils just pounded the dirt hard under their desks, took a pointed stick, and wrote on the ground.

After school the children practiced writing words and numbers on the ground in front of their homes. One afternoon when Burleigh and I were visiting a village, we heard a child sobbing. Burleigh went to him and asked what was wrong. The boy was crying too hard to reply, but a friend said, "He's crying because he's lost his ABC's."

"Well, Mama Uya Koi will write them again for you," Burleigh told the little boy. "She's a real teacher."

I hated to think of the pastors struggling to teach without materials or books. Not only were there no books for the students, but the teachers had nothing with which to prepare the lessons. When I had taught in the teacher-training school at Wembo Nyama, I had learned what books were considered essential for our teachers. So I sent off a big order for teachers' books.

As we visited the villages, we made plans to open new schools and to equip those that were already opened. When our order of books and supplies came, we made a special trip to deliver them. It was a joy to see the children's eyes as we brought out pencils, paper, slates with slate pencils, and crayons. And sometimes, even a volleyball!

We were especially pleased with the bright and colorful books for the teachers. At the first village, when I handed the pastor his new books, his eyes lighted up.

But when he opened one, he asked, "Are they in French?"

Suddenly it dawned on me. I had ordered books that not one single Congolese pastor could read. Still, the children could enjoy the pictures.

Now that the most pressing immediate needs had been met, we had time to ponder just what was our over-all job at Lomela. We soon found that the Congolese expected us to take over the supervision of all the work. We were the missionaries who had come to direct them. We resisted this idea, wanting the Congolese themselves to take responsibility. But during the first few months, we had the same type of experience over and over.

A Congolese pastor or teacher would ride his bike up to our door. "Uwandji Utshudi A Koi, I need doors on my house down at Omba."

"Who has been seeing about doors for the houses?" Burleigh would ask.

"The Congolese district superintendent."

"Then the district superintendent will continue to see about doors," Burleigh would say.

On another day, a pastor proudly announced, "Here's the offering from my village," and he held it out to Burleigh.

"Who has been taking the money before I came?"

"Ndjukendi, the postal clerk, has been the treasurer of the church," the pastor replied.

"Then Ndjukendi will keep on taking the money."

Over and over Burleigh explained, "What progress would we make if Mama and I do what you were already doing? We will do what wasn't being done."

Slowly they realized we really meant it.

We found, too, that we had much to learn about the church in the Congo. "Would you help me with the communion?" the district superintendent asked me one day. "We haven't been able to have it often. It's too hard for me to prepare away from home, and the village women don't know how."

"All right, I'll help your wife prepare it, and we'll bring it out to the village in our station wagon."

We took a red unsweetened berry juice to the village. It was the first time communion had been served there. The preacher explained the meaning carefully, making it very clear that this was no magic potion that was being passed out. Then he explained the rules of the church concerning those who would be permitted to take communion. A group of women had just knelt at the altar when a loud feminine voice called out from the back of the church, "Is that you, Dembo, at that altar?"

There was a pause. A woman at the altar turned to look back.

"That *is* Dembo," the voice said.

Marching down the aisle with great authority, the accuser shook her finger at the kneeling woman and said, "You know you've been drinking palm wine. Get up from that altar."

Without any argument, Dembo rose and went back to her seat.

Whenever we came to a village, the children always crowded around. Many of them had never seen a white person.

One afternoon a little boy about three years old was

standing beside Burleigh, naked except for a cord around his waist with a small leather pouch tied to it. Burleigh stooped down to talk with him.

He pointed to the pouch. "What's that?"

"That's medicine," one of the bigger children answered.

"What's it for?"

Everyone stood quiet for a moment. We sensed that the boy was thinking of an answer to give the missionary. He seemed to find it. "That's to tell if a child is a boy or girl."

Raffia loin cloths were the accepted dress in the region, but in most villages we always found some young men in Western dress, sometimes even in a coat, shirt, and tie. These were members of the *Evolue* or elite group. We never could tell exactly how they had arrived at this distinction, but everyone seemed to accept them as being above the rest of the village.

We were to spend the weekend in a village where the Belgian government was making its first effort to select Congolese leaders. We were hardly settled in our guest house when a big group of well-dressed young men came to greet us. Even in the hot afternoon sun they were wearing heavy woolen suits and ties.

"We are the elite group of this section," the leader said.

"Are you having a meeting here?"

"Yes, we have come to select someone to work on the co-op program. The state man sent us the rules for making the selection."

They went back to their meeting and not long afterwards, we could hear angry voices shouting at each other though we couldn't understand what they were saying.

Walking to the door, Burleigh called to the sentry, "What's all the noise about?"

"They're just trying to select a leader. The state man sent over the rules. One rule says the leader must be able to read and write. None of them can read or write."

Turning to me Burleigh said, "No wonder our pastors with third-grade education are such respected leaders." In the villages where they were serving, these pastors were the real elite.

This was further borne out one afternoon in a small village where we had stopped for service. The village was full of children, who ran and crowded into front log seats in the little church. Most of them had a cloth draped about their waists, though some wore only a large leaf. All of them were dirty, with scaly hands and big scabs that stood out in knots on their heads. Their stomachs were distended. It distressed us to see children in such condition. "They need teachers and nurses," I said to Burleigh.

"Yes, they do." He nodded to one side of the church. "But look at that little girl."

There sat our pastor's wife dressed in a pretty, bright African print, with a gay kerchief on her head. Before her stood a little girl, her hair cut short and so thoroughly scrubbed that it shone even in the dimly lighted church. Her hands were clean and smooth; her dress was of unbleached muslin made with a simple yoke and a full, gathered skirt. Across the yoke were rows of vari-colored cross-stitching, and in the center was embroidered the child's name, "Ngandji," which means "Love."

"Her name fits her, doesn't it?" Burleigh said.

Not only our pastors but their families, too, were the examples to the villagers of a new way of life, the way of love.

The pastor's wife spoke to me after the service. "Couldn't we have a women's school here? My husband could teach reading and writing. I could teach sewing."

That very afternoon we opened our first women's school. Several months later we came back to visit. The pastor was teaching reading to a class of about twenty women. I noticed one very old woman in a grass skirt sitting on the front log with her skirt pulled between her legs exposing her thighs. Her skin was flabby and wrinkled. She shifted her book around, straining to find the best position to see. I walked over to her.

"Why do you want to learn to read?"

She looked up at me in surprise. "Why, they tell me if I learn to read this book, then I can read God's Word."

Determination such as this was a source of much satisfaction to us in our work.

Many of the pastors' wives had moved to Lomela district several years before. Since then, they had had no contact with the Christian women in other districts. I knew they felt isolated.

"Could we arrange to take some of them to the Woman's Conference for Central Congo?" I asked Burleigh. "It meets in about a month in the Lodja District this year."

"I need to take our radio transmitter to Wembo Nyama to have Al check it out," Burleigh said. "Margaret can go with me, and we'll drop you and some of the women off at Lodja and pick you up when the Conference is over."

The women chosen to go with us were excited over the prospect of the trip and of the chance to meet Christian women from all over Batetela land.

I knew just how the delegates from isolated Lomela felt getting back among their friends. I felt the same way. The village people at Lodja cleared some of their houses so the missionaries could set up their cots, and they furnished beds for the Congolese delegates. We ate together under a palm-branch arbor. All the water had to be carried from the spring in gourds on the women's heads. We dared not use one drop more than we absolutely had to. A real bath was out of the question.

On the third day of the Conference some of us were sitting in front of our house following the afternoon service when a group of Congolese delegates came by. "Where're you going?" one of the missionaries called to them.

"Down to the stream to bathe," they replied.

Just the thought of a bath made us all feel grimy.

"Let's go along," someone suggested.

Four of us grabbed towels, soap, and clean clothes and started down the path after them. Every village has three distinct areas for water. One is for drinking water, always upstream; another is for the women to bathe, and the third belongs to the men.

We came to a shallow, but swift-flowing, stream, with a white sandy bottom and high dark-green bushes growing on the banks. It was a little exposed for those of us accustomed to small walled-in bathrooms, but we began to undress. The Congolese women smiled and glanced from one to the other. We waded out into the stream with them, splashing ourselves with water, and the women smiled more broadly. As we began to work up a white lather with the soap, they broke into laughter.

"What's so funny?" I asked.

One woman controlled her mirth long enough to say, "It's just that you're so naked with your clothes off."

We had to laugh, too, for it was true. Our white bodies stood out in stark contrast against the dark-green leaves. The Congolese did not look nearly as naked as we did.

When the Conference ended, Burleigh came from Wembo Nyama to take us home. He was full of enthusiasm about the hospital.

"Did you get your radio fixed?" I asked.

"I'm bringing back a stand-by rig. We didn't work on the Lomela set." He smiled sheepishly. "Al and I spent the time talking about our hospital."

"Our hospital," he had said. I knew he would always feel that way about it even though he had left before it was completed.

Margaret had enjoyed playing with her missionary friends in Wembo Nyama, but we were not off the ferry at Lomela until she was excitedly greeting her Congolese friends. Her special playmates were the three children of our cook and the daughter of Simoni, Burleigh's Esongo Mena protégé, a little girl with hobnailed face and filed teeth. Sometimes they all joined Margaret for kindergarten in the morning. In the afternoon, they would move her toys out under a shade tree to play. Later they would come in and ask me to read one of her storybooks, which I translated as I went along. They loved to hear the Christmas story any time of the year.

One April afternoon after quitting time on the workline, I looked out to see some workmen trimming the palm trees. When Burleigh came in, I asked him if he had told them to.

"No, I didn't," he said, and we went out to investigate.

"You're working overtime, aren't you?" Burleigh asked.

"A little," a workman answered. "Amena (Margaret Ann) wants some palm branches for her Christmas play." He pointed to one corner of our yard where the grass was the thickest.

There, two more workmen were sticking palm branches into the ground, forming a semicircular backdrop. "We need to hurry," the workman said. "The pastor down in Olua has already beat his drum. The people will soon be coming."

"Coming up here?" Burleigh asked.

"Yes, we sent the pastor word," the workman said.

Obviously some stage production was under way that neither Burleigh nor I knew anything about. We could see Margaret Ann and her four little friends busy in the palm branch semicircle.

"Maybe we'd better just wait and come with the rest of the audience," Burleigh suggested.

It wasn't long before about twenty-five people and their pastor arrived. They went directly to the area the workmen had prepared and sat down on the ground.

Burleigh and I sat behind them.

The play began with Margaret Ann lying on the ground. Another little girl appeared draped in one of my bed sheets—obviously, an angel. The scene changed. Margaret Ann and two little girls sat around some sticks piled up for a make-believe fire. Their heads were wrapped in bright kerchiefs. When two more sheet-draped angels appeared, the audience knew they were the shepherds.

There were several more scenes before Margaret came out with her baby buggy. The one little boy in the group stood beside her. From behind the palm-branch screen came a little girl with a long shepherd's stick. Beside her, crawling on her knees, was the little Esongo Mena girl. Just her hobnailed face showed from under a sheet draped over her back. "Baa, baa," she bleated as she crawled up before the buggy-manger—a gift lamb for the Baby Jesus.

At the end of that scene, the shepherd went back behind the palm branches, but the little lamb stood upright, wrapped her sheet tightly about her body, and went over to stand behind the manger. A moment later the shepherd returned, and two little angels sang "Away in a Manger."

Margaret Ann stood up and lifted her little black doll out of the buggy. She tied it on her back with a long cloth and followed Joseph off to Egypt.

The play made a hit with the audience, who clapped enthusiastically.

All this time we still lived in "Aluminum Haven." In building it, Burleigh had carefully used vines and poles so that there would be no nail holes in the materials. He planned to use every piece in future permanent buildings. The first of these to go up was a two-bedroom guest house where we would live until he could build our permanent residence. At the same time Burleigh started a pastor's house near the church. "They need their house as much as we need ours," he said.

I doubted it but did not dare to say so!

As these houses progressed, Burleigh needed more and more of "Aluminum Haven." Soon he literally began to take out the planks I was standing on. I became accustomed to shifting things about so he could get to that special two-by-four he needed.

The bathroom end of the house was walled with boards. While taking a bath one afternoon, I heard some discussions just outside. Then I heard Burleigh shout, "Esso, let's go! Bring me that wide board."

Before I realized what was happening, the top board of the bathroom wall disappeared, and bright black eyes were peering down at me—in the tub.

I was ready to move into something more permanent. As soon as the concrete floors were set, even though not really dry, we began to move into the guest house. The carpenters hung doors, nailed in screens, and puttied the glass windows around us.

As always, Burleigh's main interest was the men who worked with him on the project. Gathering their cloths about them against the early morning cold, they came for a service before the day's work began. Their off-key, but enthusiastic, singing carried across the station and into the valley. Then Burleigh would speak to them, giving them simple but sincere explanations of the Christian life. When work assignments were given, Burleigh, by working among the men, illustrated the Christian life of which he had spoken.

At the close of work one day, Nonga, one of the most dependable block makers, came to him. "Uwandji, I will be leaving next payday."

This came as a shock to Burleigh. "Leaving? Aren't you happy here?" Burleigh asked, fearing that more tribal tensions were erupting.

"*Elu*, I'm very happy here. But God has spoken to my heart in our morning services. Now I want to tell my people about God's love. I am going up to Tokondo as village pastor."

Burleigh laid his arm upon his worker's shoulder. Nonga had no more than a second- or third-grade education, but it was very likely that no one at Tokondo had that much. And Nonga had something precious to share.

Each Sunday we went to some out-village. It was only natural, therefore, that a few months later Burleigh suggested, "Let's go up to Tokondo this Sunday. I'd like to visit Nonga."

We had heard good reports of his work. The state administrator had said to Burleigh one day, "He surely fits my idea of the 'shepherd of the flock.'" He explained that New Year's Day the State Post had received an urgent call to come to Tokondo because the entire village had become drunk on some very potent palm wine. When the state men arrived, there seemed to be one great drunken brawl, and many were seriously wounded. Then the administrator heard singing coming from the crude mud church. "That's the village pastor and his group of Christians," someone explained. "He called them to early morning prayers. His wife cooked food, and he tied the church door shut. They've been singing and praying in there all day."

When we arrived at Tokondo for our visit, we easily found the church with its neatly trimmed leaf roof and red flowers blooming at the door. A crowd quickly gathered about us. We admired their church, and Burleigh asked, "Where's the pastor's house?"

A woman dressed only in a raffia skirt, with fetishes on her wrist and ankles and red mud packed in her hair, pointed with pride. "The house there. The one with a window."

Down the village were two long parallel rows of mud-walled houses. Believing that evil spirits enter a home at night through any openings, the people built homes with no windows and only one door, which the entire family guarded by sleeping in front of it. But there among the windowless houses stood the pastor's house with one small window, a witness in that village to confidence in God's love.

CHAPTER TWELVE

The Elephant-Hair Bracelet

IT WAS LONELY AT LOMELA. LOCATED AT THE NORTHERN extremity of the Batetela tribe's territory, the district stretched for one hundred fifty miles from Lukavukavu to Itana. The Lomela government post stood about half-way between these two villages.

The one road between Luluabourg and Stanleyville ran in front of our station, so getting supplies was no problem. But as the only missionary family, we felt isolated. Often three months would pass without our meeting anyone who spoke English. Still, we found our work challenging and rewarding, and we were proud to be pioneers.

For Lomela represented a new type of mission program, called "Village Centered Work." The station was not to become a center to which the people would come for school, church, and hospital, such as we had in most stations. Rather Lomela was to serve as the hub, with the work itself being done in the villages where we would build small churches, schools, and dispensaries close to the people. At the hub we had plans for building residences: two for the missionaries (additional personnel was to come), one each for the Congolese district superintendent, the district school director, and the treasurer. Burleigh also built a carpenter's shop and dental office.

This new plan of working directly in the villages required that we travel out to them. When we moved to Lomela, Margaret Ann was only five years old, but we took her with us on our trips. Everywhere we went she received attention. Many villagers had never seen a white child, or a white woman for that matter. "What do you put on her to make her skin so pale?" they would ask.

They wanted to touch her or feel her hair. "How do you grow it straight? Was she born like this?"

It was amazing how well Margaret Ann took all this attention, but she didn't like to be touched. Burleigh or I would suggest, "Here, touch my hair. She's my little girl so she's just like me, the same as your child is like you."

One weekend we went to visit the village of Uhekeli, about fifty miles north of Lomela. This was a new village, several miles from the road. The villagers had cleared a narrow path through the forest, barely wide enough for our station wagon. We jostled over big roots, short stubs of bushes, turfs of tough grass, and freshly made holes where the people had removed trees to widen the path. We weren't at all sure the tires would stand up under such treatment.

The villagers had moved to Uhekeli to start new rice gardens. Now they were building homes. Looking down the wide street, we could see houses in varying degrees of construction on either side. The pastor had sent word that we were to stay in the chief's house, one of the few that was completed. Since there was no plains grass readily available, the roofs had been made of small leaves brought in from the forest. This wasn't as easy as it sounds, for it wasn't simply a matter of cutting down the trees to strip off the leaves. A man caught doing that was in disgrace for using his grandchildren's leaves.

Before each house, three long logs were arranged on the ground like spokes of a wheel, and a fire was burning in the middle. The ends of the logs were kept smoldering in the hot coals, replacements being added when necessary. It was considered shameful to let the fire ever go out.

The dirt on the street was still dark and rich looking. In time it would become bleached and clean swept. In the yards we could see that someone had recently been digging out roots. A few cannas drooped in the hot sun, planted but not yet at home in the new beds. Palm branches and fresh flowers showed us we were welcome.

We were slowly making our way up the street, waving in the characteristic broad sweep of the Congolese, when Pastor Samba signaled for us to stop. When we got out of the car, the villagers crowded around, clapping their hands together in slow, firm claps, their equivalent of an American handshake, and calling, "*Moyo, Moyo*, Welcome, Welcome."

"How long have you been here?" Burleigh asked Pastor Samba.

"We came at the end of the harvest. It has been eleven moons. Our new gardens are about ready to harvest." He pointed to a small rectangular building, roofed but without walls. "That's our church. We will get it finished soon."

"What about your own home?" Burleigh asked.

"I'm building it. It is there, just this side of the church. But I need my wife's help, and these days she must stay in the garden to frighten the birds away."

Chief Uhekeli invited us to his house. His wives had cleared a large room, making a place for our cots. Behind the house the villagers had built a cookhouse equipped with a table (four poles driven into the ground and a top of palm branches, flat sides up), an already smoldering log fire and a good wood supply, and three small round anthills, looking like stones, to hold up the drum top we carried for a stove.

A path led through the high underbrush to another palm-branch hut—our bathhouse and toilet. A row of large brown gourds holding about a gallon of water each stood along one wall. A low bath platform, only inches from the ground, gave us a clean place to stand while the water ran off into a trench dug beneath. The toilet was a deep hole, with the fresh dirt left beside to be thrown back in as needed. The villagers had really worked to meet our needs.

The chief's house had one long center room with doors at either end opening on the yard. We set up our cots in this, and the chief stayed with one of his four wives in her small house nearby.

On the wall of our room hung a board with black-and-white photographs of Congolese, several of the chief himself. There were also a few brightly colored pictures cut from some American magazine, including one that said, "I Dreamed I Went on a Safari in My Maidenform Bra."

As Burleigh and I sat on the porch waiting for the evening vesper service, we saw a group of women coming up the village street. Strapped to their backs were wedge-shaped baskets piled high with produce from their gardens and with pieces of firewood. On their heads were gourds filled with water. Several women also carried babies in their arms. They moved at almost a smooth trot, without a jolt to all that load.

"A long day in their gardens and now supper to cook," I said.

Margaret Ann, followed by three children about her age, ran up to Burleigh. "Look, Daddy," she said as she held out a small object. She pointed toward one of the boys. "Djamba made it all by himself." It was a kind of pull toy, with round hard fruits the size of oranges for wheels, a soft reedlike wood body, and a long stick handle. Each time the axle rotated, a piece of tin made a "tink, tink, tink" noise.

Burleigh tried it on the floor, and his face broke into a broad, pleased grin. "You must be a mechanic, Djamba." The little boy beamed.

The sun was beginning to set when we heard the ekuli calling the people to worship. The sound of this small drum reverberated from the forest, which closed tightly around us. The drum was made from a small log hewn out by a master drum-maker, and it had great meaning for the Christian people. Years before it had been the victory drum for war. Today it is used only for calling people to worship.

We sat with the others on log seats in the open-sided church. An occasional chicken joined the group, and a mother goat, bleating for her kid, ran through the congregation and out the other side.

Mid-way through the service, we heard in the distance a mournful chant, one voice and then many voices. The sound came nearer and nearer until we could see a strange group of men passing the church. They were dressed in loin cloths, hanging low on their hips and reaching just to their knees. Around their ankles were bracelets of dried seeds, which rattled as they moved along in rhythm. They wore wreaths woven of delicate vines, and their faces and bodies were decorated with wide streaks of whitewash. Each man carried a small brown gourd marked in white which was used as a rattle to keep time as the men chanted and stomped the ground. The leader of the group was a jester, dressed and marked in the same distinctive way, with the addition of a black and white monkey skin on his head and a small leopard skin hanging in front of his loin cloth. We watched them continue up the road to the chief's house.

As we finished our service, an elder came and called Pastor Samba outside. They talked for a moment; then the pastor returned to announce, "You women must go cook food. These people who passed by haven't eaten today."

The women rose and went without a question. This seemed strange to me. It was late in the day, and preparing food for so many people would mean hours of work and a drain on the food supply.

"Where are they from?" I asked.

"From Ukedi," Pastor Samba said.

"That's not far from here," Burleigh said. "Why didn't they eat before they left home?"

"They couldn't. Eating was taboo," the pastor answered.

This was something new to me. "Why?" I asked.

"Their rice is almost ready to harvest," the pastor explained, "and ground moles are eating the roots. The whole crop is threatened. Their witch doctor called together the spirits of those moles and put them in the gourds, and the men had to leave the village without eating. They must take the gourds just beyond our boundary where they will break them and let the spirits out."

I still felt there must be some other reason why the women would prepare food without any question.

"But couldn't you refuse to feed them?" I asked.

The pastor looked shocked. "And have them break those gourds and let the evil spirits out here in our new village?"

Burleigh and I went back to the chief's house, and from the porch watched the women hurry back and forth bringing food to the crowd gathered under the palaver shed. The chief joined us later, and we lit our lantern and sat talking to him.

Margaret Ann came out with her favorite doll to say good-night to Burleigh, who gathered both doll and girl into his arms and kissed them. Turning to go, Margaret stopped and shook hands with Chief Uhekeli and then stretched out her doll's hand which the chief grasped and shook.

The next morning while I straightened up our room, Burleigh sat on the porch reading his Bible and thinking about his message for the next service. The chief approached. "Would you sell me your child's dikishi (idol)?" he asked. "I'd like it to guard my little girl."

Burleigh was puzzled. "Dikishi? Margaret doesn't

have a dikishi." The chief pointed to the favorite doll. "That one there."

Burleigh tried to explain that this was only a toy. But how does one explain that a doll is not the same as an idol, a wooden figure the village carver has tried his best to make look human? After that experience the doll was replaced by cars and trucks.

We started back to Lomela after lunch. About five kilometers from the village there was a mark across the road. "It's pounded charcoal," Burleigh said. "The boundary line."

Just a few feet beyond were the smashed gourds, broken to free the spirits of the moles in another clan's territory. I was glad I didn't have a rice garden in that area!

Shortly after our return to Lomela from Uhekeli, we had two visitors. English-speaking guests were a treat for us. To have Methodist lady tourists all the way from the States was especially pleasant.

We knew that visitors were always interested in seeing the unusual. "If you'd like, on your way to Katako Kombe Station tomorrow, you could stop off at Okaku for a while," Burleigh said. "I'm going up there for a pastors' meeting." He smiled. "I should warn you—it's pretty primitive. The women don't wear anything but a G-string."

We sent word to the pastor that we were coming and drove with our guests as far as Okaku. The meeting had begun before we arrived, but the pastor ushered us to seats up front.

We looked around the crowded, little mud church

and had the sensation of being in a dry-goods store. There was cloth everywhere, not one bare breast. In fact, nothing was bare except the women's faces. We had never seen anything like it.

After the visitors had gone on their way, Burleigh and I discussed the service. We couldn't understand what had happened to the G-string fashions. Burleigh chuckled, "I'll bet the ladies are saying, 'That poor, prim missionary. He doesn't even know what is primitive dress.'"

I went again to the church for a special service the women were having at two o'clock. As I walked in, I found everything as usual. G-strings in abundance. My curiosity had to be satisfied. "Where did all the cloth come from for this morning's service?" I asked.

"We rented it. From the local vendor. To please our American visitors," one explained proudly.

They had no need to impress me. I was home folks.

Sometimes we made our out-village trips in just one day, visiting several nearby villages. Wherever we went, the people wanted Burleigh to preach, so he prepared what he called his "Circuit Sermon." But it was never given as he had prepared it, for in each village something unique was bound to happen.

One Sunday afternoon Burleigh had just begun his sermon when an old man came in and walked directly to the front of the church. In his hand was a bowl of djese—cassava leaves pounded fine and cooked in palm oil. Djese and rice are the Batetela's main food.

Standing before Burleigh, the old man interrupted in a pleading voice. "Will you take the taboo off this food for me?"

The congregation watched intently. Burleigh waited, looking thoughtfully at the old man. So much depended upon his reply.

"What harm does the taboo do to you?" Burleigh asked.

"It makes me afraid to eat djese, so I'm hungry."

"I can't take a taboo off the food," Burleigh told him, "for I have never known anything about this kind of taboo. But I can pray with you that God will take away your fear of the taboo. God loves you. He would want you to eat the good food He has put here for your body to get strength."

At the end of the prayer the old man rose smiling and went out with his bowl of djese. We hoped he ate it!

Burleigh went back to his sermon, but it wasn't the same one. God's love became God's taboos. "God's taboos never forbid something that is good for us," Burleigh assured them.

Burleigh and I made many trips, and the Congolese district superintendent, Ona Dinga, spent almost all his time in the field. We often arranged to meet him in a certain village. Mama Ekoko, his wife, would travel with us and see about the women's work.

One weekend we met Ona Dinga at Lukavukavu, a large, new village at the farthest point south in our district. The streets and walkways were carefully laid out and bordered with a red-leafed, low-growing plant. The small cement-block houses were plastered in rainbow shades, had metal roofs, and even proper windows with panes of glass in them. The village bore the definite mark of some Belgian administrator, and the houses were the product of a Belgian contractor.

The men of Lukavukavu worked on nearby rubber plantations owned by the village. Each man also had a section of his own to work. The village drummer called them to the plantations each morning before daybreak. We learned that they gathered the white rubber sap for two weeks at a stretch. Small oval-shaped cups hung from each tree to catch the sap. They emptied the contents into a bucket and that, in turn, into large cans, similar to milk cans, each bearing a worker's number. The truck from the rubber factory came later to pick up the day's output.

At the end of two weeks, the cut on the tree began to dry up. It was then time to clear around the trees, to work in the new plantation not yet producing sap, or to work in the rice gardens. There were always a few days of rest, time to hear palavers or have a feast before work began again.

Rubber was not only the money crop for Lukavukavu but also the security for government loans used by the co-op in building the village. Every month each man had a sum taken out of his pay. Although it had all been carefully explained, such a way of borrowing money was completely new to the Congolese. Every payday was a day of wrangling, and some poor state agent had to explain the deduction all over again.

I was greatly impressed with Lukavukavu, with the clean, neat homes and the orderly plantings. Walking along one of the streets, we saw a young man standing in front of a pink house. Instead of a loin cloth, he wore a cloth of raffia looped over his belt in front, running between his legs and looped again in back, with a small yellow and black leopard skin hanging down in front.

On each wrist he wore several copper bracelets, and around his neck was a leopard-tooth necklace.

He was holding the chain to a bicycle that stood upside down in front of him. Somehow that modern-looking pink house and bicycle and the man just did not go together.

Burleigh walked over to him. "Having trouble with your bicycle?"

"Yes, Uwandji. I can't get this new chain on."

"I'm an utshudi. Let's see if I can."

While we waited for Burleigh, the district superintendent's wife and I walked around to the side of the house. Out back stood a stick-and-mud house about as big as the pink house. "What's that?" I asked.

"That's where the owner of this house lives," Mama Ekoko answered.

"Then who lives in the pink house?"

"No one. It is to sit in and visit with friends. If someone important comes, he sleeps here."

Burleigh had quickly slipped the new bike chain in place. As we walked on down the street, I noticed that behind each pretty block house stood another brown mud one, obviously the one the family lived in.

We were invited to the pastor's home for supper. A table in the back yard was set with six metal bowls, each about the size and shape of a pie plate, and large tablespoons. In the center of the table was a bowl the size of a large wash basin, piled high with steaming rice, and smaller bowls filled with djese and chicken cut into small pieces and cooked in oil.

"Here is water to wash your hands," the pastor's wife said, holding out a cup of water. She slowly poured a few tablespoons of water over my hands, just enough to wet them, and handed me the soap. I worked up a thick white lather, then extended my hands to her. Slowly she poured water over them until they were completely rinsed. Less than one cup of water had been used.

The others all followed suit, and we took our places at the table. Margaret Ann looked around for the pastor's little girl with whom she had been playing. Dembo was sitting nearer the kitchen on a large straw mat, a dish of white rice and a small helping of djese before her. With her hands, she gathered a little rice, added a little djese, and pressing this into a firm ball, she put it into her mouth. "I want to eat with her," Margaret Ann said.

"But they put a place for you here at the table," I told her.

Though she didn't understand English, the pastor's wife knew something wasn't right. "What does she want?" she asked me.

"She wants to eat with Dembo," I said.

The pastor's wife smiled. "Then if you don't mind, I'll fix her plate down there."

Margaret sat down beside her friend on the mat, and the pastor's wife filled her plate and placed it and the big spoon in front of her. We said grace, and I turned toward the mat to see how everything was going. The spoon lay unused. Margaret was busily trying to get a rather unwieldy ball of food into her mouth.

The food was good, and we were hungry, yet we kept a fast conversation going. Suddenly we heard a young girl's high-pitched voice screaming and shouting. Burleigh and I could not understand her words.

The pastor explained. "She is saying 'I don't want to go!' It is a young girl being taken to her husband's home."

The screams drew nearer. As the girl passed the house, we could see she was not more than ten years old. Leading her by each arm were two young men, one carrying a long-handled ornate copper spear, highly polished and glistening in the dimming afternoon sun. Behind trailed several other men and an old woman.

"Who is the man carrying the spear?" Burleigh asked.

"Her older brother," the pastor said. "That's the spear that the groom's family gave years ago to bind the marriage agreement. Now that he is bringing the girl, the brother returns the spear and will receive the dowry."

"Who is the old woman with them?" I asked.

"That's her grandmother, the one who decided to complete the marriage. Now she is going to get her special gift for letting the girl go."

The screaming slowly faded in the distance. No one said anything for a while. "Is she really going into a marriage at that age?" I asked.

"Yes," answered Mama Ekoko. Sensing the question I hadn't adequately expressed, she added, "She'll now be a wife in every way that you and I are."

Margaret Ann came up to me. "Why is that little girl crying, Mother?"

"She's unhappy."

"Are those people mean to her?"

"They don't think so," I answered.

Margaret stood thinking for a moment. "Maybe she'll soon be happy."

"Yes, maybe so," I agreed. Within my heart I emphasized *maybe*.

The following morning we began with a six-o'clock service, and at nine we had a service with the women. A drum called us to the church, a long building closed in only to window level and plastered in light green. The low benches inside were without backs but were still a real improvement over logs. I sat on the front bench, thinking of the little girl we had seen the day before. On the bench behind me was a row of girls, none of them much bigger than yesterday's bride. Two of them were nursing babies.

"Why aren't you girls in school?" I asked.

"Our husbands won't let us go," one replied.

"Are you already in your husband's home?"

"Yes."

"How old are you?"

"I don't know."

"Have you seen blood yet?" I asked each one. Except for the two nursing mothers, they all said "No." From the pulpit I counted them, twelve little girls, already married though not yet through puberty. When we drove back home to the Lomela station, we carried with us the memory of those little girls.

"We must get back up to the northern end of the district," Burleigh said to me one day. "When could we go?" We checked the calendar for things already planned.

On the first of May, the Africa Missionary Tour Group was coming from America, and John Wilkins, the leader, had asked us to arrange for some of them to

visit the district out-village work. We decided to plan
our trip for that time.

"You'd better write to John and tell him what it will
be like," Burleigh advised me. "We'll need hearty people in body and spirit to take this trip."

When they arrived, it was obvious John had done a
grand job of selection. There were five, including
John—three ladies and another man. All of them were
excited to be going to an isolated, relatively untapped
area.

Since our group would number nine (Paul was home
on vacation and would go along), it was too much to expect the pastor's wife in each village to take care of us.
We sent to other stations to borrow additional cots and
utensils. We had chosen Itana as our destination, a village at the very end of the north road. We traveled
slowly, stopping often in villages for services under a
palm tree and making one overnight stop. Late on Saturday afternoon we arrived at Itana. The village pastor
was there to greet us, bringing gifts of food from his
people and seeing that we had wood and water. He was
a lay preacher who had studied for a short time under
the Scottish missionaries at the Plymouth Brethren
Mission at Kole. These missionaries do excellent work
in Bible training. But their customs of worship differ
from Methodists on at least one point. They accept
literally St. Paul's admonition that a woman should
have her head covered while in church. If you visit their
mission and have left your hat at home, they have by the
front door a collection of hats from the "missionary
barrel" for your use.

Saturday night we had a campfire service. Then early

Sunday morning the pastor came to the house at the edge of the village where we were staying. "Mama Uya Koi, I hope you brought your black hat."

He had seen me wearing my big black milan straw hat at Conference, the only time I wore it all year.

"No, I didn't. I didn't think I'd need a hat here."

"I had so wished you would be an example to my women. I have trouble getting them to understand this rule."

Here was a problem. What could I do? "I could wear Uwandji's sun helmet."

"It wouldn't be a good example to wear your husband's hat."

"I could wear a kerchief on my head."

For lack of something better, this was accepted, and the three visitors followed my example.

When the drum beat for the morning service, we went to a coffee grove where we would hold the service. The little church could not hold the crowd that had gathered to hear our visitors. When the villagers arrived, every woman had a bright kerchief on her head but wore nothing else except a G-string. I couldn't resist commenting to one of my guests, "What a pity St. Paul didn't think of a blouse!"

On our return trip, when we had stopped to eat our lunch, we saw a man running toward us, shouting, "Don't leave. I have a message from the chief."

Not even waiting for Burleigh to reply to his greeting of "*Moyo*, Uwandji," the runner said, "Chief Ohambi has sent me to you. He and his people want you to come. No missionary has ever been to our village."

He drew a deep breath and continued, "We'll feed all

of you and give you a place to sleep. The hunters have
gone for meat."

"Where is your village?" Burleigh asked.

He gave Burleigh the directions.

"Do you have any gasoline there?"

"No, we don't," the man said.

"We'd like to go, but we have just enough gasoline to
get us back to Lomela. It would be a long way for our
visitors to walk if we ran out. We'll come to see you
some other time. (And we did.)

On our way once more we rounded a curve and came
upon a large village. Standing across the road blocking
us was a human barricade. The chief approached us.
"We want a preacher," he said. He handed a piece of
paper to Burleigh and pointed to the signatures and
thumbprints. "Here are forty people who want to join
a catechism class if you'll send us a preacher."

"Is there any way you know that we could divide one
preacher into several?" Burleigh asked.

The chief looked puzzled.

"We have only twelve preachers for all of Lomela
district," Burleigh explained. "These preachers are
serving three and four, maybe more, villages each. We
can't cut them into more preachers, and we don't know
how to get any more."

"Mete, truly that is hard," said the chief.

"We want you to have a preacher. Send some of your
boys to our school at Shutsha, and let them come back
to be your preachers."

We drove on taking with us the paper so carefully
folded. It spoke for itself of our opportunities.

It is no longer the missionary who brings news of other worlds into a simple society. The transistor radio had reached Lomela district. Villagers who knew nothing of their neighbors a few miles distant now heard daily, in Swahili, the "World News"—from Moscow, Cairo, or Peking. The news was often confusing. But talk of freedom for African nations was in the air.

It was Christmas of 1959. David and Paul were home from boarding school although the district schools were still in session. Each afternoon the boys went out to Shutsha to play soccer with the students. They became interested in a Christmas pageant the youth fellowship was preparing, written by one of its own members.

"It's really great, Dad," Paul said at supper one evening. "Too bad that only the people at Shutsha will see it. Can't we take the youth group in the truck to some out-village and let them give the play there?"

Burleigh pondered a moment. "I'll talk with the youth counselor at Shutsha and see what he says."

The counselor thought it was a fine idea. So the Law family went to Okaku with the youth group the Sunday before Christmas. The play was a great success. Afterwards we went to a house that had been cleaned out for us and set up camp. By the time we finished, it was dark and a bright moon was shining just above the treetops.

"Let's build a fire out in the yard and sit in the moonlight," suggested Paul. Some of the youth group helped our boys build a blazing fire. We pulled our chairs up close, and as word of the fire spread, a crowd began to gather. The village elders joined us in the circle.

I remarked how pretty the moon was.

"Does this same moon shine at your home?" asked one elder.

"Yes, the same moon shines in America."

Our thoughts came abruptly back to earth when one of the elders called, "Uwandji, is Little Rock near your home village?"

What news had these people, without any concept of history, any frame of reference, heard about the incidents of Little Rock?

"No," Burleigh answered. "But it is in the territory of our Chief. It is in the same country."

"Is it true that the white people there mistreat the black?" the spokesman asked.

"I haven't been to Little Rock," said Burleigh, "but I have heard over the radio, just as you have, that some white people haven't been very kind to some black people."

Everything was still. Burleigh was leaning forward in his chair, his chin cupped in his hands, his eyes searching the fire as if to find some answer. Then he said, "It's there as it is here. Here some Bahamba aren't kind to the Esongo Mena. Some Esongo Mena treat Bahamba badly. Here it is the clans that mistreat each other. In my country it is the races that sometimes don't understand each other."

Again Burleigh paused. No one spoke. He went on. "I didn't come to the Congo because everything was perfect in America. There are many Christians in America who are working to bring peace to our country. We are here to help you find peace, too."

Then another elder spoke. "How far is it from here to your home village?"

Burleigh figured for a moment. "Do you know how far it is to Lodja?"

"*Elu.*"

"Then go the two hundred miles to Lodja and come back. Make that round trip eighteen times. That is about how far my village is from Okaku."

It took time to grasp that. Then the elder spokesman stood. "We are amazed at how far you have come from your home village. Who paid your way?"

"Your Christian friends in America paid our way."

The spokesman went on. "Last year we wanted a rubber contract. All of us paid our part for Okito to go by truck to Lodja to get it for us. We paid his trip, but we got our rubber contract. What do those people get out of sending you here?"

"These are your Christian friends. Some are black, some white. They don't get anything for themselves," Burleigh said. "Some of them are poor. Some do without things they need to give the money. They know how many blessings they have because their land has heard the message of Christ. They want you to hear it, too."

It was quiet again. Then slowly the leader spoke. "These young people said tonight that God loves us. Never until now could I believe that. People who don't even know me pay your way for so long a trip just so you can tell me that God loves me. They don't get anything out of it. Now I can believe God's love for me."

Our second furlough was approaching. "I simply

have to get down to Lowo and roof their church before May," Burleigh said. "I've been promising for months."

I started immediately to prepare for the two-day stay at this out-village, for I knew Burleigh would just suddenly decide one day to go. Sure enough, he came in one noon. "Do you think we could go to Lowo tomorrow?"

At Lowo we set up camp, and Burleigh went to work at once on the church roof.

At the end of the first day, Burleigh rested with the men under the palaver shed. "Have you planted your new rice gardens yet?" he asked.

"We aren't going to plant rice this year," the chief answered.

"Aren't you going to eat rice next year?" Burleigh asked.

The chief spoke confidently. "Oh, yes, we'll eat rice. But we are going to be independent by then. We won't have to plant gardens. Nobody can make us work when we are independent. We'll buy rice from the trader."

Burleigh felt he must help the chief understand that independence would not magically bring food.

"You've seen the trader loading the sacks of rice he bought from you onto the river barges at Lomela. Do you know where the rice was going?"

A young man spoke up. "To Léopoldville."

"That's right. You are paid five francs a kilo for rice here. The people who live in Léopoldville pay seventeen francs for that same rice. If it has to be shipped up here to you, it would cost thirty francs a kilo, and maybe you couldn't get it sent up here at all. If you stop growing it, there might not be enough rice."

No one said anything. "How much rice will your children eat when you are paying thirty francs a kilo?" Burleigh wondered out loud.

Nothing more was said about the rice. The next morning we heard the village drummer pounding away on his big drum. "What's all that drumming about?" I asked my helper.

"He's calling the men to their rice gardens."

Once the church roof in Lowo was finished, Burleigh had another promise to fulfill—the construction of a new school at Shutsha. Since this school was only eight miles from our station, Burleigh could drive out each evening after his regular work for an hour or two. The work progressed well not only because of Burleigh's close supervision, but also because of the work of Kalonda, the very capable village carpenter. Although he did not do really professional work, it was "true and straight" and Burleigh was pleased. Often the two of them would go hunting in the forest nearby after their evening's work.

The school was just about completed when Chief Shutsha died of a ruptured appendix after only a few days illness. He was an important and much-loved chief. The people were shocked, and all work stopped.

Just at dusk one evening a week later, a student came to our home on his bicycle. "Come quickly, Uwandji," he cried. "The village is about to have a trial by poison for Utshudi Kalonda and two others."

Burleigh went immediately to Shutsha. He found the village pastor and all the village elders sitting around a fire before the council house. A little isolated to one side sat Kalonda and two other men. Burleigh quietly joined the circle, and as they talked, he learned the story.

Chief Shutsha had died suddenly of poisoning, according to the state health officer. The villagers reasoned that if it was poison, then someone had poisoned him and that someone must be a person in line for the chief's place. Why else would anyone want such a beloved chief to die? Kalonda and the two others were in line. One of them had to be guilty. To determine which one, three cups of water would be set in a row. In one cup would be poison. Each man would choose a cup, and whoever drew the poisoned one was guilty and would die.

Kalonda showed complete willingness to drink from any cup. "I'm innocent," he said to Burleigh. "It won't kill me."

"But poison will kill you even if you're not guilty," Burleigh explained.

"Not if I'm innocent," Kalonda said with conviction.

Quietly Burleigh spoke to the group around the fire. He explained how the Chief had died of poison from inside his own body. It was his appendix that had killed him. If he had gone to a doctor, he probably would have lived. The elders listened intently but said nothing.

The village pastor spoke up. "A trial by poison will prove nothing."

Still no one else spoke. Finally, they began again— the same thing over and over. Hours passed. Burleigh tried again and again to convince them to forget the trial, but he seemed to get nowhere.

At last Burleigh stood to go. He shook hands with the elders, then with the three men on trial. When he came to Kalonda he said, "I wish there was something I could do."

Later the pastor reported what had happened. After Burleigh had gone, the elders sat in silence for a long time. They all sensed Burleigh's distress over the trial. Then a senior elder of the village said, "Let's put a lamp on the chief's grave at night. Then his departed spirit can see for himself and poison the killer." That proposal was accepted.

For months we saw that lamp glowing when we visited Shutsha at night. Burleigh contributed some kerosene to keep it burning. Then a villager died of rabies, and the case was closed.

It was only a few weeks now until we would leave for our second furlough. We wished we could turn back or stop the clock. There were many villages we wanted to visit or revisit, but there was just not time.

"But you must come down to Lukavukavu for at least the weekend," Ona Dinga, the district superintendent, insisted.

We went, arriving in time for the Saturday evening service. Crowds had gathered. The revival meetings so successful in the Lodja district were spreading into the Lomela district, and crowds attended. After the service we gathered around a campfire, and one by one new Christians stepped up and threw on the fire some fetishes they were surrendering. One man had an armful. Turning to Burleigh, he said, "Uwandji Utshudi A Koi, I'm an utshudi, too. My father was an utshudi and his father, too. I want to give you these witch doctor fetishes. My father used them, and so did his father. Beyond that, I don't know. I have used them, but I use them no longer. God has given me peace in my heart. Take these to America. Show the people there these useless items we utshudis depended upon before you came to Lomela." Those fetishes still witness in our home.

We could not stop the clock, and our departure date arrived. Most of the jobs were done, not to Burleigh's complete satisfaction, but done just the same. The day before we were to leave, a stream of people came to tell us good-bye.

Next morning the alarm went off at five. As we got up, we heard a crowd outside in our yard. Some people were weeping.

"Don't leave," they begged.

"We must go back to see our families," Burleigh explained. "My wife's family would be unhappy if I didn't bring her back to see them."

They could understand a husband's needing to take his wife home for a visit.

"Will you come back after you've seen them?"

"It is a long trip. We must spend a year in Belgium studying French. Then we will go to stay a few moons with our families. After that, we'll be back."

"Do you promise us that?"

"Yes," answered Burleigh. "I promise you that."

A village elder stepped up. In his hand was an elephant-hair bracelet woven from stiff tail hairs. He slipped it on Burleigh's arm. "Tell your family and friends that we need you here. This bracelet is to remind you of your promise to come back," he said.

It was our Lomela "good-bye." Our two years there had been hard, but fruitful, years. Now the Congo faced its independence, just six weeks away. We felt uneasy about what lay ahead. We had seen impossible expectations in the hearts of the Congolese. We knew how few of them were prepared to govern. But no matter the future, the elephant-hair bracelet reminded us that we were still needed in the Congo. We expected to come back.

CHAPTER THIRTEEN

Working in the New Congo

SLOWLY A SMALL PLANE CIRCLED ABOVE OUR HOME IN TALLA-hassee, Florida, banking and turning in the clear fall afternoon sky.

"Mother, is that Daddy?" Margaret Ann asked.

The plane was too high for me to tell for sure, but it could be the Aronca Champion in which Burleigh was taking his pilot's training. "Maybe so," I said.

Just a year before, Bishop Booth of our Central Congo Conference stopped in Brussels, where we were taking our twice-postponed French instruction. "I'm sure you've heard that the Indiana Conferences gave our mission a Cessna 180," he said to Burleigh. "There aren't many landing fields, and our Central Congo Mission is a long way from any service area for the plane," he said smiling. "But we think we've handled the servicing problem. We voted for you to study aircraft mechanics on furlough next year."

Burleigh was delighted. The bishop went on. "We hope to have a full-time pilot for the plane, but we also need a good relief pilot."

He looked at Burleigh with a twinkle in his eyes. "We voted for you to be that pilot."

Now Burleigh was excited. "That's great! I've always wanted to fly."

When our year of language study was finished and our French exams passed, we left Belgium and went to Tallahassee. I enrolled at Florida State University, David was in high school, Paul in junior high, and Margaret Ann in grammar school. Burleigh went to Lively Technical School, where he had taught auto mechanics for a year before we went to the Congo. And two afternoons a week, he took flying lessons.

The time had passed rapidly and happily, and now we were thinking about our return to the Congo. Our twelve years there had been wonderful years. We had seen our five-year-old David grow into an athletic seventeen-year-old football player. Our little three-year-old Paul was now doing his best to push past six feet. And our Congo baby, Margaret Ann, was an eight-year-old mirror watcher, always trying to see whether a new tooth was coming in yet. Congo was home to all of us, and we wanted to return in spite of the fact that the Congo was now in turmoil.

Independence had been granted by Belgium in 1960. But civil war and bloodshed had resulted. All our missionaries had been forced to leave and had been out for almost a year. During that time roving armies had entered and occupied Batetela land. Some of our mission stations had been looted. There was no way to get the details, but we did know that Wembo Nyama station, our first Congo home, had suffered terribly. Almost daily we heard of some further tragedy in the Congo.

"Surely you aren't going back," friends would say, shocked that we would even consider returning while conditions were so unsettled. Many of our missionary friends were scattered over southern Africa, waiting until they could return to their stations. Some had gone to Southern Congo, and were caught in the middle when the fighting between Katanga soldiers and the United Nations forces began in Elisabethville. One woman wrote of having to stay with her four small children under their beds for days while the bullets whizzed overhead. She suggested a new policy: "All beds should be high enough to sit under comfortably."

We chuckled at this, but the situation was grave, and we wondered what we should do. We had our own family to consider, especially eight-year-old Margaret Ann.

Just at this time, an offer of an excellent job in the United States came to Burleigh. I felt that this might be the answer. "I could teach, too," I said. "That would help us replace all our household things." We still did not know what had happened to our home at Lomela.

We talked with the children about the future, but none of us ever discussed the job in the United States as a permanent arrangement. It would be only a fill-in until the Congo situation became more stable.

Our minds and hearts were full of anxiety and concern when Burleigh and I accepted an invitation to the Annual Meeting of the Methodist Board of Missions in January at Buck Hill Falls, Pennsylvania. We were looking forward to talking with Bishop Booth.

The very day of our meeting with him, the headlines of the day's paper read "Fifteen Congo Missionaries Slain."

Just a few weeks before, a group of Italian airmen working for the United Nations had been slain at Kindu near one of our Methodist stations. And now fifteen Catholic fathers not far from Tunda, another of our stations.

We discussed the situation frankly with Bishop Booth. He told us of a recent survey trip he had made with two missionaries into our territory, Batetela land, where he had great hopes for the future. "But the picture doesn't look bright right now," he said.

This was no time to save face or feelings. There were many displaced missionaries from the Congo.

"Would the Board like us to take a leave of absence?" Burleigh asked, and he told of the job opportunities we had.

Bishop Booth shook his head. "Congo desperately needs technical assistance right now." He looked at Burleigh. "I'd hate to let you out of my hands."

"Frankly, what is the chance of our getting back into the Congo?" Burleigh asked.

The bishop hesitated. "You know I never advocate the separation of families," he said. "But unless families separate now, the Congo won't have any missionaries for a long time. We just can't risk sending women and children there."

When we left the Bishop, nothing had been decided. A big question for me was whether we could return to such a changed situation. I knew that the missionary's role would be different in a Congo that was conscious of itself as an independent nation. Could I return, see my possessions in another's house, and not resent it?

But this was only skirting the urgent question of

whether we were willing to separate as a family—willing for Burleigh to go out alone. This was the question we could not reason through. That night we prayed, we talked, we cried, we prayed some more, until long after midnight. Then Burleigh said, "Sweetheart, you know I'd never leave you and the children for just some advancement or personal gain. I can't imagine what it would be like in the Congo without you." He went on haltingly, "But I am sure God has not changed His purpose for me. I've put my hand to the plow. I can't turn back now."

I knew he had made a decision. I remembered the elephant-hair bracelet he often wore and the promise it symbolized. Then I remembered my own promise of years before: "I'll never stand between Burleigh and God's Call for him."

The next morning we told Bishop Booth that Burleigh would return to the Congo alone. We thought it would not be until September. But the Congolese leaders were pleading urgently for technical help. They needed trained personnel to operate machinery and to teach technical skills. In March, Bishop Booth cabled Burleigh asking whether he would come in June. We heard by the grapevine that after being closed two years, Central School would reopen in August. David and Paul were anxious to go. They were old enough now, and they knew the Congo. There were many jobs they could do until school opened besides being company for Burleigh. "We know the Board will approve if you'll write a good letter," the boys told me.

I agreed to write the letter, and the Board did approve. So Margaret Ann and I began preparations to get our three men off to the Congo in June. Burleigh doubled up his hours at Lively School and completed his course. He also got his pilot's license.

David and Paul continued with their school activities which included football training. David had played on varsity that year, and the coach now told him he would be eligible for the first string in the coming fall.

David told him, "If I can't go with my dad to the Congo, I'd love it. But if I can go with Dad, I'd rather do that."

When telling the story to Burleigh, the coach said, "Imagine a boy who would rather go to the Congo with his dad than play first-string football in America."

As June drew near, Burleigh and I decided to attend the Furloughed Missionary Conference at Greencastle, Indiana. Directly from there Burleigh and the boys would go to New York and fly to the Congo.

The night before they left, we all went to a special service for missionaries from all over the world. After a short devotional the leader said, "We want to give each of you a chance to share with us. Speak of anything you feel you'd like to tell us."

Many spoke—missionaries with years of service, missionaries just going out. Burleigh stood at the back of the chapel and was the last to speak. Many turned in their seats to look at him.

"How wonderfully God has led my life!" he began. "Why He should have called me to the Congo I shall never know, but I thank God for all the opportunities this service has brought me. Tomorrow I am returning to the Congo."

He went on. "I realize the unsettled situation, the

dangers, even the possible death that may wait for me. But if somewhere, someone must raise a white cross over my grave, I'd rather it would be in the heart of the Congo, fighting with Christianity as my weapon, than on any battlefield of the world. I am confident this is God's will for me."

Early the next morning Burleigh, Paul, and David left. Returning to my room I prayed earnestly, "God, give me the grace I need."

God's grace did sustain me. Yet I was restless. Despite all the rumors and reports I had heard from the Congo, I couldn't believe that it would be unsafe for me to be there with Burleigh.

"As soon as I see for myself whether I think it is safe for you, I'll let you know," Burleigh had promised. I waited for that word.

I knew he wouldn't make a judgment until he had reached our territory, but I told myself, "Maybe he'll write something encouraging from Léopoldville. He'll get there on Monday. He'll mail a letter on Tuesday— or Wednesday at the latest. In a week surely I'll know something."

Two weeks later a letter finally came, mailed ten days before. Burleigh didn't say much about the Congo, and I didn't find his silence encouraging. Again I waited. I knew he was now making his way inland to Central Congo for the meeting of the Annual Conference. Six weeks passed before additional word arrived. "We've talked it over here at Conference. It certainly isn't going to be an easy life for any of you wives, but we feel it will be reasonably safe. Our Congolese friends are so eager to have you come back—not to mention us husbands."

So I was to join Burleigh!

The letter went on to tell me that he and the boys would be working at Lodja for several weeks, trying to get a home ready for the families and single women coming there. Then they would be moving down to Katubwe, and I could join them. I was to teach, and Burleigh was to be the supervisor of maintenance at a secondary school operated jointly by the Presbyterians and Methodists. It was the only secondary in a large area and desperately needed to prepare Congolese for responsible positions. Located just twenty-five miles from Luluabourg, it was in a relatively calm area and had managed to keep going during all the troubles of the past two years. We could not yet return to Lomela.

I called the Board of Missions in New York. They had received no instructions from Bishop Booth. I waited and called again. Still no word. Finally, I received the State Department forms to apply for my Congo visa. My application had to go to Washington and then to Léopoldville.

August went by, and we were well into September. School in the Congo started without me. Burleigh tried to find out from Léopoldville what the delay was. "How foolish!" I remarked to a French teacher over from France for a year. "The Congolese government is desperately in need of teachers. I can't understand such a delay in getting one on the job."

"I know just how you feel," she said. "I waited six months for my United States visa."

October was just beginning when my visa came. Immediately I sent two cables, one to Burleigh and another to a friend in Léopoldville, giving our arrival time in the capital. Two days later Margaret Ann and I were on our way.

On the long flight from New York to the Congo, I wondered just what was awaiting me. Burleigh's letter had said very little. He had written the most about Wembo Nyama:

"We are now at Wembo Nyama. What a sad sight! Refrigerators, stoves, washing machines still lying about where someone threw them. Dr. Bob White's house is burned to the ground. Our old home torn up. The windows and doors are all gone, even the window frames. But the hospital and school are not seriously damaged. The looters seem to have turned their fury against the residences of the missionaries.

"I hear that Minga station is as bad, but Lodja not so looted. Lomela seems to be all right.

"It is a sad picture. But when foreman Wembo Lua came over to visit with me and told me of God's presence with him and his family during the terrible days of fighting, my faith was lifted."

I knew Paul had caught his dad's spirit when he wrote to me, "Everything the white man brought is gone except the Church, and it has actually grown."

Although I had declared a lack of fear, I felt very apprehensive as I walked off the Sabena plane at Léopoldville. I scanned the crowd on the observation platform, but I saw no tall, wavy-haired man waving to me. From the customs room I looked out and saw my friend, but no Burleigh. I struggled to get my bags lined up and cleared. There was no order anywhere; everyone seemed to be yelling and pushing. I felt completely dismayed. Then beside me I heard, "Hello, Mama."

I turned, and there stood Pierre Shaumba, Executive

Secretary for the Congo Protestant Council. He attended to all the details and saw me quickly and safely through customs and outside.

After greeting my friend I said, "I thought Burleigh would be here."

"If you sent his cable the same time you sent mine, he wouldn't have it yet. It will probably take about two weeks."

Outside the airport terminal, crowds of people were trying to force themselves into the few available cars and buses, all of which looked battered and unreliable. As I waited for my friend's car, I looked about, and I had the strange feeling that I was in a place I had never been before. My impression was one of complete confusion.

There were seven of us in Pierre's Peugeot station wagon. I felt uncomfortable as we passed people walking toward Léopoldville, twenty miles away, many with suitcases on their heads. Yet I knew that if we stopped and offered one person a ride, we'd be surrounded by an unruly crowd.

"We were able to get you a room at the mission hostel," my friend said. "To find a hotel room in Léopoldville is impossible now."

This suited me fine. I would feel safe there, and for some reason, I was looking for some place that would be safe.

Since Burleigh had not come to Léopoldville, my first concern was to get on to Luluabourg. "I have my through ticket," I said.

"That doesn't mean a thing. We'll see tomorrow what we can get for you."

The next morning I found out what he meant. It was

then Tuesday, and I could not get on even the reserve list until Saturday. "You could take a chance and go out every morning at five. Sometimes a plane takes off almost empty."

"I'll wait until Saturday. If I don't make it then, I'll start going out to take my chances," I said.

Secretly I kept hoping Burleigh would arrive, but Thursday came and still no sign of him. Our friends, the Shaumbas, invited Margaret Ann and me to dinner that evening.

I was standing on the lawn talking when a car drove up, and it was Burleigh, at last. Three Batetela men who had worked with him at Wembo Nyama had brought him from the airport and insisted on seeing that he found me so they could witness our reunion.

"Did you get my cable?" I asked.

"No, but Pastor Shungu was in Léopoldville when it arrived. He went home to Lodja, and yesterday the mission plane brought me a note congratulating me on getting my wife out to the Congo. I rushed in to Lulua-bourg, and a Mennonite missionary said he had heard you were here. This morning I was at the airport before dawn and begged my way onto the plane. It didn't take off until three o'clock this afternoon." Even in a chaotic Congo, it was wonderful to be together again.

At dinner that evening when several Congolese friends were present, we discussed the new Congo. All of them had graduated from our Methodist schools and now had important jobs with the government in Léo-poldville. Only Mr. Shaumba was a college graduate, one of the twelve in all of the Congo. I remembered how we had complained through the years when a teacher or preacher had left our mission work to go into government service. Now I thanked God for everyone who was in any position to help the Congo stabilize its government. These men from our schools reflected the lasting part of our work.

Someone said, "We didn't have to fight the Belgians for our independence. They granted it to us. But there is a price to be paid for freedom. And we Congolese neither are trained to govern nor are we united as one people."

"I think we missionaries will have to pay our share of this price, too," Burleigh said, and I knew he was right.

Saturday morning, before daylight, we sat in the airport waiting for the plane to Luluabourg. Most of the passengers were Congolese, many carrying bulging briefcases and wearing large black horn-rimmed glasses. They shook hands, greeting each other with great formality, and spoke titles of respect in loud voices. With each dignitary were usually one or two porters carrying his bags and boxes. "The new elite," I commented to Burleigh.

There were a few women dressed in long colorful African prints. When we were told to board, they gathered up their huge handbags, stuffed to absolute capacity, and lifting them onto their heads, walked to the airplane. Some women carried long, slender baskets made of two palm branches woven together. Between the twisted plaiting, chicken heads stuck out. Occasionally a loud squawk announced displeasure with modern travel.

Stewardesses of Sabena Air Line had been replaced by Air Congo stewards. "Would you like a drink?" one asked.

"Yes. Some Bako, please."

He brought us three glasses of a cola drink on a tray covered with a very soiled napkin. It stuck to the last glass and fell to the floor. Quickly the steward picked it up and carefully spread it on the tray. He continued with his job, serving passengers the way white men had taught him. I sat holding the uncooled Bako drink and pondered the future of a Congo that tried to imitate the white man. I remembered the statistics I had heard in Léopoldville. Only twelve college graduates, and not one Congolese doctor or lawyer or engineer in all the country. And no one with experience in governing a nation.

In Luluabourg we picked up our car where Burleigh had parked it in the United Nations guard camp and drove into town. No matter what anyone might have told me, I simply could not have been prepared for Luluabourg as I now saw it. Two years before, it had been a modern miracle town in the heart of the Congo. I remembered a lovely fountain at one end of the boulevard, throwing water thirty feet into the air. At night we had watched the colored lights play on this fountain. Flowerbeds and bordered paths arranged in intricate designs stretched for over a mile down the boulevard. Gardeners had worked constantly keeping the plants and shrubs pruned and trimmed. Halfway down the lighted boulevard, a fine hotel had been built. Tourists from Europe and America had often marveled, "This is better than home." We in the Congo had been proud of all this. That fountain, that park, and that hotel proved that the Congo was part of the modern world.

Now looking about me, I felt physically sick. The stench of the decaying trash in the stagnant fountain filled the air. Paper and debris lay everywhere in the park. The nicely trimmed borders were now top-heavy bushes. Here and there a dead dog or cat lay rotting in the street.

"Shall we eat lunch before we drive out to Katubwe?" Burleigh asked.

I had misgivings but said, "I guess so."

As soon as we parked our car, the beggars crowded around. They were ragged and dirty. They were hungry, too. "Don't give them anything now," Burleigh warned me. "Wait until we come out and are ready to leave. Otherwise, they and all their relatives will be waiting for another gift."

I had never seen beggars like these before in Luluabourg. I wondered if they had always been there but had been kept off the main street, hidden from travelers.

The hotel was crowded and noisy. I remembered it as quiet and dignified. Prices had doubled or tripled from what we had ever paid, but this seemed no deterrent. Rounds of drinks were offered to anyone gathered at a table. Men ordered in loud voices. I had the feeling it was very important for everyone there to register his presence upon others. And why not? Many of the Congolese had not been allowed to enter this lovely hotel before 1960.

A sign above the bar read, "It is necessary to wear a coat." At one table a man obeyed the rule and wore an ill-fitting coat but no shirt.

There were Congolese women at some of the tables, several puffing on cigarettes in elaborate holders. Sheer white blouses revealing all beneath were the rage that year. Some wore African wrap-arounds. Others wore very short, very tight skirts. Freedom seemed to mean to them imitating European vices. They moved from table to table, pulling at men's arms, whispering in their ears.

Two very well-dressed dignitaries entered the room, each escorting gaudily dressed women. I found out later that these women were brought to town to act as hostesses for the officials. Why, I asked myself then and many times later, did these men feel they needed such women for official functions when many of them had lovely and gracious Congolese wives? Could we help those wives who still cooked and ate out in back of the big new official residences to come out and claim their place in the new Congo?

Hardly were we out of Luluabourg before we began to pass car after car abandoned beside the road. Some of them were recent models, now standing stripped of everything that would come off. Passing a big Chevrolet, Burleigh commented, "Palm oil just won't keep a motor running."

As we passed a village, Burleigh remarked, "Here's where our Katubwe driver was killed. He was driving the white Chevy pick-up. A child ran out in front of it, and he hit him. He stopped as quickly as he could, but before he could explain, the village people jumped on him and killed him."

"What about the child?"

"He was just scuffed up," Burleigh said.

"I guess the moral of that story is, in Congo, don't stop if you hit someone."

"I hope I never have to decide that," Burleigh said.

I hoped so for I knew what his decision would be. We rode for a while in silence.

"I saw Nguwa last week here in Luluabourg," Burleigh said finally. Nguwa had worked as a student mechanic and driver with Burleigh at Wembo Nyama. "He's the driver for Okito, the merchant from Katako Kombe. You should *see* that truck. He really does baby it. He asked me to check it over, and I didn't find a thing not right."

When we saw the next abandoned pick-up truck, I thought of Nguwa, one of the very few in the Congo who knew anything about trucks.

Riding home we passed rows of lonely palm trees along the road where villages had stood not more than three years ago. Sometimes a few huts were still standing, their roofs collapsing. Other times there were only heaps of fire-blackened debris. Large sections of land stood bare and deserted. This was the price of tribal war that boiled up when there was no strong central government, I thought. There was no shortage of land. So why did the Baluba and Lulua tribes fight so cruelly, burning and killing, sticking cadavers on sticks along the road as a witness to their hate and revenge? Not a Baluba village was left in the area.

Burleigh broke into my contemplation. "Saturday I helped get the soccer goalposts up on the athletic field at the school."

"You did?" I wasn't very interested in soccer goal-posts.

"Two students came over and asked for some nails and a hammer. They wanted to fix it up. I didn't know until we were almost finished that one of them was a Baluba and the other a Lulua."

Now I *was* interested in soccer goalposts! Imagine a Baluba and a Lulua working together to fix a goalpost when they could look out across a plain dotted with blackened monuments of the conflict between their tribes!

From a distance we could see Katubwe standing on an elevated plain. Vari-colored stuccoed block homes with gray stone trim faced each other across a wide central lawn.

Six missionary families and five single women made up the teaching staff of the school, with Congolese looking after the secretarial work and the boarding department. A Congolese was also pastor of the congregation. The students came from twelve different tribal or clan groups. It looked quiet and safe. Burleigh and I were to serve here for a year, hoping that then we could go home to Batetela land.

The entire station at Katubwe was less than ten years old. All the homes had been built from an architect's plan from the ground up instead of growing up by accident like most missionary residences in the Congo. They were comfortable and attractive.

The barrels of household goods we had packed away two years before in the attic at Lomela were now sitting in the living room at Katubwe. I stared, unbelieving.

"Pastor Ona Dinga guarded the house while the two

armies fought in the yard. There were dead and dying soldiers everywhere,'' Burleigh explained.

We took Margaret Ann to Central Boarding School, where her brothers were both in high school, and before the week was up, I began teaching classes at Katubwe.

Each time before, when we had arrived in the Congo, there had been the feeling, "Well, we're here for four years." Now it was different. Unspoken, but very real, was the feeling, "I hope we're still here next week." The United Nations-Katanga situation remained serious. We were far enough away not to be directly involved, and no Katanga students could cross the barriers to come to our school. Also we did not have either the time or the knowledge to argue the issues. But when we heard that the Congo Army was on the move, we hoped they wouldn't come past Katubwe. We had heard that the soldiers lacked discipline. Whenever missionary women saw a jeep driving on the station, most of them hurried inside and limited their contact with the army to peeping out from behind the draperies.

Commercial transportation into Luluabourg was nonexistent. When we had to have some part replacement, drugs for the hospital, or supplies for the school, we asked the United Nations Command to get them for us. It sometimes took weeks, but they usually managed. Perhaps we did not try to see beyond our own needs, but we couldn't imagine what would happen to the school without the United Nations forces to keep order among the hostile tribesmen.

With so many tribes represented in our student body, we caught the ripples of unrest wherever they started. Often when tensions heightened between two clans, we had in our dormitory students from each side. How does one carry on as if there is no cause for alarm, knowing full well the fuse is burning on a stick of dynamite?

The land upon which the station was built had been granted by the land-owning Lulua tribe. Now periodically the school director received a note from the Lulua chief demanding that more of his students be accepted in the school. Acceptance was always on the basis of very stiff competitive exams, and some Lulua students just had not made the grade. Certain of the students from other clans felt threatened and often were afraid to sleep in the dormitory. It was not uncommon for several of them to appear at a missionary's door, begging to sleep in the attic. At such times the ripples of uneasiness swelled to high, overpowering waves.

Food was also a problem. Villagers nearby had fled, leaving gardens behind, and some who remained didn't bother to plant. The shortages increased the prices, and although the highest bidder usually can get what he wants the world over, how could we, as missionaries, bid up the price of an egg or banana in competition with villagers who needed them, too?

"It seems to me something ought to be done about the egg shortage," David commented, when home on vacation. Upon investigation, he found that through Church World Service he could get five-week-old biddies already innoculated against disease. This he did, and the village chiefs were supplied with eggs and brood chickens.

Just as we would get used to one source of tension,

we'd be driving to town and find a new army barricade across the road. Why it was there no one ever seemed to know. Where would the next one be? We never knew. At one time in the 125 miles between Lusambo and Luluabourg, there were eleven such barricades. The soldiers always said they were looking for something. We needed a "permission to pass."

Since Burleigh went to town weekly for supplies that might have arrived or to pick up cases from the United Nations, he went to the authorities at army headquarters and got a permit, duly stamped and signed. But this was of little help. The guards always wanted another color, a different date, another signature.

Once when we were stopped, the guard demanded another pass while he was holding Burleigh's official pass upside down. He obviously couldn't read it. Finally Burleigh produced his Florida driver's license. It looked official enough to satisfy the guard, and he let us through.

"And to think," Burleigh commented, "that is the only authority keeping the Congo from complete chaos. If only the Luluabourg area had one battalion of men who could read and write."

There was no use attempting extensive new building at Katubwe. Building supplies were nonexistent. But mere maintenance was a full-time job. The power plant had to be kept operating at night so the students could study. The water system kept filling up with algae; the toilets didn't flush. The plaster fell off the walls. Windows got broken. From six in the morning until ten at night, Burleigh was on call. Some student always

seemed to be standing at our door wanting something—
a nail, a screw, a hammer, a saw, a ride to town, a letter
to be mailed, or a chance to work to earn some money.

While we were coping with the situation as best we
could at Katubwe, other Methodist missionaries had returned to the looted stations in Central Congo. Since
the stations were so terribly isolated, one plane could
not possibly serve them all. In February, the mission
was able to buy a second plane, a Cessna 210, and Burleigh began making regular weekly flights up to Batetela
land in addition to his other work. When he'd leave
for overnight, I always held my breath for fear the light
motor would go out, but it never did.

As June grew near, we began to look forward to going
back home to Batetela land. The year at Katubwe had
been in many ways more rewarding to me than to Burleigh. After building a hospital at Wembo Nyama and
opening a new station at Lomela, what he'd done to
keep the school operating did not seem very challenging. Then, too, he had to use sign language with most of
the workmen, for he didn't know the Tshiluba dialect,
and his foreman could speak neither the native dialects
nor the little French Burleigh had learned. He felt
limited in communication with the men.

So with little sense of accomplishment we went to
the closing banquet for the graduating class. They had
prepared a farewell to each missionary leaving for a
furlough and to us as we left for Lodja. Some were hu-
morous, some were full of satire, some subtly critical,
and some were real tributes.

I wondered what they would say to Burleigh who had
had no classroom contact with them. They thanked

him, commenting, "For the first time in the history of the school, the lights and water have not been off a single day."

Then they spoke of his patience and kindness toward the students at the barricades, his willingness to drive out of his way to pick up a student in town, his spirit of humility toward his fellow missionaries. They closed with, "You are the kind of missionary who merits all the respect paid you by your fellow man."

Burleigh was genuinely surprised. But after all, the students understood that he had done more than just pump water and generate electricity.

The next day eleven seniors, representing four different clans, were graduated. That same day near Luluabourg, a warring chief was burned to death by his tribal enemies. Listening to the shortwave radio broadcast coming from across the world that night, we heard the gory details of his death. Not one word was said about our graduates, the future leaders of the Congo.

Classes were just out when, as a family, we faced a new separation. The time had come for the boys to return to America. David was ready for college, and Paul would go to boarding school. At the end of the vacation we packed them up and sent them stateside. Margaret Ann went back alone to Central School, and Burleigh and I moved to Lodja where he had been appointed industrial missionary.

Our new home at Lodja was quite unlike the one at Katubwe. It had been built as a grass-roofed house years before. As time passed, partitions had been knocked out, rooms added, changes made until no one could take credit for the architecture. Then it had withstood the looting—screens torn off, toilets clogged, walls blackened. We went right to work. The beds were so dirty that I took the mattresses out and scrubbed them. After sunning them for a week I still complained, "I can smell them."

Burleigh pointed out, "They don't smell when you sleep on your back."

Slowly we turned the house again into a home. But now I faced a new problem. Night after night I was left alone. Although Burleigh was supposed to make only emergency flights while another pilot flew the regular runs, an emergency seemed to arise every day. "I don't see how you stand to be alone at night," my friends said.

"Do I really have a choice?" I asked. "Can Burleigh refuse to fly on some mission?"

Burleigh felt torn, too. He had been appointed to Lodja, but we were also missionary advisers for the village work around Lomela which was 150 miles away. His flying duties came last. "But," he often lamented, "I don't get anything done but flying."

He realized that I was alone more than I should be in such troubled times. Batetela land was now torn with intergroup conflicts just like Katubwe had been. All around our mission station stood deserted villages. Only a few months before there had been a mass exodus of the "plains people."

Years ago, long before most of the people could remember, a group of the Basambala clan from the open plains near Wembo Nyama had invaded the forest area. Having better weapons, they had conquered the "forest people" and settled down, building their own villages among the forest villages. Side by side they had lived for years—but not in love and brotherhood.

When our church began work in the area, we went first to those villages that asked for our help. When a village built a church, we sent a pastor; when they raised a school, we sent a teacher, and we opened dispensaries. Not by our own choice but because of the response from the people, most of our work was with Basambala villages or the "plains people."

No one knows just how it began, but in May, 1963, a few months before we came, fighting started between these two groups, the plains people and the forest people. Actually the number killed was not large, but people all over the area were terrified. Whole villages crowded in upon our Lodja station, living in the schools and church until they could get into trucks that would take them to the plains country. Just over the Lodja district border sprang up Ndjalu, a large refugee village in the original land of the "plains people."

What this conflict did to the people was heartbreaking. Students at Katubwe had to write home to find out where they should go at vacation time. The better-educated leaders were in the "plains clan" and so were suspect to the "forest people." There was constant uneasiness in the local government. For months Lodja was the center of a fierce political battle, and we never knew who would be in power from day to day or even from hour to hour.

Waiting at the airport one afternoon, I met one of our former teachers who was now working in the government. He greeted me coldly and said, "I hear you have deserted our Batetela students."

Since I was then teaching a full secondary school load and had been since returning to the Congo a year before, I was startled.

"You have chosen to teach people who are *not* our people," he continued.

I thought perhaps he was referring to my being at Katubwe the year before. "I don't understand that. I had Batetela students at Katubwe. And now I'm home so all my students are Batetela."

He contradicted me sharply. "No, they're not. You won't be teaching *Batetela* students until you go back to Wembo Nyama."

I stood dumbfounded. There was no question in the mind of this "plains person" that the only Batetela were those living in plains territory. And he was an official of the Congolese government.

It was little wonder, therefore, that when Burleigh was flying, I always grew uneasy when dusk fell. I listened for the plane and, then, as the sky grew darker, I was afraid I *would* hear it. Too many times Burleigh came in with the aid of his landing lights alone because no one was manning the field. All that year he seemed to be racing with time, racing with the sun to get home.

The flying was telling on Burleigh. He came home exhausted. For the first time in his life, he needed his back rubbed before he could relax and sleep. "You can't keep up this pace," I warned him.

Yet, when a rumor of danger at any station reached us, I agreed that he must investigate. News was so unreliable and communications so inadequate that we never knew what the situation might be. One day we heard that there was serious trouble in Wembo Nyama.

When Burleigh landed at the air strip there, one of the missionaries came running out and greeted him, "Am I glad to see you! We've been hearing terrible reports from Lodja."

Another time the noon broadcast from Luluabourg in the Otetela language reported that there was tribal fighting at Katako Kombe. "More people were killed than one could count," the announcer said.

In spite of a busy schedule Burleigh flew off to see what had happened there. He returned later in the afternoon. "There were two soldiers killed," he told us. "One forest man and one Esongo Mena."

"What did the broadcast mean by saying more than one could count?"

Burleigh shook his head. "I guess no one could count as high as two."

So it went. Rumors galore, but no facts.

We also had medical emergencies. A missionary had appendicitis; a Congolese woman had trouble in child-birth; six persons were bitten by a rabid dog. It was always Burleigh who flew in vaccine or whatever was needed.

And there were financial emergencies. Pastor Shungu, serving as field treasurer for the mission, needed money from the Luluabourg bank so he could pay our teachers for the first time in more than two years. As legal representative Pastor Shungu also had to go immediately when official problems arose. He had to have reliable transportation.

For three months there was no mail service into Lodja. Imagine the difficulties of administering a provincial government under such conditions. Burleigh flew load after load of mail up from Luluabourg. Only in this way could the local government get official instructions.

No matter how much I wanted him home, I knew Burleigh must go when such crises arose.

At Lodja we were close to the village people. What we saw shocked us. I had always been troubled about their diet, but now I saw real suffering.

Most of the little children wore only leaf-woven loin cloths. In the rainy season they coughed and shivered without anything to keep them warm. When a sixth-grade boy comes to school with his entire bottom exposed, you know he has nothing to wear. When, out of fifty-two pastors, not a single one has on a whole shirt at their district meeting, you know that there are no shirts to be had. Part of the trouble was lack of funds, but bare shelves in the stores were the principal cause. Supplies just were not delivered. The ancestors of these people had dripped salt from a swamp plant, but the present-day Congolese knew no more about dripping salt than I did. In village after village there was neither salt nor soap. Those people were asking neither for an industrial revolution nor for technical advance. They just wanted salt and soap.

Missionaries might have stayed in relative safety on the mission stations. But we found ourselves drawn out to those suffering villages to do what we could. There we saw the real life of the Congo church. For more than two years the members had carried on without the support of missionaries. During the persecution and abuse by invading armies, leaders had arisen among the villagers. One chief had been arrested and placed in prison because he was a Christian. Another chief, chosen to succeed him, tried to convert the people to a new prophet movement sweeping the country as a nationalist religion and decried Christianity as a "foreign" religion. Two years later the old chief was freed and reinstated by the very same villagers who imprisoned him. "He loves this village," they said of him. "He is a Christian."

Mama Podina had become the only Christian in the northern part of the Lodja district just a few months before the evacuation of the missionaries. As part of the ritual of the prophet movement, every person had to drink a holy oil. She refused. She was threatened, and terrible pressure was put on her. When her grandchild died, the village said the threat had been carried out. Every disaster in the village was blamed upon her, but she never wavered. Two years later the villagers asked for an evangelist to come, saying, "We want the kind of faith that Mama Podina has." It was impossible to visit her village and not wish for more of this faith for oneself.

So despite the uncertainties, we wanted to meet our responsibilities. "We've got to take a trip through the Lomela district," Burleigh said. "I think we can make it in the truck."

We left just after Easter, during spring vacation. It was now four years since we had left Lomela. We had been there only for two years as the only missionaries that had worked in the area. The Christians had been under great pressure. We were anxious about what we would find.

On the way we stopped at a big Bahamba village and were amazed to find the largest out-village church we had ever seen. There had been none when we left. Burleigh marveled at how straight and level the grass roof was. As we waited for the pastor to come, we saw a small, short man running down the road waving his arms and crying, "Oh, Oh, Ohooo U-wandji, Uuuu-wand-ji!" It was Nonga, the block-maker whom the state official had called the "shepherd of the flock." It was five years since he had left Burleigh's workline at Lomela.

Next we stopped at Mukamadi where we had left a strong church in spite of a drunken chief. Now we found a new and bigger church and a new pastor's house, but, even more important, the chief came to church, sober and alert, bringing his Bible and songbook. During the fighting, while hiding in the forest with Pastor Ukunda, Chief Mukamadi had become a Christian. Sitting with us, clear-eyed and happy, he told us all about it, making the story sound new again.

In village after village we found new hope. Even seeing and hearing for ourselves, we could hardly believe it. As Burleigh said again and again, "And to think I ever doubted the strength of the church!"

We began to see that our doubts were not really for the faith of the church but for a church caught up in political chaos.

The local tribal conflicts continued, and now we were hearing more and more about the rebels. Their revolution broke out in the Kwilu. Who were these rebels? What were their aims? Few seemed to know. Reports came that some of the Congolese mission employees were involved in the movement. The movement seemed to be feeding on the needs of the people. It promised salt and soap.

The Mission Boards in the United States realized that the lives of their missionaries could be in danger. It was difficult to know what to do—rumors were so rampant, communications so impossible. Men and women dedicated to their calling did not wish to leave their responsibilities on the basis of rumor. No one had hard facts to report about specific conditions on the various stations. We tried to get interstation radio communications set up but often failed. Impassable roads made visits to stations impossible. Thus, we could only push on with our jobs, day after uncertain day.

Two years had now passed since Margaret Ann and I had returned to the Congo. We could still not foresee the political future. As someone said, "It is like a pot of boiling clothes. Punch it down on this side, and it boils up on the other."

Once again our local problem of the "forest" versus "plains" people erupted. It was the "plains" villages, where the missionaries had worked for some time, that sent students to our schools to become preachers and teachers. When the missionaries had been evacuated from Lodja three years before, the shortage of teachers had become acute. The only solution was to persuade "plains" teachers to teach "forest" students. Several of our very best teachers had the courage to agree to do this.

One of the outstanding teachers of our entire Conference came back to Lodja as director of the primary

school. Realizing that we were in a vicious circle as
long as weak students had weak teachers, he volunteered to direct the school and also to teach sixth-grade
math and French. By taking on this double work load,
he hoped to get at least some students through the stiff
competitive examination and into the secondary school
at Katubwe. The need for educated Congolese leaders
was so urgent. For most of the other classes he simply
had to fill in with whatever teachers could be found.
Some of them were almost completely unprepared. Still,
the school was operating, and the director was doing an
excellent job.

Then, without warning, the "forest" teachers demanded that their "plains" director be dismissed and
replaced by one of them. As legal representative, Pastor
Shungu met with the teachers and tried to show them
how much the school would be hurt by such a change.

How the problem ever became such a complicated
affair I still do not understand, and I followed it day by
day. Before we realized what was happening, the "forest" teachers had gone to the state authorities, written
threatening letters to Pastor Shungu, and threatened
the missionaries and the director to their faces. The situation was so dangerous that Pastor Shungu asked for
soldiers to guard the station.

Burleigh was away on an emergency flight, so I was
at home alone one evening when Pastor Shungu
knocked at my door. "I have a guard for you tonight,"
he told me.

After he had gone, I went out on the porch, and a
short, little man jumped to attention, saluting me by
stomping the ground in a hard kick. "*Moyo*, Mama

Uya Koi," he said. "Do you remember me?"

I stepped back inside and turned on the porch light. There was Simoni, Burleigh's little Esongo Mena shadow from Lomela. I was delighted to see him. At least here was a soldier who could read. I had taught him myself.

As days went by, we realized that this conflict was more than a mission-teacher problem; it had suddenly become a political problem. Pastor Shungu was under real pressure to accept the demands. The fact that he was from the "plains" made it difficult for him to be regarded as unbiased. Threats against him increased.

The threats made no difference to Pastor Shungu. Although the missionaries actually feared for his physical safety, time and again he rode his motorcycle to the state post, seven miles away. He made it clear to the local political leaders that he would not accept interference in operating our schools.

With the same courage, he tried to impress upon them just what was happening to the Congo because of this narrow tribalism. He was a "plains" person, true. He didn't have to be at Lodja. He could have moved to the safety of his own clan. Instead, he, his wife, and their children stayed on the Lodja station unprotected while he tried to keep the school open so all Congolese could have opportunities. Somehow he made the political leaders see that the church was there to serve any tribe and any clan. Unless it could do this, it could not serve at all. Whatever his words, they reached the leaders who withdrew their demands and threw their support to him.

A few days later the students and teachers marched

past our house, singing and waving their flag. "Well, it looks as if school is back to normal," Burleigh said. "The future of Congo doesn't look nearly so tragic when we see leaders like Pastor Shungu." He did not know that within three months Pastor Shungu would be Bishop Shungu, head of the entire Methodist Church in the Congo.

A few weeks later, Conference came. At this time we celebrated the fiftieth anniversary of the opening of Central Congo Methodist work. We listened to preachers, teachers, and nurses discussing the future, making plans that included people of all the different tribes and clans within our Central Congo Conference. We saw delegates from all over Batetela land worshiping together though we could tell by their facial markings that they came from opposing clans. We realized that the church had more leaders dedicated to the welfare of all Congo than did the government itself.

During these years the role of the missionary had changed markedly. When it came time to elect delegates to the Central Conference for all of Africa south of the Sahara, the nominations were listed on the blackboard. Ten years before there would have been one list of missionaries and one of Congolese. Now there was one combined list. The only division was between ministerial and lay delegates, as is the rule in all Methodist Conferences around the world.

This particular session of the Conference was my last. As soon as Burleigh returned from a trip, Margaret Ann and I were going to America for a brief special vacation, a surprise trip given to me by the Congolese government in recognition of my service as a teacher.

When I entered the meeting, I read Burleigh's name among the list of nominations. I hoped that his being absent would not limit his chances of election. When the ballot was counted, they announced, "Uwandji Utshudi A Koi is elected." The smile that spread over the faces of the Congolese delegates told me they had voted for him and were pleased that he would represent them.

When I left the Conference, I felt that missionaries were still needed but that the leadership of the church was now in the hands of the Congolese. We knew and they knew that many serious difficulties lay ahead. But we had confidence in the future of the church in the Congo.

CHAPTER FOURTEEN

White Cross

JUST TEN DAYS AFTER LEAVING THE CENTRAL CONGO CON-
ference, Margaret Ann and I were at my parents'
home in Tallahassee, Florida. David, who had completed his classes, joined us, and Paul was due from
school in a few days.

One morning as I sat enjoying a cup of coffee and
chatting with Mother, the phone rang. Dad answered.
"Yes, she's here. Just a minute." I knew it was for me. I
was receiving many 'Welcome Home' calls. Then I
heard Dad's voice change. "A message from the State
Department?"

Something had happened to Burleigh!

Dad handed me the phone. I heard the Board of Missions Secretary at the New York office say, "The State
Department has notified us that Burleigh was killed
August 4th by a rebel soldier." He talked a few moments longer, but I heard little of what he said.

I hung up the phone and stood staring at it.

"Who is a rebel soldier?" I wondered.

I gathered Margaret into my arms, and David gathered us both into his.

"Maybe there's a mistake, Mother," he ventured.

"No, there's no mistake. I know it's true."

We had so many questions. When? Where? How? But my biggest question was one I did not voice. Why? I looked down at my new diamond.

David, now nineteen and looking painfully like his father, cried out, "If only we knew how Dad was killed! If he was beaten, tortured, shot with an arrow. It would help to know."

I sat numb. Then it came to me so forcibly that I could say positively, "But I know it was not a terrible death. No matter what he had to face, God was with him. I know he knew that."

We found comfort in being together, sharing each other's grief. David spoke again. "I'd rather have Dad killed by a rebel soldier than in some plane crash or something. I know he died like a Christian, and the rebel will remember that."

We waited until Paul had finished his last examination before I phoned him about Burleigh. "Oh, Mother," he cried, "I just can't take it." Then his voice quieted. "Yes," he said, "with a dad like mine, I can take it."

It was months before we had all the details, but slowly we pieced together the story.

It had happened just ten days after Margaret Ann and I had waved good-bye at the Lodja airport. Burleigh was working at home when a missionary neighbor burst in with the news he'd heard from a soldier—the rebels had taken Wembo Nyama station and the missionaries were under arrest.

Burleigh stood thinking for a moment. He knew that Dr. Hughlett, the missionary who had met us when we first came to the Congo, was there. So were his wife and two missionaries with young children and one whose wife was pregnant. Burleigh must go. He asked his neighbor to help service the plane. As they worked, they talked of the dangers involved and discussed the signal Burleigh should use before landing at Wembo Nyama airstrip.

The report had said the missionaries had been under house arrest since the rebel soldiers had appeared suddenly at their breakfast table two days earlier. The station Landrovers and trucks had been confiscated, so every means of escape was cut off, and they were being threatened.

As Burleigh approached Wembo Nyama, the captive missionaries heard the drone of the plane motor. They knew it was Burleigh, and they knew he would be in great danger if he landed.

He flew low, circling the station. A note tied to a rolled-up newspaper fluttered down. "Sit down if in immediate danger. Stand straight if OK for now. Wave if safe to land."

The missionaries gathered in the center of the station grounds. They stood straight, giving no signal for Burleigh to land. They didn't want him in danger, too. As slow and as low as he could, Burleigh circled again and again. Then the plane flew off, and the missionaries hoped he was returning to Lodja.

A few minutes later, one of the confiscated Landrovers manned by a stranger drove up to missionary Larry Pliemann's house.

"Come out to the airstrip," the driver called. The strip was about two miles from the station.

Fearing some trick, Larry hesitated. The driver urged, and Larry realized he had no choice. He climbed in, and they started toward the landing field. Excitement rose among the people along the road. In Wembo Nyama village, they had gathered in small groups. Just at the end of the village, Larry saw the high tail wing of the Cessna standing above the plain grass. "Oh, my God, no!" he cried.

When they drove into the clearing, Larry saw Burleigh lying by the plane. There was blood on his clothing. Running to him, Larry called, "Burleigh, what happened?"

"I'm shot." He was groaning in pain.

Seeing Larry start toward the soldier standing by, Burleigh added, "Don't blame him. I couldn't speak his language. He didn't understand me. I tried to keep the keys."

"Did you get our signal not to land?"

"Yes—I tried to fly away three times but—I couldn't leave you here without trying to help."

Dr. Hughlett arrived a few minutes later. The two missionaries lifted Burleigh into the Landrover and drove quickly to the hospital.

Four hours later, after blood transfusions, surgery, after every effort possible, Burleigh died in the hospital he had spent eight years helping to build.

The news spread quickly among the Congolese people. "Uwandji Utshudi A Koi is dead!" No one could believe that this tall, smiling missionary, known to them as Chief Leopard of the Artisans, had been killed by a rebel soldier's bullet! Then news was passed that the rebels refused permission to bury him.

The carpenters Burleigh had trained went to the carpenter's shop he had built. They sawed boards on the

sawmill Burleigh had installed. They smoothed these
boards on the planer he had set up. The planer wailed
its own grief across the Wembo Nyama station where
groups of people who loved him sat about weeping.

They placed Burleigh's body in the coffin they'd lovingly made, and it waited for almost a day in a missionary's home for permission to be buried. Suddenly the
rebels agreed there could be a Christian burial with
grave-side service.

In the small cemetery where the baby, the two Portuguese merchants, and the young missionary were
buried, and where only two months before, Pastor
Ngondjolo Moise, the Billy Graham of Central Congo,
had been buried, the workmen dug a new grave.

It was almost five o'clock when the Congolese pastor,
teachers from the schools, nurses, workmen, and villagers gathered with the missionaries for the grave-side
service. The pastor spoke in Otetela, Burleigh's second
language. He spoke of Burleigh's life among them—his
courage, his unselfish service, his abilities as a builder,
his love of laymen's work, his strong body, his persever-
ance. Many times he repeated, "He was here to serve
us."

Then the pastor spoke of Burleigh's love for the Congolese people, his love for his own fellow missionaries.
After a long pause, as if speaking to himself, he said,
"Greater love hath no man than this, that he would lay
down his life for a friend."

There was more than grief at the grave side. There
was a question, "Why did it happen?" Pastor Ndjati
said, "When God said to Uwandji, 'Go ye into all the
world,' He did not promise that this would not happen

to him. But He did promise 'Certainly I will be with you.'" He paused, then added, "And a crown of life if he was faithful unto death."

Chanting an Otetela song, filled with the love of a breaking heart, the Congolese workmen lowered Missionary Burleigh Law into Congo soil.

Even when I knew all that had happened, I was left with the same question, "Why?"

"Why did Burleigh land where there were rebel soldiers?" But Burleigh had done exactly what I would have expected him to do. His fellow missionaries were in danger. Burleigh had gone to help them. It was as simple and as complex as that.

Yet I questioned. "Couldn't God have protected him?"

I remembered an earlier time. Burleigh had been flying from Wembo Nyama to Katubwe, a flight mostly over tropical rain forest. If trouble arose, the only place to ditch was a treetop unless the plane happened to be near one of the two emergency landing fields in that large area.

With Burleigh was a young student nurse going to Luluabourg to take an examination. She was uneasy about her first flight. Burleigh tried to ease her fears.

He flew just a little off course to the right to show her a big village she would recognize. Later, he veered still a little more to the right to show her one of these emergency landing strips. These detours took only about five minutes, but that five minutes saved their lives.

Directly over the landing field, the motor developed a strange sound, and Burleigh smelled gasoline. He cut his power, banked around, and glided the plane safely to the ground. It was a freak accident—only once in a lifetime does a cylinder burst. Yet it happened to his plane. And it happened directly over that isolated landing field.

I thought, "Couldn't God have acted at Wembo Nyama? Couldn't He have saved Burleigh from that rebel's bullet somehow—caused it to jam or misfire?" My heart cried out, "Why didn't He?"

My thoughts raced on. "*If* Burleigh hadn't gone to Wembo Nyama, *if* he had been away on another trip when the word came, *if* he had come stateside with us." The *If*'s that would have made it all different were endless.

Then quietly I came to understand that one never finds the answers to all the *Why*'s and *If*'s in this life. I knew I would just have to trust them to God, trust that somehow in a way I do not see or understand now, through Burleigh's death, his witness will do more than twenty or thirty years added to his life would have done. His life was not wasted, though it was cut off in its prime.

I recalled a conversation Burleigh and I had had a year before. The political situation was at another peak of tension. Tribal fighting had broken out again, and our students were upset. As their fear increased, they wanted to run home to safety. Yet, often, going home meant going through enemy territory. No one knew what to do.

At the Sunday afternoon English vesper service, the leader shared with us a tape recording that had been sent from her home church Youth Group. I do not recall all that was said, but the closing remarks went something like this: "Who knows but that God might honor you with a call to be a missionary?" The youthful voice went on. "He might even honor you by letting you die a missionary martyr."

Walking home in the fading light, I had said, "This idea of being a missionary martyr sounds noble. I suppose most Christians can get excited to think they might die for their faith. But it's living this routine of strain and stress that's getting me down."

Burleigh patted my arm. "Well, you can't die a martyr for some cause unless you have lived for it," he said.

As the children and I sat together on the following Sunday afternoon at the memorial service held in St. Paul's Methodist Church in Tallahassee, we heard the tribute that had come from the Methodist Board of Missions. It was read by a fellow missionary from the Congo:

"No man could have loved his church or mankind more than did Burleigh Law, nor could one have loved Africa and her people more than did this quiet, persuasive missionary whose life and work were the personification of complete dedication.

"Burleigh was a builder. . . . As a layman he ministered to the total needs of the people. . . . No task was too small or too great for him to attempt for the Lord. . . . He was a person of great patience. . . . He was proficient in more trades and professions than most men and was always seeking to broaden the scope of his service.

"He helped any person who came to him. . . . He was interested in the lives of all the workmen and made a special effort to see that the workmen on the projects received training not only in building but also in the Christian faith. . . . He was a person who lived his Christian faith day by day. Now he has given his life for this faith.

"The Board of Missions is highly honored to have had the privilege of being related to this servant of Christ."

After the service Margaret Ann said, "You know, Mother, I believe that Daddy would have gone to rescue those missionaries even if he had known that the rebel would shoot him."

"We don't know that, Margaret. But we do know that when Daddy took off from Lodja, he knew it wasn't safe at Wembo Nyama."

I remembered what Burleigh had said at the Greencastle meeting the night before he returned to the Congo. "If somewhere, someone must raise a white cross over my grave, I'd rather it would be in the heart of the Congo, fighting with Christianity as my weapon, than on any battlefield of the world."

Three months later we were in the chapel at Asbury College attending another memorial service. Memories crowded in. I could see Burleigh as a senior on the platform of this chapel, taking part in the vesper service. I could remember kneeling beside him at the altar to take Communion.

Paul, now a freshman at Asbury, had been chosen to speak for the family. He was tall, six feet three, with his father's soft brown eyes. In my son I saw Burleigh here at Asbury, twenty-three years before.

"My heart would be filled with grief today," Paul

said, "if it weren't so full of pride. Pride in my dad. But more than that, pride in the cause he lived and died for. God honored Dad when He called him to be a missionary. Dad honored this call when he served, faithful unto death. He forgave the rebel soldier who killed him. Surely I can, too. The Congo still needs missionaries. I hope I may return to Congo and be a doctor—in the hospital my dad built, in the hospital where he died."

I would never find all the answers to my "Why?" But I could find comfort. I knew that Burleigh's influence would live on.

Epilogue

WEMBO NYAMA STATION STOOD DESERTED, SILENT. THE missionaries had all been evacuated. The Congolese teachers, nurses, students, and workmen were gone, too. The Congolese National Army had moved on after driving out the rebels. Most of the village people were still hiding in the forest, hiding from both rebels and the national army. Personal belongings had been looted and taken away. Only a few objects lay about here and there, dropped in haste or thrown away in disgust because they couldn't be used. One lady's shoe, a hair brush, a book of old used stamps, a hymnal.

A tall elderly Congolese man walked slowly from his home in the village up across the station. He hadn't gone to the forest with his wife and children. At his age it seemed useless to flee.

He had been just old enough to start working when Wembo Nyama mission station opened fifty years ago. In fact, he had helped to open it. He had been among the first to push a cart to Lusambo and back, loaded with supplies for the men building the station. He could still feel the jolt as the iron wheels fell in and out of the holes in the road.

The roads were wider now. Dirt still and often rough,

but cleared back so cars could travel. Even smooth in places. But was it better? The rebels came in over those improved roads. The old man shuddered at the memories. No matter what he thought of, his mind turned back to the rebels. It was as if their spirits haunted him day and night.

The last five missionary men left over those roads, fleeing from the rebels. The missionary wives had gone earlier by air. The old man shook his head in wonder as he remembered the plane. He had never dreamed that he himself would fly. Even as foreman of the workmen at the station, he did not expect a plane ride.

But he had been given one. His spirits soared as he remembered. How strange Batetela land had looked from the air—his village so small, his house like a goat shed. Uwandji Utshudi A Koi had laughed at him when he said that.

Remembering that laugh the old man stood still and rubbed his chest where it hurt. The pain tightened as he thought of his plane trip.

For six years he had managed to earn enough money to keep his oldest son, Kasongo, at the secondary school in Katubwe, and now Kasongo was graduating. Himself just a workman, and his son graduating.

He had gone out to the airstrip one day with a load for the plane. Uwandji Utshudi A Koi had just flown in a supply of medicine. When he saw the old man, he said, "Wembo Lua, I want you to be ready on Saturday to fly with me to Katubwe. Kasongo will graduate on Tuesday, and Sunday they have a special sermon for him. I didn't get to attend the graduation of either of my sons. I know how much a father wants to go to his son's graduation. So, I want you to see Kasongo get his diploma."

On Saturday the old man was ready, dressed in one of Uwandji's suits. Not many missionaries' clothes were long enough but Uwandji was tall and it fit him just fine. Most of his villagers went to see him off. Laughing and teasing, everyone had to shake his hand, from the smallest child to the oldest man. Then Uwandji said, "Let's go."

He had climbed in, and Uwandji leaned over him to fasten his belt. Someone called, "Aren't you afraid?"

"No," he said, "not with Uwandji flying."

Uwandji had laughed. That same laugh. Not loud. A chuckle. It told him that Uwandji was pleased.

When they arrived at Katubwe, the students crowded around the parking area. Looking out at them, he felt uneasy. These were smart secondary students. He was only a mission workman who couldn't read or write. Would Kasongo be ashamed of him? Should he have come?

He climbed out when Uwandji came around and loosened the belt. "Thank you, Uwandji, with dirt on my head," he had said. He thought he should not really get down and put the dirt on his head as he would have done at home. Not here before these students.

Uwandji took his arm. "This is just one way I can say 'Thank you' for helping me when I was a new missionary and you were the foreman of my workline."

Uwandji had glanced at Kasongo. The boy was smiling. The students were smiling, too, friendly and with welcome in their faces.

The old man suddenly stopped remembering. He felt

full of shame. If only he could do something to lift this shame! As he walked he had to force his lungs to fill with air. His chest had hurt ever since the day a workman had run up saying, "Uwandji Utshudi A Koi is shot."

The shock of it had dug into him. He had just stood there in silence. He didn't need to ask who shot him. He had known it was a rebel soldier.

He found himself at the small cemetery. Standing over the mound of red clay dirt, he noticed a few runners of grass beginning to climb up the side.

He let his mind run back. He remembered when they had built the sawmill, the brick press, the kiln, the carpenter shop, the maternity, the hospital. These buildings still stood but were empty now. Into each of the buildings had gone something of Uwandji. He could see Uwandji at work.

Then thoughts of the rebels came back. He remembered when he had first heard of rebels. They were far away then, over beyond Kibombo close to Albertville. One of the young men of his village had brought tales of their strength. They were said to be working for Lumumba's cause. Was not Lumumba his own tribal brother who had become the Congo's first prime minister? If other tribes were fighting for Lumumba's cause, should not his own tribe in Batetela land join with them? The young man made promises. Help the rebels get power, he had said, and the Congo would be united as a great nation. The tribal fighting would end.

There were other promises. Salt and soap and cloth would come again to Batetela land, the young man had said. Where the rebels had been, he had seen wives with new clothes. He had seen people washing with soap. If you joined with the right people, you could get it, too. The young man was persuasive. Each man in each village would have a chance at these good things, he told the villagers. And they listened. Was this not a Christian idea? To share good things?

The old man had joined with the villagers, saying, "What can we do to help?"

"Wait until these people come," the smiling young man had said. "Then receive them. Feed them. Help carry them on to the next village. Soon they will unite all Congo."

The villagers waited for this new hope to become reality. Then the rebels came. The old man was a village elder, and he went out to meet them. Why should he not help get good things for his village?

Three days later the workman brought word that a rebel soldier had shot Uwandji Utshudi A Koi.

The old man rocked back and forth in grief beside the grave. Why could he not have known what the rebels would do? At least he had warned other villages, sent runners to tell that the rebels had killed Uwandji. He thought of those villagers tearing down the flower branches and arches of welcome, stomping them in the ground. Then the villagers themselves had gone into hiding, leaving villages empty of people and food. Without food the rebels could not move on. They had come a long way, but they were stopped in Batetela land. The people would not carry them. They had killed Uwandji.

"Why did it take Uwandji Utshudi A Koi's death to show us the rebels would not bring us peace? Someone had to die before we could see the truth," the old man said. He looked again at the mound of dirt. Uwandji's grave needed a cross. He would make a white cross in the carpenter shop. He would bevel the edges and point the ends, the way Uwandji had taught him.

Then he remembered something he had forgotten in his grief. A second workman who had been at the place where Uwandji had been killed had said, "Uwandji asked us not to blame the rebel soldier. He said the soldier hadn't understood."

The old man stood for a long time in the middle of the empty mission station. Finally the tears came. The hate drained away. "Uwandji forgave the soldier. Help me to forgive him," he prayed. "Help me to forgive myself."

He went to the shop and made the white cross. He planted it firmly at the grave.

In the distance an ekuli drum was beating. The sound came from deep within the forest. Somewhere a Christian pastor was calling his people to worship.

The old man started toward the sound of the drum. He would find his people hiding deep in the forest. He needed to worship with them. As he walked the pain in his chest eased.

A few months later the silence at Wembo Nyama was broken. First a few, then more and more Congolese teachers and workers returned. The station was cleared of rubble. Word went out that the schools and hospital were open.

In February, 1965, one thousand twenty-four students paraded up the main street at Wembo Nyama. Leading the group were four students carrying large wreaths of flowers. They approached Dr. Melwin Blake,

Secretary for Africa of the Board of Missions, and a group of returning missionaries. Presenting their wreaths, one student spoke for the group.

"With much joy I stand before you in the name of the Methodist Church in Central Congo to bid you welcome.

"We thank you for your coming to us in these days of trouble. You remembered us in prayer, and God heard your prayer.

"Truly you heard and you have seen that many things of the mission have been destroyed. But in spite of it all, the Church of Christ is here. The Church was and is; and we pledge that the Church will be."

An old man, clutching a bunch of flowers, joined them. Dr. Blake recognized the foreman who had worked with Burleigh Law. Together they walked to the small cemetery and laid the flowers on Burleigh's grave.

As the students sang, "Praise God from whom all blessings flow," they did not yet know that the Church in America was raising funds to build a new secondary school at Wembo Nyama, to be named *Ecole Utshundi A Koi*. Through the years to come students from this new school will pause at the grave. They will read on the grave marker:

Burleigh A. Law
Missionary to Batetela
1950–1964
Nduku untu la ngandji kuleki
Kene ka mvwela engenyi andi*   John 15:13

and they will ponder their own Appointment Congo.

*"Greater love has no man than this, that he lay down his life for his friends."

Walking Into Eternity

Twelve years is a long time. Twelve years without any new clothes — without any feast. Twelve years to go daily down to Uwandji Utshudia Koi's grave to sweep away the leaves and place fresh flowers by the cross. Then to just sit and grieve, twelve years is a long, long time. Papa Wembo Lua had lived those painful twelve years at the Wembo Nyama Mission Station.

Even one year seems a long time when you are putting together a new life in a new place and you aren't even sure what form that life should take. Crying out to God in my pain I wept, "As if it isn't enough to lose Burleigh, my home, 22 years of accumulated presents, my friends who are now scattered all over Africa — but to lose my place of service! I am no longer a missionary. I can't return to Congo with eleven-year-old Margaret Ann." I sat sobbing. Then quietly in my heart I heard so certainly, "All my sheep aren't in Congo."

There came to my mind a student who sat by me each day in Scarritt College Graduate School in Nashville, where I was studying to receive a degree. She needed a friend. I could be that friend. I arose to begin searching for a new life, although I had no idea what kind of a life I would find.

Life turns on seemingly insignificant events. I was invited to speak to the United Methodist Women at West End Methodist Church. I didn't know what to share. I decided to simply share my pilgrimage of faith through Burleigh's death, and the conviction that serving Christ faithfully was worth whatever it cost. I had no feeling of elation or pride over a job well done.

The next day my phone rang. Dr. Ben St. Clair, pastor of West End Church, was calling. "Would you speak again for us?" he asked.

Thinking that he had another small group he wished to have hear me speak, I replied, "I guess so. When do you want me?"

"On March 4," he said.

Still thinking it was a Sunday School class or youth group I asked, "What time?"

"At our eleven o'clock church service," he said.

"Oh, Dr. St. Clair," I said. "I can't do that. I've never spoken at a morning church service. What would I say?"

"Say just what you said to the women, as nearly as possible."

Neither Dr. St. Clair nor I knew that on that particular Sunday the church would be full of conference and jurisdictional officers of the United Methodist Women from all over America.

Within two weeks I had all the invitations I could accept to speak on missions. I needed to work to help with expenses. My honorariums would be better than part-time work, and the interruptions of my study time would not be as great. We already had a student living with us who could care for Margaret Ann. I decided to accept this opportunity.

Graduation drew near. Offers for employment as a director of Christian education came unsolicited. Invitations to speak continued to come faster than I could accept them. The first edition of this book, *Appointment Congo* was coming off the press. I was approached about teaching English in a Japanese school. With so many open doors, which should I take? A dear friend counseled me, "Take the doors that will close if you don't enter now. The others will be there later if you still need them."

I decided to accept the invitations to speak, even after graduation. I expected them to slow down or even stop. But they didn't.

Week after week I shared the story of Burleigh's life. Over and over I told the story until it became rote. "I'm getting weary of that story," I confided in a good friend.

"I've told it so much I often can't remember if I've just told an incident or if it's the next story to tell."

Continuing my confession I said, "I need to stop all this speaking. I need to stop being Burleigh Law's widow. I want to move on into my own life."

"I'm glad to hear you say that. I'm tired of hearing the same old stories too," my friend replied. Then waiting a moment he continued, "I agree you need to stop being 'the widow' but not the speaker. Can't you share your own witness? Hasn't God done anything in your life since Burleigh's death? Why don't you talk on family life. I'd love to hear some of your experiences in child rearing."

"But I'm invited to talk on missions. I can't just go talk on family life," I excused myself.

"Try just giving your own witness. Share about your life with Burleigh but stop telling *his* story."

With great fear I ventured a few days later to try this

out. When I had finished I received as many words of appreciation as ever except for one lady who came up to me saying, "I did wish you would have told us about Brother Law's death."

"That's in my book *Appointment Congo*," I replied. "You can read all about it there."

Strange, but God was actually already preparing me for an emphasis on family life. Margaret and I had moved to Wilmore, Kentucky, where David and Paul could live at home. Paul was attending Asbury College. David was at the University of Kentucky in Lexington.

In late October, 1966, David took Leveda Bailey out for dinner at the Campbell House in Lexington. He had reserved a special table where the full moon shone in the window. As they waited for the dessert the organist played their special song with the message, "When we fall in love, it will be forever." The vocalist sang it. Then once more the organ played while the waitress sat before Leveda a plate covered with a lace napkin. Slowly she lifted the napkin for Leveda and there sparkled a diamond engagement ring on a black velvet cushion. What a perfect evening that was, just as David had so carefully planned and arranged!

"Who could beat that?" Paul asked.

"No one could beat it, but someone could equal it, possibly," I said.

Marty Stoneking came for our Christmas party. For her birthday Paul had given her a nice gift with the warning, "For Christmas it will be one rose."

As we completed our gift exchange, Paul handed Marty a florist box. She opened it and admired the beautiful dark red rose. She lifted it to her nose to smell its fragrance and suddenly cried out, "Is it real?"

We enjoyed her genuine surprise to discover a *real* diamond engagement ring carefully wired in the rose. We
were having two weddings in one year.

Shortly after Christmas I overheard David and
Leveda discussing pre-marital counseling. "You know
who I'd rather talk with than anyone I know?" she said.

"No, who?" David asked.

"Your Mom. She knows more about raising Law
babies and making Law men happy than anyone I
know," she answered.

So it happened that we began a weekly discussion
about Christian family life every Thursday evening
around our supper table. "How did you and Dad have
such a happy marriage? Did you ever fight?" Often I
heard expressed, "I want the kind of marriage you had."

From those honest, frank discussions, I began to share
on family life as I accepted invitations. More and more I
was invited to share on this subject as I moved away from
being the "Missionary Speaker."

The missionary message began to be picked up by
Paul. Between his junior and senior year in college he
directed his own Witness Africa team to Congo. Paul and
Becky Petrie and David Persons, the son of missionaries
from southern Congo, joined him for a three-month tour
of ministry to students. Paul returned convinced more
than ever that God had called him to serve in Congo.
Upon completing their senior year he and Marty were appointed to Wembo Nyama as teachers in the high school.
Later they were moved to Lodja but still as teachers.

David was struggling to find his area of service. He
felt he wanted to be an agricultural engineer. Yet the fur-

290 APPOINTMENT CONGO

ther he went the more he realized that there was more engineering than agriculture in his program. David loved the out of doors, with animals and farming. Through a wonderful guidance of God he found his place at Moorhead State University where extension service was a strong major. He had found his niche. Leveda completed her home economics degree. Before they moved to Moorhead, little Michele was the first grandbaby born into our Law family. Christmas time two years later at Moorhead, Margaret and I spent snowbound with Leveda while we eagerly awaited another baby. Paul was born on January 7, his Uncle Paul's birthday.

Healing was taking place in my heart. I was far enough down the road to look back and see my journey. As much for my own good as anything else, I decided to record my pilgrimage through grief. I wrote *As Far As I Can Step*, which was published by Word Books in 1969.

More invitations than I could accept kept coming for me to speak on family life. Then suddenly, and unsolicited, an invitation came to be interviewed for a position as Director of Family Worship in the Upper Room Section of the Board of Evangelism of the now United Methodist Church. I didn't even know the position had been available.

Frankly, I did not want it. I had so recently purchased my comfortable home in Wilmore and had spent months getting it decorated. I had just completed the job. I felt safe and secure there. Margaret was enjoying school and her friends. I did not want to move her back to Nashville. Sitting in my living room the day before the interview, I looked around. "Father, I don't want to go to Nashville. I want to stay here," I prayed.

"Lovest thou Me more than these," I heard in my heart.

"But it isn't fair. This is the first home I have ever
had. I have friends who have lived their entire married
lives in the same home."

"Lovest thou Me more than these?"

"But you shouldn't require me to move Margaret
back to the city."

"Lovest thou Me?"

On and on went the spiritual battle. Until today I do
not remember ever having a more painful decision. Peace
would not come until, from the bottom of my heart I
cried, "OK, Lord, if You want me there, I'll go."

Soon after my move to Nashville, David and Leveda
were off to Zaire with Michele and little Paul who were just
about the ages of David and Paul when they first went to
that land. They were missionaries at last. There had been
many changes in Congo since independence. One of the
most significant changes was that the name "Congo" had
become "Zaire."

For four years while I served in Nashville, David and
Paul with their families served in Zaire. Little Stephanie
and then, two years later, little Burleigh David joined
Paul's and Marty's family.

Margaret Ann grew into a lovely young lady, active in
school and church, having inherited the best of both of
her parents. She was fun to live with and love. We enjoyed each other. Then she was off to Asbury College. I
had to urge her to go, for she felt she should stay and take
care of me. "But no," I insisted, "time has come for
mother to learn to live alone." I had decided that in spite
of interesting opportunities I would be alone. There was
not to be another Mr. Right for me.

Just another of those invitations. They came so fast

and so crowded that I often almost lost count of where
I was. "This must be Troy, New York. This is
Tuesday.

"I'm sorry, I can't take you back to the airport
tomorrow afternoon," my hostess said as we rode in from
the airport to the motel. "I have a conflict. But there is a
gentleman who has offered to drive you for me."

Nothing different in that situation. I was quite accustomed to being chauffered about by strangers. Becoming aware again of how very weary I was I asked, "Would
it be possible for me to rest tomorrow and come to the
meeting after lunch when I am on the program?"

"Well, I don't know," she said. Then she began to
wonder out loud how this could be arranged. I didn't pay
too much attention as she considered that perhaps the
gentleman who was taking me back to the airport might
come by the motel and drive me over to the meeting.

Suddenly I came fully alive when I heard her say, "I
think he has a crush on you anyway."

"Who in the world is that?" I asked, shocked.

"Donald Shell," she answered. "Do you know
him?"

"No, I don't know him," I answered. "But I have
heard of him."

Heard of him indeed! Heard *from* him was the truth.
Several months earlier a box of candy had arrived at my
office. Taped to it was a letter saying in part:

The Holy Spirit often leads us to do strange
things. I trust this will not be too much of a shock
to you. I have read your book *As Far As I Can Step*.
I am tremendously impressed with you and the

book. Please accept this candy as a token of appreciation for the faith which we share.

Sincerely,
Don Shell

I wrote thanking him for the candy and suggesting I could understand why the Holy Spirit was called the "Sweet, Sweet Spirit" if He was prompting a gentleman to send candy. I suggested I would like to know more about this prompting. He replied, but the letter was so completely lacking in information about himself that I threw it in the wastepaper basket. I said to a friend, "I don't need another pen pal."

I had completely forgotten the incident until here suddenly I was hearing the name of Don Shell. Immediately I realized, "That's the Candy Man!"

"Tell me something about him," I said, trying not to appear too interested.

"How old is he?"

"Around 50 I would imagine," she said.

"What does he do?"

"I'm not sure, but he's a big shot over here at General Electric. His picture is often in the paper for some honor or another."

"How tall is he?"

"Pretty near six feet, I think."

"How well do you know him?"

"I knew him mostly through his wife, Alice. She was a conference officer when she became ill with cancer. Don would take off from work to bring her to meetings in the wheel chair when she became unable to walk. He even handled all the materials for her while she sat at the School of Missions and visited with her friends. We voted him "The Most Desirable Husband."

Stopping for only a moment, she continued, "I just love to hear him pray. He seems to be a really wonderful person."

I liked what I was hearing. My hostess came into my motel room to call Don. They arranged for him to take me to the meeting. Since I didn't need to be there until after lunch, Don would come to join me for lunch at the motel. Life was suddenly very interesting. I didn't feel nearly so tired.

I was dressed in plenty of time for Don's early arrival. He called me on the house phone. I walked down the hall, around the corner, and there stood this attractive, neatly dressed man with a fringe of greying hair around his bald head. "Well, I get to meet the Candy Man," I said.

"Oh, you remember," Don said.

"Sure I do."

"Well, just in case you didn't, I brought you another box," and he handed me a box of Schenectady's famous Uncle Sam's candy.

We had ordered our meal when I asked him, "How did you get my book?"

He told me a rather detailed story. A minister he knew had been a great influence upon his life. This minister's wife had died and he had trusted God to bring another wife into his life, if it were God's will. Don knew the second wife and admired her very much. This wife, Ellie, had heard me speak at a Good News convocation in Cincinnati, and had purchased a copy of my book. In fact, I had autographed it for her. Ellie had liked the book and had given it to a mutual friend, Doris.

Several months after Don's Alice had died with cancer, he was spending part of each week in

Washington, D.C., with General Electric. Doris and her husband invited him to share a guest room in their home instead of staying alone at a motel. One evening Doris completed reading a book and slid it down the couch to Don.

Looking directly at me, Don continued his story: " 'Don,' Doris said to me, 'I think you should read this book. I believe the author should be your next wife.' "

There was a long pause. Still looking directly into my eyes, Don said in a clear, strong voice, "I have read the book, and I fully agree with her."

I gulped, "How interesting — " was all I could say. Soon the conversation moved on to other subjects.

Don drove me to the meeting. I spoke, greeted people and was finished by 2:30. My plane didn't leave until 5:30. We had time to sightsee, visit his church and drop by his home. As we drove into his yard, a note book slid off the dashboard. I picked it up. The name on the front, Dr. Donald L. Shell, struck my eye. "Are you a Ph.D.?" I asked.

"Yes," he answered.

"In what field?"

"Mathematics."

"From what university?"

"Cincinnati."

I could tell he considered the subject closed. There were just lots of things I would still like to know about this man.

Then it was out to the airport and off on my plane. What a day! I was still stunned by such open, vulnerable candor. I found myself praying, "Dear God, don't let this man get hurt."

Ten days later Don flew to Nashville. He brought the same open, vulnerable spirit. He had decided that I was the lady he wanted to marry. The decision was up to me and we had lots of getting to know each other to do. "Let's talk about the things we did in our first marriages which we'd like to repeat should we ever remarry," I suggested. Our first evening was spent in sharing the good things out of our lives as married persons. It was fun to recall the happy, fun events. It also introduced us to each other as a married person.

"Let's agree to ask and answer questions. Any question you wish to ask is OK and deserves an honest answer," I suggested. Don often teases me that he had no idea what he was letting himself in for in agreeing to this idea. I had been a widow for over eight years. I had dated several men and had already asked some questions. I knew much better what I wanted to know than he did, with only a year of being a widower. Perhaps I did have an unfair advantage, but Don will also admit that very quickly we knew more about each other than many married couples ever do. From time to time, without realizing it, I said, "That's a good sign." Don was reassured that he was passing my stiff test. I was most impressed with this gentleman.

On Sunday morning we attended the communion service. As we sat there I suddenly became aware of my actions. I was playing it safe. I was not needing to risk, for Don was taking all that. "That isn't really very fair," I realized. "If he were not so open I would be doing everything I could to get his attention. I must let him know how tremendously impressed I am with him. He really is a wonderful person," I resolved.

Suddenly I knew as certainly as I could possibly know, "This is the man you have been waiting for."

Hearing of our engagement, Margaret wrote to Don,

"There is a little girl in me who will always need a Daddy." Mr. Right had come for both of us.

We planned a quiet wedding in the chapel at McKendree United Methodist Church. In our Christmas letters we both shared our good news. There were to be no formal invitations, but we would welcome friends to join us, "Just let us know," we said. They did let us know — 135 out-of-town guests wrote that they would be coming. We reserved an entire floor at the Holiday Inn. Friends of mine prepared our rehearsal dinner, while others prepared the punch and hors d'oeuvres. We invited all 135 to share the happy occasion. Locally so many were coming we moved from the chapel into the church, and 450 guests attended our wedding.

There were many things about our wedding that were special, but to me our Covenant of Love was unique. For after all, we were putting two families together. David and Paul were home from Zaire with their families. Margaret and Don's son, Peter, were our attendants. Paul and Don's son, Allyn, were ushers. David escorted me down the aisle. At the close of the ceremony all our children with their families joined us at the altar for communion.

We closed the service by forming a circle in a Covenant of Love:

> We believe that God is love and the source of all true love. Today we are aware that we are the product of all the love we have known. With gratitude for this love we now covenant together to let God's love fill our hearts, that we may enter a new family relationship where we will love each other as

Christ loves us. Amen.

Don and I were off to Japan for a wonderful honeymoon before we settled down to make a new family in Don's Schenectady home.

Just two years later we gathered again for another wedding. Margaret Ann was marrying Andrew Howell, an Asbury College classmate. As we joined hands in the bride's room, David led us in prayer. As I remember his prayer, he said:

Dear Father, years ago Paul and I asked You for a baby sister. We promised You that if You gave us a sister we would love her. We have loved Margaret as much as it has been possible for us to love her. Today we turn her over to Andy to love, and we believe that she is more beautiful than when You gave her to us.

There was not a dry eye in the group. It had been eleven years since Burleigh's death. A friend said to me, "Burleigh would be happy to see all of you with Margaret, and Don being such a loving dad."

Yes, I believed Burleigh was rejoicing that all of us had moved out of our grief into a new life as we waved Margaret and Andy off to their work as youth director for a church in the Florida Conference.

———————o———————

"But the Zairians can't leave their grief until you come back to Zaire for them to 'Pandjula Utanda — kill the funeral,' " David and Paul told us.

I was aware of this African custom. At an appropriate time following the death of an important person they plan a feast. All the family and friends gather to remember the departed loved one. The killing of the funeral is the ending of grief. One is not permitted to grieve any longer. New clothes are purchased and worn. An abundance of food is prepared. Drummers are hired. The celebration is for everyone.

There had been no such occasion for Burleigh. "We must go out to Zaire," Don said. "The Africans need you there for this."

It had been twelve years since Burleigh's death when Don and I arrived at the Lodja station to be welcomed by our African friends. A day's visit there, then we were off with Paul to the ranch about 40 miles away where he and Marty lived with their family.

While Paul had served as a missionary teacher at Lodja he often passed the agricultural extension station called the Olembia farm. Years before, the Belgian government had built this model ranch as a training school for African agricultural agents. They had done considerable research and development for that particular region of Congo. Also, they had invested large sums of money in buildings and equipment. It was amazing that after more than ten years with no European director and no programing, the facilities at this ranch were in such excellent condition. Seeing such need all about him, realizing the potential for this station, and also wanting to be involved with village work, Paul began to dream his dreams. He wrote his ideas up and presented them to the Zairian government, but without encouragement from his fellow missionaries. "The day of the white man is a limited one," many said.

They had not considered that Paul's father was buried in Zairian soil. In Africa a son belongs wherever his father is buried. The Zairian government gave Paul a grant of $60,000 per year for four years to reactivate the center.

Don and I arrived to find cattle grazing on the plains, a hydroelectric system which Paul had built producing electricity, a water wheel pumping water across the plains to the cattle, and a promising young agriculturist, Nzeza, working with Paul. Marty was busy giving medical care to the workmen. It was an exciting operation, and yet terribly isolated.

David was living about 100 miles away at the Katako Kombe station. He too was working in agriculture. His special project was training oxen as beasts of burden. Leveda was working in nutrition. We could see what an understanding of the people and their needs both David and Paul had. We could also see their frustrations. They could understand the people, for they could understand Otetela better than the missionaries of my day. They had grown up speaking it as children. They saw what was happening to a church dependent upon American support, with no plan to become self-supporting. They knew how money corrupted leaders when it reached the field with no accountability. They could choose to speak out or stay quiet. Either way, my sons were headed for trouble with the hierarchy. We did not understand what was happening, but there had begun a subtle change in the philosophy of missions. Some changes were perceived as good, for they encouraged African leadership. Yet while leadership was encouraged, no training was given for the responsibilities being assumed. The attitude toward missionaries discouraged long-term commitments or learning the language, and contributed to the opinion that missionaries were spying on the Africans. Unfortunately, national liberation was being interpreted as freedom from all that had gone before, both good and bad. Literally, "the baby was thrown out with the bath."

Although we could appreciate their dilemma, we were not there to resolve their frustrations. We were there to "kill Burleigh's funeral." It was to be a celebration of a great life. Nothing would hinder that.

Over 600 invited guests came to Wembo Nyama — all Burleigh's former workmen from both Wembo Nyama and Lomela with their wives, plus dignitaries from the government and Catholic Church as well as the Methodist Church. The wives of the teachers, pastors and nurses prepared the feast for us. The year before Papa Wembo Lua had planted a huge garden of cassava. He harvested sacks and sacks of the fresh green leaves. The women pounded these, added palm oil and cooked big pots of "djese." Three-fourths of a ton of dry rice was also cooked along with a beef, a buffalo, ten goats, three pigs, an antelope and thirty chickens. It was a feast in the true African sense. Each guest brought his own large bowl for eating. After eating all he could hold, he took his bowl home with him heaped up with food. That was a *good* feast!

We gathered first in the church for a service before the feast and before the drummers began their music for the celebration. A surprise awaited Don at this service. The leaders conferred on him an African name, Uwandji Koi. Interpreted it meant, "the inheritor of Burleigh's affairs." This was an appropriate name.

I spoke, sharing Burleigh's witness. Many had never heard the details of Burleigh's conversion, nor how he came to be a missionary. A pastor spoke of his life among them. A workman spoke of his work. Lastly, a nurse spoke of his death. I had heard bits and pieces from different missionaries. Now I was hearing the African version. This story was what they believed to be true. After the service I called the nurse over to the house. I wanted to check his details again. I realized I would never get a guaranteed accurate account. I would simply choose to believe the story the Africans believe.

Nurse Ulumbu was on duty at the hospital when Dr. Hughlett came by on his way to the airstrip. "I rushed out and insisted that I go with him," he said. Dr. Hughlett agreed.

"When we arrived at the plane, Uwandji was lying wounded on the ground. We lifted him up into the bed of the jeep. He laid his head on my lap. All the way into the hospital he never lost consciousness in spite of his heavy bleeding," he told us.

"The doctors began to prepare to give Uwandji blood transfusions. There was a terrible noise at the door. 'What is that?' Dr. Hughlett asked.

"It's the soldier who shot Uwandji," a nurse answered.

" 'Let him in,' Uwandji Utshudia Koi said. 'I want to tell him I forgive him.'

"The soldier came in and Uwandji told him he forgave him. As the soldier left he said to the nurse at the door, 'He was one of us.' " Nurse Ulumbu paused, then proceeded.

"The doctors needed more blood. People were crowding around in the hall outside. They wanted to give blood.

" 'You aren't going to save me,' Uwandji said to the doctors. 'I'm going to die. Don't keep trying to get more blood. I'd rather we would have prayer.' "

Sadly, Nurse Ulumbu shook his head. "The doctors knew this was true. They stopped. Each of them prayed. I prayed and then Uwandji prayed.

" 'Father, I'm glad that I'm not afraid to die.' he began.

"Then he prayed for his family, for Mama Uya Koi, that God would take care of her, for Davidi and Paulu and Amena. He called them all by name. Then he prayed for his grandchildren, although none of them had yet been born. He asked God to let his faith be passed from generation to generation in the Law family. He died."

Shaking his head as if he still found it hard to believe, Nurse Ulumbu added, "I have seen hundreds of people die in our hospital but that is the first man I ever saw **WALK INTO ETERNITY.**"

We went from the church to the feast. It was held in the Burleigh Law High School auditorium. As I sat at the head table on the platform I could look through the center front door. Directly in front of the door, some 200 yards away, I could see the white cross marking Burleigh's grave. Then I noticed Papa Wembo Lua, dressed in a new suit, sitting with his family enjoying a real feast. Twelve years of grieving is a long, long time but they were over.

The grieving is over, but life with its frustrations goes on. David and Paul came, by different experiences, to realize that the door of service as Methodist missionaries was closed to them. When they were able to overcome their bitterness, new doors began to open.

During their years in Africa, and most especially as Paul worked to reactivate Olembia farm, they had made friends with an outstanding Zairian, Col. Omba, the head of security in the government. Suddenly the fickle fate of political power turned and he was thrown into prison on false charges. For 22 months he lived in an underground dungeon with no sanitation, no covers, no clothes except the underwear he was wearing, and often days with only bread and water to eat. Yet into that dungeon came a most remarkable revelation of God's love to this nominal Catholic layman. God touched him, healed him and assured him that he would survive. He did.

Out of jail after four years, he wrote asking Paul to come out to Zaire. Col. Omba offered to pay his expenses. "I need you to instruct me in the Christian faith," he wrote. David joined Paul. Spending hours together in Bible study and prayer, God began to give them a vision of a new mission.

So little of the church was growing in African soil, they observed. Practically all of the lay leaders were employees of the church. As employees, they were subject to the authority of the church. David and Paul saw that the power to assign jobs was the power to make or break a person. They knew teachers and pastors who had their assignment changed after their garden had been planted — they were financially ruined for the year. David and Paul knew that none of the money coming from America was contingent upon local support. The leadership in Africa was not accountable to any authority. Both David and Paul felt there was a need for responsible decision making beginning in each village among the villagers, and not the pastor only. These people needed to provide for their pastor in such a way that he looked to the villages and not to the American church for his support. This would be possible only if the African layman prospered enough to support and train church leadership. If only they had some laymen who were not church employees or family members of church employees serving on decision-making committees. Having themselves served on the field committee, where finances from America were processed, David and Paul believed such a change there would bring a sense of ownership in the church. The church could begin to grow in African soil. Col. Omba had seen this vision even before Paul and David talked with him. What a confirmation of God's leading this was!

Out of their dream, Christian Lay Ministries was born. David and Leveda prepared to return to Lodja. Their children, Michele and Paul, were now teenagers, Danny, who had been born while living at Katako Kombe, was already three years old. Their ministry would be to help develop the agriculture of the region and assist the farmers in marketing. Also, they would conduct a rural health program to teach the people basic hygiene and nutrition. Paul and Roxann Rule, both having grown up as missionary kids from the Presbyterian mission, joined them. Paul was a master mechanic with many useful skills.

Paul Law felt led to continue his seminary training at Asbury Theological Seminary. The experience of isolation at Olembia farm gave Marty and him a vision of the need for team ministry. Paul increasingly felt drawn to John Wesley's concept of class meetings and bands. He involved himself diligently in Wesleyan theology, gaining an understanding of our Methodist roots. This naturally brought him to become active in the Barnabas Foundation, which gave him valuable experience in leading Wesley-type groups. Increasingly, Paul saw how important community building was if we are to mature in our Christian faith. How exciting to learn that he had been approved for Ph.D. studies at Perkins School of Theology at Southern Methodist University!

After three years as a youth director in Florida, Margaret's husband, Andy, joined Paul at Asbury Seminary. Margaret taught school to "put hubby through." They often spoke of the mission field, but it was always at some future date. It seemed in the dim future when they returned to the Florida Conference as a pastor. How exciting when first Kimberly Virginia and then, two years later, Andrea came to bless their home.

While our children were moving about the world, Don and I also made a major change. Before we married, Don had left General Electric Company to work in developing robots for a new company, Robotics. After only a few years, when Don had made his major contribution to this young company, he returned to General Electric. This time he went to Rockville, Maryland, to work in General Electric Information Services business. We left our friends who had so warmly welcomed me into their fellowship and settled in Potomac, Maryland. We enjoyed nine wonderful years in that challenging city.

While serving at the Board of Evangelism I had participated in the developing of a new program, "Marriage Enrichment." As soon as we were married, Don received training for leadership. This gave him a direct involvement with people, which he wanted. It gave us, as a couple, a ministry we could share together. In Maryland it provided us a real opportunity to bring both the program and the ministry to that area. It became our open door of service. Looking back, we could understand why we had moved to Maryland.

We saw this so clearly in September of 1983 at our farewell party. After 30 years of service, Don was retiring from General Electric, and we were leaving for Zaire for a three-month missionary tour. Thirty-five friends who had been active in the Marriage Enrichment program came to wish us well. During the time of sharing, 31 of these shared that it had been through our ministry that they had come to accept Christ as their personal Lord. It had been a fruitful nine years, and we were grateful.

After Don retired our attention turned to David and his work in Zaire. We had known that David's work had become far more complex than he had expected. He had gone to Zaire knowing that the farmers isolated in central Zaire had no market for their coffee and rice, nor encouragement to produce any cash crop. David needed to go out to the villages to help farmers get seeds and encourage them to work their crops. This took time. He began to operate a rice mill to pound and clean rice because the women were having to spend long, tiresome, unproductive hours pounding what rice they were able to produce. Transportation was absolutely essential for any improvement in the living standards of the people. Roads often had to be repaired before trucks could pass over them. Even bridges had to be built. This took time and energy, as well as supplies. Areas with potential for an abundance of rice existed not too distant from diamond mining camps filled with hungry people. Money they had, but not food. Roads linking the areas were non-existant, but rivers did connect them. So David began to operate a 50-ton river boat to haul food supplies.

A deficency of protein in the people's diet was evident. Especially among the young children. Leveda saw this need as she visited villages with her nutrition program. In response, David began to develop fish ponds, helping the village people in construction and providing the fish to stock them.

Beyond these projects, there were constant demands from Africans who were trying to build their own commercial enterprises. Trucks constantly needed repairs, from simple bolts to complex wiring and welding. "Where can we get these?" the Africans would ask. "At Uwandji Ona Koi," (David's). In addition to volunteers who gave from a few months to two years time, Paul Rule and David were working from dawn to dusk trying to keep ahead of their own and everyone else's demands. Every need presented an opportunity. Every opportunity gave a bigger vision of what was possible. His ambitions for his work had outgrown his personal resources. The tasks, especially those of keeping records, had become overpowering. His deep convictions of financial accountability made it difficult to live with anything less, and the urgent taking precedent over the important created unbearable tension for him.

Added to this tension was a concern for his own family. The limited resources and high cost of educating the teenagers in Kinshasa made it imperative that they be taught at home. Both the accounting and teaching were jobs Don and I could do temporarily. We volunteered. Once more I was in the land that had become a part of me.

Don spent hours helping David get his accounting system arranged and caught up. Both of us spent happy times teaching our grandchildren. We experienced the pain of seeing suffering, and the joy of watching very sick children, even unto death, revived with Leveda's rehydration fluid of water, salt, sugar and lime juice. So simple and yet so vital. We understood anew why the reward of God is for service "to the least of these."

All too soon our visas expired. We returned stateside. "Paul and Marty are not going to S.M.U.," a friend told us. "They believe God is calling them to return to Zaire as missionaries."

"You've got to be kidding," I said.

"No, I'm not," she answered, and sure enough she wasn't. We learned that in our absence God had confirmed to them a sense of call that had been lingering in their hearts for several years. They were preparing to return with their children, Stephanie, now 14, Burleigh already 12 and their stateside little girl, Stacy, who was five.

Sitting in his family room one evening, Paul shared his vision with us. At the time Don and I went to Zaire, a most wonderful miracle had happened. The Zairian government had agreed to sell the Olembia farm to Christian Lay Ministries for an unbelievably low price. Paul's years of work were returning as bread upon the water. While we were there David began to arrange to move to the Olembia farm. This would make possible much more of his vision of agricultural development.

Years ago there were strong churches in the Olembia area, but the tribal fighting between the forest and plains people had all but destroyed them. Unaware of what was happening, the missionaries, years before when they were opening the work in that area, had worked with the people who responded best. These people happened to be the invader tribe. When they fled they took their church with them, leaving only empty buildings. The unevangelized land owners, or forest people, moved in from other villages, occupying the land, but they brought no church with them. Now there existed thousands of people in small villages surrounding the ranch who had never heard the Gospel. Paul's heart had been moved by these people when he had last visited Zaire. He also saw the wonderful opportunity to begin building a church using the John Wesley concept of small family-oriented bands and village-wide class meetings, where discipling the people would be as important as preaching. This approach would fit the African sense of community and assist in maturing the church in native soil. It would not look to America for any of its support. Local leadership would be the decision makers.

We listened carefully. I also listened painfully, for I saw my dream of Paul's ministry of bringing renewal of Wesleyan theology to the United Methodist Church going down the drain. Slowly Don spoke, "There are many people who can earn a Ph.D. in Wesleyan Studies. But with your ability to speak Otetela, your knowledge of and love for the people, and your experience in discipling ministries, you are the only person who can do what God is calling you to do in Zaire."

The matter was settled. Paul would begin to raise the support he needed to fulfill God's call.

"Who will teach the children." I asked.

With a knowing smile Paul replied, "God will provide."

And *indeed* He would. Margaret and Andy had heard just such a call. "We have always felt eventually we would go to Zaire," they told us. Andy would work in discipling with Paul. Margaret, with her elementary education degree, was fully qualified to be the missionary teacher for the missionary children.

Their dim, distant vision was now most present. Andy had been granted a special appointment by Bishop Hunt. They would need to raise their own support in order to serve under Christian Lay Ministries. "If God wants us to go He will provide," they said.

I had to agree, and admired their faith. Amazingly, God was calling others to join them — a builder, a nurse, a pilot, a business man! Who knows what God had, and still has, in mind?

Zaire is a needy land. What deterioration the past 25 years have brought! Nothing seems to function. The mails are unreliable. The roads are washed out. Inflation is now over 60 percent. Corruption and bribes are constantly reported in the international news media. When we returned to Zaire to help David, although I already was aware of this, the reality was painful to me.

Now that I faced two more Laws accepting God's call to serve in Zaire, I suddenly remembered an experience Don and I had had when we were there only a few months before. While visiting with David and Leveda in Zaire we often sat out in the yard after supper. One of our favorite pastimes was watching for satellites as they streaked across the sky. Early in the evening, when it was dark around us, the sun just below the horizon would shine on satellites passing high overhead in the sky. We could often spot one looking like a fast-speeding star. At other times the bright moon reflected from the smooth sides of a satellite, and we could follow it on its eastern journey.

While visiting in the moonlight one evening, watching for just such a satellite to flash across the sky, I was aware of the contrast between America and Zaire. These two countries were quite literally worlds apart. Yet here was our son with his lovely family freely choosing to live in this isolated, undeveloped part of the world, rather than in progressive America that sent satellites streaking across the sky. As much as I loved Zaire and her people, the situation seemed hopeless to me. It must have seemed even more so to Don. "David, what do you hope to accomplish here?" he asked.

After a long moment of silence David replied, "I bring hope to these people."

He talked of real opportunities he could have in America for a good, secure job with excellent pay. "But," he said, "I would spend my life, and what would I gain but money and material advantage?"

Another silence followed. He appeared to be weighing the contrast as he continued. "Here, I can't ride my motor bike down to the Lodja Center that everyone I pass doesn't have more hope for tomorrow just because I am here."

Don and I knew that he was right. He did have the opportunity for security and remuneration in America that he talked about. We also knew he was certainly right in his reason for being and staying in Africa. He and Leveda *did* bring hope to these people.

Now we faced the reality that Paul and Marty, with Margaret and Andy, were also freely choosing to answer God's call to go serve in that same needy land. We knew

that the same hope brought by David and Leveda would
be brought by Paul and Marty, Margaret and Andy.

As I look back, surely I can reflect that God has led us
all the way. As we closed our circle of prayer at our
private family New Year's Eve worship service a few
years ago, Paul turned to Don and said, "I just realized
again, Don, how God did answer Dad's prayer for Mom.
He asked God to take care of her. God couldn't have done
a better job of taking care of her than to bring you into her
and our lives." I agreed. Could it be that Burleigh's
prayer for his children was also being fulfilled in their
renewed call to serve in Zaire?

Don and I call beautiful Lake Junaluska, North
Carolina home. Here the Laws and the Howells, as well
as Allyn and Carol Shell with Matthew, and Peter and
Pattie Shell with Craig and Kris, can come "Home."

Our lives are busy with retreats, conferences, lay
renewal weekends and mission emphasis. Don works on
developing computer programs for mission projects. I am
writing a regular feature, "From the Heart," for *Good
News* magazine. We both serve on the Good News Board
of Directors. Don is part of the Advisory Council for the
E. Stanley Jones School of Evangelism and World Mission at Asbury Theological Seminary. Our home is
available to friends for rest and refreshment. To the very
best of our ability we are living our lives in response to
God's call as we hear it.

Paul was asked recently, "What is it that has drawn
all of you Law children back to a place where there are
only a few missionaries, and no second-generation missionaries at all?"

He reflected and responded, "Two things. First, the

attitude toward the people there that Mom and Dad sowed into our lives from the beginning. Our freedom to befriend village children, play, eat, sleep and hunt with them. We grew to love their language and culture.''

Then he added, ''Secondly, and finally, because God has called us. When Dad died he didn't leave me any material inheritance, but what he left me was priceless. He gave me an insatiable desire to do the will of God.''

Burleigh Law's story doesn't end here. For:

As long as God keeps calling,

As long as we keep heeding His call,

As long as friends support us,

So long will faith and hope keep passing from generation to generation through our family and through our Zairian family. We will each discover our own Appointment Congo until

WE ALL WALK INTO ETERNITY!

Paul and Marty Law, Stephanie, Burleigh and Stacy

Andy and Margaret Howell, Andrea and Kimberly

**David and Leveda Law,
Michelle, Paul and Danny**

**Workmen bearing Burleigh's casket. Foreman Wembo Lua
leads, wearing the white coat given him by Burleigh. PHOTO:
DOUG CROWDER**

Burleigh levels the floor for "Aluminum Haven."

Villagers return the honor paid their isolated village by bearing Burleigh and Virginia in the *kipoi*: a type of sedan chair.

ZAIRE, AFRICA

The Law family standing before the Lomela guest house.

Burleigh Law "turning through the prop" at the small two-family mission center on Lake Kafakumba in the Katanga area of the Congo. PHOTO: DON COLLINSON

Missionary builders of Lambuth Memorial Hospital at
Wembo Nyama studying the plans. Left to right: Lawrence
Lundeen, electrical engineer; Burleigh Law; and Al
Burlbaugh, construction engineer. PHOTO: DON COL-
LINSON

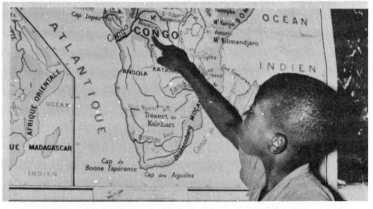

This is Batetela-land. An elementary school boy points to it
on a French-titled map of Africa. French will be his language
tool for all of his schooling. PHOTO: DON COLLINSON

Donald and Virginia Shell